ENV BOOKS SERIES

WATER RESOURCES

MAPPING, MONITORING AND MANAGEMENT

Editors

Dr. Pawan Kumar Tyagi
Managing Director
ECON Laboratory & Consultancy
Inderpur, Nawada Road
Dehradun - 248 005 (Uttarakhand)
(INDIA)

Dr. Avnish Chauhan
Associate Professor
Phonics Group of Institutions
Roorkee (Uttarakhand)
(INDIA)

Dr. Pawan Kumar 'Bharti'
Vice President
Society for Environment, Health, Awareness of Nutrition & Toxicology (SEHAT)
1775, Sohan Ganj, Near Clock Tower
Delhi - 110 007
(INDIA)
E-mail: gurupawanbharti@gmail.com

DISCOVERY PUBLISHING HOUSE PVT. LTD.
INDIA

Published by:

Namit Wasan

DISCOVERY PUBLISHING HOUSE PVT. LTD.

4383/4B, Ansari Road, Darya Ganj

New Delhi-110 002 (India)
Phone : +91-11-23279245, 43596064-65

Fax : +91-11-23253475

E-mail : discoverypublishinghouse@gmail.com
namitwasan9@gmail.com
sales@discoverypublishinggroup.com

website: www.discoverypublishinggroup.com

First Edition: **2017**

ISBN: 978-93-5056-861-3

Water Resources: *Mapping, Monitoring and Management*

Printed at:
Infinity Imaging Systems
Delhi

ENV Books Series, (India)

Calls lengthy and error free chapters for further volumes of books on various environmental issues. (Send your manuscripts to envbooks@gmail.com)

Founding Editor (Editor-in-Chief)

Dr. Pawan Kumar 'Bharti'
Society for Environment, Health, Awareness of Nutrition & Toxicology (SEHAT-India)
1775, Sohanganj, Near Clock Tower, Delhi-7, (India)
E-mail:*gurupawanbharti@rediffmail.com*

Other Titles by Editor-in-Chief:

1. **Advances in Biotechnology and Ecological Sciences**
   Bharti, P.K., Chauhan, A. and Ray, J. (eds.)
   (ISBN: 978-93-5056-358-8).
2. **Advances in Agriculture and Ecology**
   Bharti, P.K.; Chauhan, A. and Ezeaku Peter Ikemefuna (eds.)
   (ISBN: 978-93-5056-362-5).
3. **Agriculture and Environmental Biotechnology**
   Bharti, P.K. and Chauhan, A. (eds.)
   (ISBN: 978-93-5056-479-0).
4. **Agriculture Development and Sustainable Environment**
   Ray, J. and Bharti, P.K. (eds.)
   (ISBN: 978-93-5056-759-3).
5. **Agriculture Ecology and Environment**
   Bharti, P.K. and Olubukola O. Babalola (eds.)
   (ISBN: 978-93-5056-480-6).
6. **Agriculture Ecology, Sustainable Development and Agribusiness Management**
   Mehta Piyush; Sharma Pankaj; and 'Bharti' P.K. (eds.)
   (ISBN: 978-93-5056-851-4).
7. **Agriculture, Environment and Nano-science**
   Bharti, Pawan K. (ed.)
   (ISBN: 978-93-5056-760-5).

8. **Agricultural Practices and Crop Disease Control**
Chauhan Alka and Sharma Anubhuti (eds.)
(ISBN: 978-93-5056-859-0).

9. **Agro-biodiversity:** ***Conservation and Sustainable Development***
Sharma, Pankaj; Singh, Narayan; and Bharti, P.K. (eds.)
(ISBN: 978-93-505-782-1).

10. **Agro-forestry and Climate Change**
Bharti, Pawan K. and Singh, Narayan (eds.)
(ISBN: 978-93-5056-514-8).

11. **Agro-forestry and Sustainable Agriculture**
Sharma, Pankaj; Bharti, P.K. (eds.)
(ISBN: 978-93-5056-786-9).

12. **Aquaculture and Fisheries Environment**
Gupta, S.K. and Pawan K. Bharti (eds.)
(ISBN: 978-93-5056-408-0).

13. **Aquatic Biodiversity and Pollution**
Bharti, P.K.; Chauhan, A. and Kaoud, H.A.H. (eds.)
(ISBN: 978-93-5056-359-5).

14. **Aquatic Ecology and Biotechnology**
Bharti, P.K. and Zaki, M.S.A. (eds.)
(ISBN: 978-93-5056-451-6).

15. **Aquatic Environment and Toxicology**
Bharti, Pawan K. (ed.)
(ISBN: 978-93-5056-236-9).

16. **Biodiversity, Biotechnology and Environmental Conservation**
Bharti, P.K. and Bhandari, G. (eds.)
(ISBN: 978-93-5056-750-0).

17. **Biodiversity of Aquatic Ecosystem:** ***Significance, Threat and Conservation*** **(2013)**
Bharti, P.K. and Kaoud, H.A.H. (eds.)
(ISBN: 978-93-5056-297-0).

18. **Biological Diversity and Ecology**
Arya, M.K.; Bharti, P.K. and Ritesh Joshi (eds.)
(ISBN: 978-93-5056-785-2).

19. **Bioremediation and Microbial Biotechnology**
Gupta, Sandeep; and Bharti, P.K. (eds.)
(ISBN: 978-93-5056-783-8).

20. **Biotechnological Approaches and Water Ecosystem**
Zaki, M.S.A.; and Bharti, P.K. (eds.)
(ISBN: 978-93-5056-779-1).

21. **Biotechnology, Agro-ecology and Environment**
Chauhan, Avnish and Bharti, P.K. (eds.)
(ISBN: 978-93-5056-757-9).

22. **Biotechnology and Environmental Management**
Arya Arun; Raaz K. Maheswari and P.K. Bharti (eds.)
(ISBN: 978-93-5056-862-0).

23. **Clean Technologies and Environmental Protection**
Chauhan, A.; Sharma, S. and Bharti, P.K. (eds.)
(ISBN: 978-93-5056-731-9).

24. **Climate Change and Agriculture**
Bharti, P.K. and Chauhan, Avnish (eds.)
(ISBN: 978-93-5056-148-5).

25. **Climate Change and Biodiversity**
Bharti, P.K. and Chauhan, Avnish (eds.)
(ISBN: 978-93-5056-360-1).

26. **Climate Change, Disaster Management and Environment**
Chauhan, Alka; Bharti, P.K. (eds.)
(ISBN: 978-93-5056-784-5).

27. **Conservation and Cultivation of Medicinal Plants**
Bharti, P.K. and Singh Narayan (eds.)
(ISBN: 978-93-5056-740-1).

28. **Crop Productivity and Plant Disease Management**
Chauhan, Alka; Bharti, P.K. and Sadana, Deepti (eds.)
(ISBN: 978-93-5056-791-3).

29. **Eco-toxicology and Eco-technology**
Bharti, P.K. and Zaki, M. (eds.)
(ISBN: 978-93-5056-313-7).

30. **Environmental Biotechnology and Application**
Bharti, P.K. and Chauhan, Avnish (eds.)
(ISBN: 978-93-5056-262-8).

31. **Environmental Conservation and Biotechnology**
Chauhan, A. and P.K. Bharti (eds.)
(ISBN: 978-93-5056-512-4).

32. **Environmental Health and Problems**
Bharti, P.K. and Gajananda, Kh. (eds.)
(ISBN: 978-93-5056-263-5).

33. **Environmental Pollution and Biodiversity**
Bharti, P.K.; Chauhan, Avnish and Kumar, P. (eds.)
(ISBN: 978-93-5056-149-2).

34. **Farming Techniques and Crop Production**
Chauhan Alka; Sharma Anubhuti; Ray Jaswant and 'Bharti' P.K. (eds.)
(ISBN: 978-93-5056-855-2).
35. **Fisheries and Toxicology**
Zaki, M.S.A.; Bharti, P.K. and Chauhan, A. (eds.)
(ISBN: 978-93-5056-452-3).
36. **Fish Habitat and Aquaculture**
Bharti, P.K.; Gupta Kr. Sanjay (eds.)
(ISBN: 978-93-5056-744-9).
37. **Food Processing, Management and Nanotechnology**
Chauhan, Avnish; Bharti, P.K. (eds.)
(ISBN: 978-93-5056-796-8).
38. **Freshwater Ecosystem and Xenobiotics**
Bharti, P.K.; Zaki, M. and Chauhan, A. (eds.)
(ISBN: 978-93-5056-299-4).
39. **Heavy Metals and Metalloids in Biosphere: *Impacts and Assessment***
Chauhan Avnish; Gupta Sandeep and Bharti P.K. (eds.)
(ISBN: 978-93-5056-860-6).
40. **Limnology and Aquatic Science**
Sharma, S. and Bharti, P.K. (eds.)
(ISBN: 978-93-5056-735-7).
41. **Medicinal Plants: *Distribution, Utilization and Significance***
Sharma, P.; Bharti, P.K. and Narayan Singh (eds.)
(ISBN: 978-93-5056-734-0).
42. **Microbial Applications and Environment**
Bharti, Pawan K. (ed.)
(ISBN: 978-93-5056-515-5).
43. **Microbial Ecology and Habitat**
Bharti, Pawan K. (ed.)
(ISBN: 978-93-5056-514-8).
44. **Microbial Environment and Bioremediation**
Chauhan Alka; K. Rathoure Ashok; and K Maheshwari Raaz (eds.)
(ISBN: 978-93-5056-856-9).
45. **Natural Ecosystem and Climate Change**
Bharti, P.K., and Kh. Gajananda (ed.)
(ISBN: 978-93-5056-745-6).
46. **Pest Management and Agro-Techniques**
Biswas, Asim; Bharti, P.K., Chauhan, Avnish (eds.)
(ISBN: 978-93-5056-794-4).

47. **Prakriti me Aushadhi (*in Hindi*)**
Singh, J.R.; Bharti, P.K. and Bharti, B.
(ISBN: 978-93-5056-200-0).

48. **Seed Technology, Plant Growth and Cropping System**
Tyagi, P.K. and Bharti, P.K. (eds.)
(ISBN: 978-93-5056-738-8).

49. **Seed Treatment, Plant Heath and Agro-technology**
Chauhan, A. and Bharti, P.K. (eds.)
(ISBN: 978-93-5056-810-1).

50. **Soil Characteristics and Agro-ecology**
Avnish Chauhan and Bharti, P.K. (eds.)
(ISBN: 978-93-5056-758-6).

51. **Soil Contamination and Conservation**
Ezeaku, P.I. and Bharti, P.K. (eds.)
(ISBN: 978-93-5056-737-1).

52. **Soil Quality and Contamination**
Bharti, P.K. and Chauhan, Avnish (eds.)
(ISBN: 978-93-5056-361-8).

53. **Sustainable Aquaculture Management**
Gupta, S.K.; Bharti, P.K (eds.)
(ISBN: 978-93-5056-797-5).

54. **Waste Disposal and Management**
Bharti, P.K.; Tabassum, B. and Bajaj, P. (eds.)
(ISBN: 978-93-5056-729-6).

55. **Waste Generation and Utilization**
Bajaj Priya; Tabassum, B., and Bharti, P.K. (eds.)
(ISBN: 978-93-5056-792-0).

56. **Waste Management and Environmental Health**
Tabassum, B., Bajaj Priya, and Bharti, P.K. (eds.)
(ISBN: 978-93-5056-777-7).

57. **Water Resources and Agriculture**
Bharti, P.K. and Ezeaku Peter Ikemefuna (eds.)
(ISBN: 978-93-5056-481-3).

58. **Waste Resources Management: *Monitoring and Assessment***
Gupta, Sandeep and Bharti, P.K. (eds.)
(ISBN: 978-93-5056-799-9).

Preface

Water resources are sources of water that are useful or potentially useful. Uses of water include: agricultural, industrial, household, recreational and environmental activities. The majority of human uses require fresh water. 97 per cent of the water on the Earth is salt water and only three per cent is fresh water; slightly over two thirds of this is frozen in glaciers and polar ice caps. The remaining unfrozen freshwater is found mainly as groundwater, with only a small fraction present above ground or in the air.

Fresh water is a renewable resource, yet the world's supply of groundwater is steadily decreasing, with depletion occurring most prominently in Asia and North America, although it is still unclear how much natural renewal balances this usage, and whether ecosystems are threatened. The framework for allocating water resources to water users is known as water rights.

The Earth is a watery place. But just how much water exists on, in, and above our planet? About 71 per cent of the Earth's surface is water-covered, and the oceans hold about 96.5 per cent of all Earth's water. Water also exists in the air as water vapor, in rivers and lakes, in icecaps and glaciers, in the ground as soil moisture and in aquifers, and even in you and your dog. Water is never sitting still. Thanks to the water cycle, our planet's water supply is constantly moving from one place to another and from one form to another. Things would get pretty stale without the water cycle!

Glaciers and icecaps cover about 10 per cent of the world's landmass. These are concentrated in Greenland and Antarctica and contain ~70 per cent of the world's freshwater. Unfortunately, most of these resources are located far from human habitation and are not readily accessible for human use.

According to the United States Geological Survey (USGS), 96 per cent of the world's frozen freshwater is at the South and North poles, with the remaining 4 per cent spread over 550 000 km2 of glaciers and mountainous icecaps measuring about 180 000 km3 (UNEP, 1992; Untersteiner, 1975; WGMS, 1998, 2002).

Groundwater is by far the most abundant and readily available source of freshwater, followed by: lakes, reservoirs, rivers and wetlands.

- Groundwater represents over 90 per cent of the world's readily available freshwater resource (Boswinkel, 2000). About 1.5 billion people depend upon groundwater for their drinking water supply (WRI, UNEP, UNDP, World Bank, 1998).

- The amount of groundwater withdrawn annually is roughly estimated at ~600-700 km3, representing about 20 per cent of global water withdrawals (WMO, 1997).
- A comprehensive picture of the quantity of groundwater withdrawn and consumed annually around the world does not exist.

Most freshwater lakes are located at high altitudes, with nearly 50 per cent of the world's lakes in Canada alone. Many lakes, especially those in arid regions, become salty through evaporation, which concentrates the inflowing salts.

Reservoirs are artificial lakes, produced by constructing physical barriers across flowing rivers, which allow the water to pool and be used for various purposes. The volume of water stored in reservoirs worldwide is estimated at 4 286 km3 (Groombridge and Jenkins, 1998).

Wetlands include: swamps, bogs, marshes, mires, lagoons and floodplains. The 10 largest wetlands in the world by area are: West Siberian Lowlands (780 000-1 000 000 km2), Amazon River (800 000 km2), Hudson Bay Lowlands (200 000-320 000 km2), Pantanal (140 000-200 000 km2), Upper Nile River (50 000-90 000 km2), Chari-Logone River (90 000 km2), Hudson Bay Lowlands in the South Pacific (69 000 km2), Congo River (40 000-80 000 km2), Upper Mackenzie River (60 000 km2), and North America prairie potholes (40 000 km2) (Pidwiny, 1999).

The total global area of wetlands is estimated at ~2 900 000 km2 (Groombridge and Jenkins, 1998). Most wetlands range in depth from 0-2 metres. Estimating the average depth of permanent wetlands at about one metre, the global volume of wetlands could range between 2 300 km3 and 2900 km3.

The Caspian Sea, the Dead Sea, and the Great Salt Lake are among the world's major salt lakes.

The present book updates the subject content of water resources of earth ecosystem, water quality monitoring, water resources management, Pollution assessment, Modeling and prediction, Monsoon and rainfall interpretations, glacier behaviour, water uses, Supply and demand aquatic flora and fauna, Freshwater ecosystem and Aquatic Science.

Thanks are due to contributors from various institutions/universities and publishers also. The book will be helpful for the researchers, academia working in the field of water resources of earth ecosystem, water quality monitoring, water resources management, Pollution assessment, Modeling and prediction, Monsoon and rainfall interpretations, glacier behaviour, water uses, aquatic biodiversity, Freshwater ecosystem and Aquatic Science.

– Editors
(envbooks@gmail.com)

Contents

Pages 1-9

WATER RESOURCES: MAPPING, MONITORING AND MANAGEMENT
***Edited by*: Dr. Pawan Kumar Tyagi; Dr. Avnish Chauhan & Dr. Pawan Kumar Bharti**
***Edition* : 2017**
ISBN : 978-93-5056-861-3
***Published by* : Discovery Publishing House Pvt. Ltd., New Delhi (India)**

Water Quality Monitoring of Umiam River in East Khasi Hills Meghalaya, India

Pawan Kumar Bharti*
Vijender Singh

ABSTRACT

Umiam river is a major river of East Khasi Hills district in Meghalaya along with many small tributaries near Bangladesh Border. It has a great importance as a natural habitat among the various ecosystems of the region, whereas there is a large scale limestone mining area and no more industrial and agricultural pollution. Anthropogenic factors mainly activities of local people and catchments runoff may influence the index of nutrients in river water and may alter the physico-chemical characteristics and also the whole water quality and the structure of biotic community. Physico-chemical parameters play an important role into niche restoration maintenance, self-regulation of water quality. Location variation in nutrients concentration of the river was studied with special reference to physico-chemical parameters and heavy metals in the river water.

Calcium and Magnesium were observed in very low range in Umiam river water at upstream as well as downstream in comparison to rivers and hill-streams of North India. Dissolved oxygen was found 9.2 to 11.0 mg/l at upstream and downstream during the study period. Heavy Metals were found almost nil or in very low concentrations at both selected site. The present study deals with the pre-liminary physico-chemical characteristics of the river water and exhibits the natural quality of water with minimum anthropogenic activities, which contribute in pollution load of an ecosystem.

Keywords: Water quality, Pollution status, Biotic community, Heavy Metals.

* Vice President, Society for Environment, Health, Awareness of Nutrition and Toxicology (SEHAT), 1775, Sohan Ganj, Near Clock Tower, Delhi - 110 007, India.

Antarctica Laboratory, R&D Division, Shriram Institute for Industrial Research, 19, University Road, Delhi - 110 007, India.

INTRODUCTION

Water is a resource circulated throughout all ecosystems and is one of the most important factors of them (Odum 1971). From the point of view of ecohydrology, for the main elements of an ecosystem including inorganic and organic compound, producers and consumers both the quantity and the chemistry of water have a decisive impact on its biomass and biotic composition. Information obtained form current hydro-chemical analyses of water specimens is very important but it is sometimes difficult to Gauge the overall situation especially the occurrence of nutrient, which may be very important to an ecosystem (Malik and Bharti, 2005a). Ecological, geo-chemical and hydrological research has been carried out in various ecosystems to understand the factors controlling the chemistry of natural water (Baron and Bricker, 1990; Malik and Bharti, 2005a). Many of such studies have been under taken during the last two decades to understand the processes that control the hydrochemistry of alpine and sub-alpine systems of North America and Europe (William *et al.* 1993 and Psenner, 1989). Similar studies were also done in China and central Asia (Xue and Schnoor, 1994).

Indian mountains are the cradle of a large number of streams and mighty rivers. In North-East region and very close to Bangladesh border, a hill-stream Umiam, 90 Km., far away from Shillong city is the study site for the accounting of physico-chemical parameters and Heavy Metals in natural water and fluctuations at the different locations along with the stream. Adequate understanding of the North-East regional streams is extremely important for the development of a realistic programme for utilizing the potential of water that exist in the form of hidden water resource in the area. The impact of anthropogenic pollution from industrial, agricultural, sources, quarrying and tourists activity on water quality has concerned environmentalists and scientists for the past three decades.

The present study reveals to characteristics the water nutrient chemistry, influenced by anthropogenic activity and quarrying of the geologically sedimental environments and to determine the nature and degree of anthropogenic impacts on qualitative and quantitative variations occurred in nutrients in relation to physico-chemical parameters and Heavy Metals of stream water.

Study Area

The seven states of North East India are quite famous as Seven Sisters, and Meghalaya is very well known for the record of rainfall, the state consists of the two places namely: Cherrepunjee and Mawsinram for maximum rainfall throughout the year. So, the maximum water resources are depending chiefly on total precipitations of the region. The Meghalaya has been surrounded by the natural beauties with lovely trees and cool climate, which is not only a pleasant place to live in but relaxing for holiday also. This is not only a popular state but also valuable or important place for tourism, Shillong is the capital of Meghalaya state. Mowlong Cherra Cement Ltd., and Lafarge Umiam Mining Ltd., are the major industries of the region.

Umiam river originated from the hills of Assam-Meghalaya basically. Upstream of Umiam is near village Dissong and Downstream near Village Pyrkan. The water of Umiam is very useful for the local people. Population of the region is completely depending upon the river water for drinking, bathing, and other activities. *Geologically,* North-east hills are enriched with various minerals and the hills near Bangladesh are rich in limestone. *Geographically*, the study area is situated in the globe on a Latitude 25° 11' 40.8" N and Longitude 91° 38' 16.4" E for Upstream site and Latitude 25° 10' 43.8" N and Longitude 91° 38' 19.2" E for Downstream site. *Meteorologically*, region has a cool and pleasant climate.

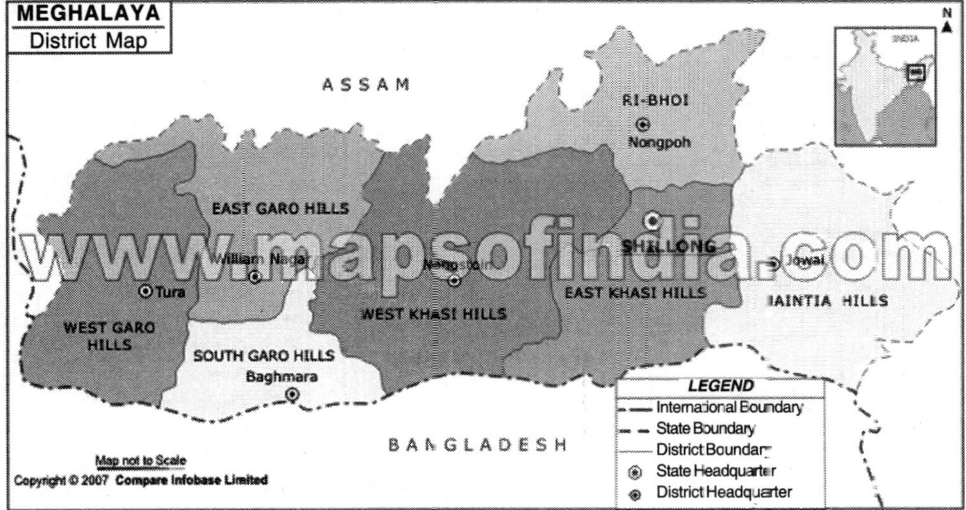

Fig. 1.1: **District map of Meghalaya**

Materials and Methods

The water samples were collected from Umiam River upstream (U/S sampling site A) Near Disong village and downstream (D/S sampling site B) near Shella Bazar according to the analytical requirement in morning period 9:00 Hrs. to 10:00 Hrs.

The samples for physico-chemical parameters and Heavy Metals were collected by using rinsed Borosil glassware, and analyzed with the help of the procedure described by APHA (1995) and Trivedi and Goel (1984). Colour, odour, turbidity, velocity, temperature and Dissolved oxygen were analysed on sampling sites. Samples were collected from selected sites and immediately preserved in ice boxes, and transfer to the lab for further analysis. Water samples were digested and Heavy Metals were detected using Atomic absorption spectrophotometer. The study of biotic community of Umiam river was carried out with the help of Schwoerbel (1991), Santhanam, *et al.* (1989). The macro-benthic biota and Plankton were identified with the help of Edmondson (1959).

Fig. 1.2: **Map of District East Khasi Hills**

Results and Discussion

Umiam river is flowing throughout a valley of North-east hills chain near the Bangladesh Border, enriched with limestone and lignite rocks, which affect the water quality of stream according to the locations. Nutrients concentration, Heavy Metals and related physico-chemical parameters from selected sites are depicted in Tables 1.1 to 1.4.

Table 1.1: Physical characteristics of Umiam river water

S. N.	Parameters	Unit	Umiam Upstream			Umiam Downstream			Desirable Limit
			Winter	Summer	Monsoon	Winter	Summer	Monsoon	
1.	Temperature	°C	13	17	16	12	18	15	-
2.	Colour	-	Clear	Clear	Clear	Clear	Clear	Clear	-
3.	Odour	-	Nil	Nil	Nil	Nil	Nil	Nil	-
4.	Turbidity	NTU	2	3	8	3	1	5	5
5.	Velocity	m/s	0.2	0.2	0.3	0.1	0.1	0.3	-
6.	TDS	Mg/l	41	43	48	46	48	55	500

Table 1.2: Chemical characteristics of Umiam river water

S. N.	Parameters	Unit	Umiam Upstream			Umiam Downstream			Desirable Limit
			Winter	Summer	Monsoon	Winter	Summer	Monsoon	
1.	pH	-	7.1	6.9	7.4	6.3	7.5	7.3	6.5-8.5
2.	Alkalinity	Mg/l	22	25	30	28	32	28	200
3.	Total Hardness	Mg/l	22	34	26	42	32	24	300
4.	Calcium	Mg/l	8	10	8	12	14	8	75
5.	Magnesium	Mg/l	1	3	4	1	3	2	30
6.	Chlorides	Mg/l	7	6	6	10	5	7	250
7.	DO	Mg/l	10.4	11.0	9.5	10.5	10.6	9.2	-
8.	BOD	Mg/l	Nil	Nil	Nil	Nil	Nil	Nil	-
9.	COD	Mg/l	4	3	5	6	5	6	-

Table 1.3: Heavy Metals in Umiam river water

S. N.	Parameters	Unit	Umiam Upstream			Umiam Downstream			Desirable Limit
			Winter	Summer	Monsoon	Winter	Summer	Monsoon	
1.	Cadmium	Mg/l	BDL	BDL	BDL	BDL	BDL	BDL	0.01
2.	Copper	Mg/l	BDL	BDL	BDL	0.01	BDL	0.01	0.05
3.	Iron	Mg/l	0.06	0.08	0.09	0.06	0.02	BDL	0.3
4.	Lead	Mg/l	0.01	0.02	BDL	BDL	BDL	BDL	0.05
5.	Manganese	Mg/l	BDL	0.03	0.01	BDL	BDL	BDL	0.1
6.	Zinc	Mg/l	BDL	0.03	0.03	0.07	0.05	BDL	5.0

Table 1.4: Pre-liminary study of Biotic communities in Umiam river

Category	Family/Phylum	Genus/Species
Neuston	**Arthopods**	*Mayfly nymph, Water spider*
Plankton	**Phytoplankton:** Chorophyceae- Bacillariophyceae- Rhodophyceae- Cyanophyceae- **Zooplankton:** Protozoans- Coelentrata-	*Volvox, Chlorella, Ulothrix, Vaucheria, Zygnema, Diatoms* *Batrachospermum* *Rivularia, Nostoc* *Vorticalla, Paramoecium, Amoeba, Chrysamocha Volvox, Cyclopes,* *Hydra, Ceratella*
Necton	Amphebia- Piscies -	*Rana* *Schizothorax richardsonii (Gray)-Asella* *Barilius barila (Ham.)*
Benthos	Macroinvertibrate- Annelida-	*Snails, Beetles, Sepia* *Pheretima, Leeches, Flatworms,*
Aquatic macrophytes	Bryophyta- Rannunculaceae-	*Moss, Fern, Weedy rooted aquatic herbs* *Rannunculus*

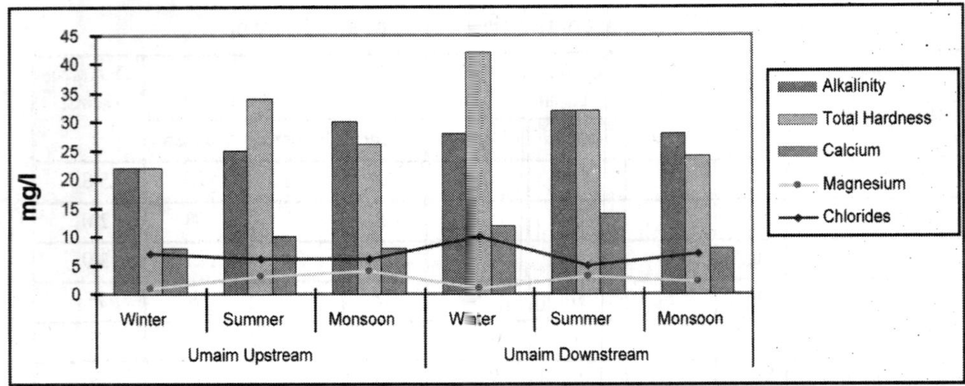

Fig. 1.3: **Showing the nutrients concentration in Umiam river during the study period**

Umiam river has the spatio-temporal variations of water temperature, which plays a vital role in all physico-biochemical reactions and self-purification power of aquatic system (Badola and Singh, 1981). Higher value of temperature was found 18ºC in summer at downstream and minimum 12ºC in winter season at downstream. Turbidity is striking characteristic of the physical status of the water bodies. Although in Umiam river water is clear because there is no more pollution, siltation was the main source of turbidity in tributaries. Detritus and other non-organic material being added to water mass due to rainfall and anthropogenic activities (Camron, 1996). Maximum turbidity was recorded 8 NTU during rainy season at upstream and minimum 1 NTU in summer season at downstream. The maximum depth of photic zone provides the better biological production for all aquatic organisms especially phytoplankton (Malik and Bharti, 2005b).

Total dissolved solids were found in the range of 41 mg/l in to 55 mg/l in monsoon season, due to the gradual increases in velocity of river which favoured effective sedimentation (Subramanian, 1979). Chemical oxygen demand (3-6 mg/l) represents chemically oxidizable organic matter load in water, while biochemical oxygen demand is only biodegradable materials (Malik and Bharti, 2005c). In the present study the values observed during monsoon months may be attributed maximum biological activities and high temperature, stimulate the growth of microorganisms (William *et al.* 1993).

The pH of natural water was controlled in a great extent by the interaction of hydroxyl ions arising from the hydrolysis of bicarbonate (Sharma, 1986). The pH of Umiam river was recorded slightly alkaline (6.8-7.5). Total hardness is mainly due to percentage of calcium and magnesium salts of bicarbonates, carbonates, sulphates and chlorides, while the value of alkalinity occured due to presence of bicarbonates. The highest concentration of hardness was analysed 22-32 mg/l during the study. Alkalinity was also found 22-42 mg/l with a small fluctuation. A positive relationship between hardness and alkalinity was recorded in river Ganga at Rishikesh (Chopra and Patric, 1994).

Maximum chloride concentration was recorded (10 mg/l) in winter and minimum in summer (5 mg/l). Chloride and hardness showed a positive relationship to one another (Chopra and Patric, 1994). Chloride was found in the form of chloride ion, and one of the major inorganic anion present in natural water (Malik and Bharti, 2009).

Calcium and magnesium the dominant cations, and these represent the main weathering products, but significant hydro-chemical differences between the two sampling sites associated with the bedrock geology exist (Jenkins *et al*. 1995) Calcium is one of the essential nutrients, which plays an important role in biological system. Maximum calcium concentration was recorded (14 mg/l) in summer and minimum in monsoon (8 mg/l). Positive relationship between, calcium and temperature was also reported by Khanna and Singh (2000) in river Suswa, Dehradun. Magnesium is also an essential element but it is toxic at higher concentration. The concentration of magnesium in Umiam river was found maximum (4 mg/l) and minimum (1 mg/l) and it was very low in comparison to Hill-streams of Uttarakhand (Bharti, 2004).

During the summer season nutrients concentration in rivers and hill-streams became more. Miller *et al.* (1997) described the nutrients availability in selected environmental settings of the Potomac River and Cameron (1996) showed the similar type of fluctuation in Fraser river of British Columbia. Bond (1979) described similar nutrients concentration pattern in a stream draining a mountain ecosystem in Utah.

Heavy Metals like: Cadmium, copper, iron, manganese, lead and zinc were not found in high concentration at both sites during any season. Cadmium was absolutely absent in all seasons, while copper, lead and manganese concentrations were also found below detection limit in maximum samples. The concentration of iron was maximum observed 0.09 mg/l during monsoon season. Manganese was found maximum 0.03 mg/l in summer and zinc concentration was 0.07 mg/l in monsoon season. Malik *et al.* (2009) described the role of Heavy Metals in the surface water of north India. The results of Bharti *et al.* (2010) were also indicated the relation of Heavy Metals and phytoplankton in a north Indian water body.

The concentrations of Calcium and Magnesium were observed in very low range in Umiam river water at upstream as well as downstream in comparison to rivers and hill-streams of North India. Dissolved oxygen was found 9.2 to 11.0 mg/l at upstream and downstream during the study period. Heavy Metals were found almost nil or in very low concentrations at both selected site. The present study deals with the preliminary physico-chemical characteristics of the river water and exhibits the natural quality of water with minimum anthropogenic activities, which contribute in pollution load of an ecosystem.

The present results conclude that significant differences in river water nutrient concentrations exist among different environmental settings within the two subunits. The environmental setting with the highest potential by more soluble nutrients, fluctuations in nutrient concentrations were the land use and carbonate bedrock that was predominated in the North East valley. The spatial variations in TDS are attributed to climatic and lithological control over the ionic concentrations. Absence or low concentration of Heavy Metals shows that the water is still industrial pollution free. However, the Indian standards are not so strict (Bharti, 2007), but Heavy Metals never cross the limits during the study period. On the basis of nutrients and Heavy Metals, the water may be considered for drinking and other purposes.

The pre-liminary study of biotic community of Umiam ecosystem was also carried out in a lengthy stretch of Umiam basin. The genera, species and their related category are given in Table 1.4 with the scientific names. Rundle, *et al.* (1993) also observed the similar species of biota in the river of Nepal. Plankton of chlorophyceae family was found dominantly in Umiam river ecosystem. Planktons are the primary producers of and aquatic ecosystem (Hynes, 1970). So, ecosystem always balanced by the presence of each and every necessary species of flora and fauna.

REFERENCES

APHA (1995). Standard Methods for Examination of Water and Waste Water. *American Public Health Association, 19th edition.* Inc, New York. pp. 1970.

Badola, S.P. and Singh, H.R. (1981). Hydrobiology of the River Alaknanda of Garhwal Himalaya. *Indian J. Ecol.*, 8(2): 269-276.

Baron, J. and Bricker, O.P. (1990). Hydrological and Chemical flux in Loch Vale Watershed, Rocky Mountain National Park. In: Biogeochemistry of Major Rivers. SCOPE 42. Wiley and Sons, New York, USA.

Bharti, P.K. (2004). Limnobiological Study of Sahastradhara Hill-stream at Dehradun, *M.Sc. Dissertation*, Submitted to Gurukula Kangri University, Hardwar, pp. 102.

Bharti, P.K. (2007). Why Indian Standards are not so Strict?, *Current Science,* 93(9): 1202.

Bharti, P.K., Malik, D.S. and Rashmi Yadav (2010). Influence of Heavy Metals on Abundance of Cyanophyceae Members in Three Spring-fed Lake in Kempty, Dehradun, In: 'Advances in Aquatic Ecology, Vol. III ed. by V.B. Sakhare, Daya Publishing House, New Delhi, pp. 107-111.

Bond, H.B. (1979). Nutrient Concentrations Patterns in a Stream Draining a Montane Ecosystem in Utah. *Ecology.* 60(6): 1184-1196.

Cameron, E.M. (1996). Hydrogeo-chemistry of the Fraser River British Columbia: Seasonal Variation in Major and Minor Components. *J. Hydrol.* 182(1-4): 209-255.

Chopra, A.K. and Patrick, N.J. (1994). Effect of Domestic Sewage on Self-purification of Ganga Water at Rishikesh. *A. Bio. Science.* 13(11): 75-82.

Edmondson, W.T. (1959). Fresh Water Biology - Rotifera, 2nd edition, Wiley and Sons, New York, pp. 420-484.

Hynes, H.B.N. (1970). The Ecology of Running Waters. *Liverpool University Press, Liverpool, 4th Impression*: 1-555.

Jenkins, A., Sloan W.T. and Cosby, B.J. (1995). Stream Chemistry is the Middle Hills and High Mountain of the Himalaya, Nepal. *Journal of Hydrology.* Vol. 166, No. 1-4: 61-79.

Khanna, D.R and Singh. R.K. (2000). Seasonal Fluctuations in the Plankton of Suswa River at Raiwala Dehradun. *Env. Conservations J.* 1(2 and 3): 89-92.

Malik, D.S. and Bharti, P.K. (2005b). Fluctuation in Planktonic Population of Sahastradhara Hill-stream at Dehradun (Uttaranchal), *Aquacult.* 6 (2): 191-198.

Malik, D.S. and Bharti, P.K. (2005c): Primary Production Efficiency of Sahstrachara Hill-stream, Dehradun, *Env. Cons. J.* 6 (3): 117-121.

Malik, D.S. and Bharti, P.K. (2009). Ecology of Sahastradhara Hill-stream at Dehradun (Uttaranchal), In: 'Advances in Aquatic Ecology, Vol. I ed. by V.B. Sakhare, Daya Publishing House, New Delhi, pp. 1-11.

Malik, D.S. and Bharti, P.K., Negi, K.S. and Rashmi Yadav (2009). Distribution of Metals in Water of an Artificial Lake at Mussoorie, Uttarakhand, In: 'Aquatic Biology and Aquaculture' edited by V.B. Sakhare, Ambajoagi, MS, *Manglam Publication,* New Delhi, pp. 77-95.

Malik, D.S. and Bharti, Pawan K. (2005a). Nutrient Dynamics in Rhithron zone of Shivalik Himalayan Stream Sahastradhara, Dehradun (Uttaranchal), *Env. Cons. J.* 6 (2): 63-68.

Miller, C.V.; Denis, J.M.; Ator, S.W. and Brakebill, J.W. (1997). Nutrients in Stream during Baseflow in Selected Environmental Settings of the Potomac River Basin. *J. American Wat. Resources Association.* 33(6): 1155-1171.

Odum, E.P. (1971). Fundamentals of Ecology. New York. W. B. *Saunders and Co.* pp. 1-344.

Psenner, R. (1989). Chemistry of High Mountain Lakes in Siliceous Catchments of Central Alps. *Aquatic Sci.* 51: 108-128.

Rundle, S.D., Jenkins, A. and Ormerod, S.J., (1993). Macro Invertebrate Communities in Streams in the Himalyas, Nepal. *Freshwater Biol.* 30: 169-180.

Santhanam, R.; Velayntham, P. and Jegatheesan, G; (1989). A Manual of Freshwater Ecology. Daya Publishing House Delhi, 3-17, 53-92.

Schwoerbel, J. (1991). 'Handbook of Limnology', *Ellis Horwood Limited, Chichester, England:* pp. 95-114.

Shrama, R.C. (1986). Effect of Physico-chemical Factors on Benthic fauna of Bhagirathi River Garhwal Himalaya. *Indian. J. Ecol.* 13(1): 133-137.

Subramanian, V. (1979). Chemical and Suspended Sediment Characteristics of River of India. *J. Hydrol,* 44: 37-55.

Trivedi, R.K. and Goel, P.K. (1984). Chemical and Biological Methods for Water Pollution Studies. Karad. Environmental Publication. pp. 1-25.

William, M.W., Brown, A. and Melack, J.M. (1993). Geochemical and Hydrologic Controls on the Composition of Surface Water in the High Elevation Basin, *Sierra Navada. Limnol. Oceanogr,* 38: 775-797.

Xue, H.B. and Schooner, J.L. (1994) Acid Deposition and Lake Chemistry in Southwest China. *Wat. Air, Soil Pollut.* 75: 61-78.

Pages 10-29

WATER RESOURCES: MAPPING, MONITORING AND MANAGEMENT
***Edited by*: Dr. Pawan Kumar Tyagi; Dr. Avnish Chauhan & Dr. Pawan Kumar Bharti**
***Edition* : 2017**
ISBN : 978-93-5056-861-3
***Published by* : Discovery Publishing House Pvt. Ltd., New Delhi (India)**

Sustainable Groundwater Management in Drought Prone Bonai Sub-division of Sundargarh District, Orissa, India

Pramod Chandra Sahu

ABSTRACT

Bonai sub-division of Sundargarh district is one of the most economically backward area of the state Orissa. The area experiences drought frequently because of erratic nature of rainfall over space and time. The agricultural lands which are mostly rainfed bear adverse effects of drought resulting in loss of crop. Rainfed agriculture is risk-prone and characterised by low productivity and low input usage. The bulk of the rural poor of the study area live in the rainfed regions. There is a need to transform rainfed farming into more sustainable and productive systems and so support the rural mass in a better way. Groundwater in the study area occurs primarily in four different aquifer systems such as: (i) weathered mantle, (ii) saprolitic zone, (iii) fractured zone and (iv) alluvial zone. The maximum thickness of the weathered mantle in the area is 20m where groundwater occurs in unconfined conditions and mostly developed by dug wells.

The groundwater resource estimation of the area (block-wise) has been calculated for the year 2015 using water table fluctuation method recommended by the Groundwater Estimation Committee (GEC-1997). According to the study, the net annual utilisable groundwater resources of Bonai, Gurundia, Koira and Lahunipada blocks are 3524.23 HM, 3935.15 HM, 3557.37 HM and 5245.66 HM respectively. The net groundwater draft of Bonai, Gurundia, Koira and Lahunipada blocks are 252.70 HM, 301.00 HM 114.10 HM and 227.50 HM respectively. The stage of development of groundwater in Bonai, Gurundia, Koira and Lahunipada blocks are

Reader in Geology, MPC Autonomous College, Baripada, Mayurbhanj Dist., Odisha 757 003, India.

7.17 per cent, 7.65 per cent, 3.20 per cent and 4.34 per cent respectively. All the blocks come under White/Safe category. From the groundwater estimation of the study area, it is evident that there exists a vast scope for its development to enhance irrigation potential, and for rural water supply. The most suitable planning for the assured source of water supply round the year can be achieved by different types of groundwater structures like: dug wells, dug cum bore wells and bore wells in favourable sites. Artificial recharge techniques play a major role for conservation of groundwater. Suitable sites for specific water harvesting structures/artificial recharge structures such as: percolation tank, check dam, gully plugs have been demarcated.

Keywords: Groundwater, Aquifer, Sustainable development, Artificial recharge, Resource estimation and budgeting.

INTRODUCTION

Water plays an extremely important role in man's life not only because it is indispensable for sustenance of life but also it determines the quality of life. The demand of water for various uses such as: drinking, irrigation and industries is increasing with time. The demand of water has been estimated to grow by as much as 100 per cent within the next two decades. The Bonai subdivision of Sundargarh district is one of the most economically backward area of the state Orissa. The economy of the area is basically agrarian. As the development of agrarian economy demands stabilised agriculture and crop insurance against natural calamities like drought; the expansion of agriculture is inevitable and groundwater can take vital part in expanding irrigational facilities. Besides, in coming years groundwater has also to cater substantially to the rural and urban drinking water supply and industrial requirement as a safe and sustainable source. Groundwater plays an important role in economic development of the district in the backdrop of ever-increasing population. A consensus is growing among scientists, water planners, government and civil societies to adopt new policies and approaches within next two decades to avoid water stress in all sphere of human development.

The study area lies in the northern part of Orissa is underlain by hard crystalline rocks of Precambrian age with very limited occurrence of alluvium and laterite. The area experiences drought frequently because of erratic nature of rainfall over space and time. Statistical analysis of rainfall data suggests that mild to normal drought is common in this area. The agricultural land which are mostly rainfed bear the adverse effects of drought resulting in loss of crop. Surface water irrigation is limited and not dependable due to vagaries of monsoon rainfall. Hence, there is a need of groundwater exploitation to save the crop and to provide safe drinking water. Besides, there is also the need of increasing crop yield by covering more areas under irrigation by groundwater exploitation. Keeping the above facts in view an attempt has been made in the present work to collect all the data, to analyze it systematically and to prepare a plan for sustainable development and management of ground water in the Bonai subdivision of Sundargarh district, which suffers from acute water crisis during summer.

Methodology

All the available data on geology, hydrogeology, rainfall, population, agriculture and other related data were collected from different agencies/publications and were suitably processed. Topographic maps of Survey of India and district planning map were used. The different thematic maps on lithology, drainage and geomorphology generated from satellite data were used. Well inventory data were collected and section of existing dug wells were examined during field work. Electrical Resistivity Method (VES) has been employed to understand the gross aquifer condition in the area. Ground water pollution potential study adopting DRASTIC Model (Aller *et al.* 1987) has been used. Water samples are collected and analysed.

Ground Water Estimation and Budgeting has been worked out employing guidelines prescribed by the Ground Estimation Committee (GEC-1997. In this method, the thickness of aquifer (T) is determined based on water table fluctuation recorded from the observation wells. Specific yield(s) of each aquifer/formation is taken from the pumping test data. By multiplying the aquifer thickness (T) with specific yield(s) and rechargeable area (A), the gross ground water is worked out. For the calculation of rechargeable area (A), satellite data have been used. In the present study, data of the hydro geo-morphological map prepared from IRS-IA (LISS II) have been used. The stage of groundwater development is calculated by using the following formulae.

$$\text{Stage of Ground water development} = \frac{\text{Net groundwater draft} \times 100}{\text{Net utilisable groundwater resources}}$$

Table 2.1: Yield potential of different litho-units

Sl. No.	Litho-units	Depth Range of Saturated Fracture (mbgl)	No. of Saturated Fractures Occurring at different Depth Ranges				Yield (lps)	
			Up to 60 m depth	60-100 m depth	100-150 m depth	150-200m 200 depth	Range	Avg.
1.	Granitic rocks	11-200.0	1 to 3 sets, very common	Mostly 1 set very common	Mostly 1 Set less common	1 set, only in one well	Negligible -20	3-10
2.	Mica schist	3.2-178.9	1 to 4 sets very common	1 set less frequent	1 set less frequent	—	Negligible -11	1-2
3.	Phyllite	18-99.5	1 to 4 sets very common	1 set very rare	—	—	Negligible -8	1-2
4.	Basic meta-volcanics	19-87	1 to 4 sets common	1 to 2 sets	—	—	2-12	3-5

Study area Profile

The study area occupies the eastern part of the Sundargarh district, lying towards the northern extremity of Orissa. It is bounded by the north latitudes 21°35' – 22°10' and east longitudes 84°30' – 85°25' and falls in the Survey of India Toposheet Nos. 73B/12, 73B/16, 73C/9, 73C/10, 73C/13, 73C/14, 73F/4, 73G/1, 73G/2 and 73G/5. It is delimited by the state of Jharkhand in the northeast, Keonjhar district of Orissa in the east, Deogarh and Angul districts in the south, Sambalpur district in the west and Panposh subdivision of Sundargarh district in the north. The total geographical area of the study area is around 2200 sq.km. The Bonai subdivision is divided into four administrative blocks namely: *(i)* Bonai, *(ii)* Gurundia, *(iii)* Koira and *(iv)* Lahunipada. According to 2011 census, the total population of the area is 276,792. The area enjoys a sub-tropical climate with very hot summer (46°C). The average annual rainfall is 1648mm. The area experiences mild to normal drought frequently because of erratic nature of rainfall over space and time. The water scarcity is chronic during summer season. Physiographically the area is marked by hills with intervening narrow intermontane valleys, isolated hillocks and flat to gentle undulating plains. River Brahmani forms the major drainage of the area. The drainage pattern is dendritic. The most common soil types in the area are Alfisols and Ultisols. The total cultivable and cultivated area are 71,585 hect., and 54,784 hect., respectively. While paddy in the principal crop, the other crops grown are: maize, mustard, Jowar, sugarcane, wheat, groundnut, blackgram, biri, arhar and other pulses. Opencast mining activities for iron and manganese ores and bauxite are restricted to Koira block only.

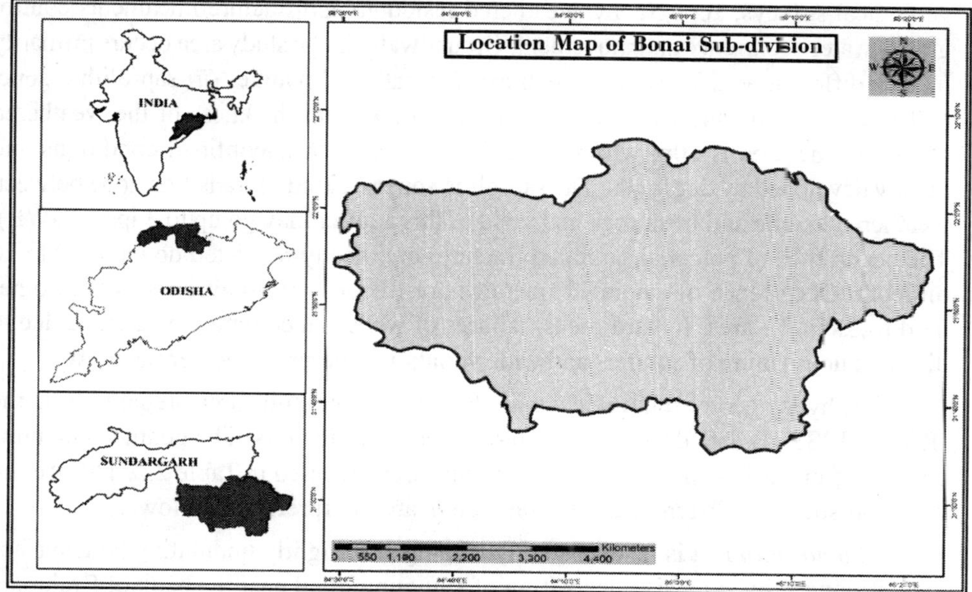

Fig. 2.1: **Location map of the study area**

The area is underlain by crystalline rocks of Iron Ore Group (IOG), Darjing Group, Deogarh Group and Bonai Granite (Mahalik, 1998). The lithological assemblage comprises of Banded Hematite Quartzite (BHQ), Banded Hematite Jasper (BHJ), Quartzite, Phyllite, Slate, Mica-Schist, Staurolite-Schists and Granite, which are intruded by dolerite dykes. These rocks are intensely folded, fractured and have been weathered to varying degree at different places. The occurrence and movement of groundwater depends mainly on secondary porosity The dolerite dykes form barrier for movement of groundwater resulting in compartmentalization of the groundwater regime. The weathered and fractured dykes at places serve as potential site for groundwater occurrence. Laterite and alluvium occur as small patches in the area. Lateritic soils of considerable thickness is a good repository of groundwater due to their high porosity and permeability. The groundwater potential of alluvium is very good.

Results and Discussions

Groundwater management requires an indepth understanding of the hydro geological set-up and also technically sound plans for groundwater development along with periodical monitoring of the groundwater regime against over-exploitation and quality deterioration through contamination. The sustainable groundwater development in the study area requires scientific management in the fields of resource location, estimation and budgeting, development, conservation and protection.

Groundwater Resource Location

The study area is characterised by varied hydro geological set-up. The hydro geological framework has been revealed through deep exploration combined with hydro geological surveys. Topography, weathered residuum and fracture lineaments control groundwater occurrence and movement. Groundwater in the study area occurs primarily in four different aquifer systems such as: *(i)* weathered mantle, *(ii)* saprolithic zone, *(iii)* fractured zone and *(iv)* alluvial zone. The maximum thickness of the weathered mantle in the area is 20m where groundwater occurs in unconfined conditions and mostly developed by dug wells. The saprolitic zone is a kind of transition zone between weathered mantle and fresh rock and yield of this aquifer may go up to 3 lps (CGWB). The occurrence of potential saturated fractures are mostly restricted down to 60 to 70 m depth. Occurrence of saturated fractures are frequent in granitic rocks than other hard rocks in the area. In hard rocks, failures of wells is a common experience due to discontinuous nature of aquifers and wide variation in porosity and permeability.

The hydro-geomorphological map (Fig. 2.2) of the study area prepared from the IRS-IA (LISS-II) data depicts the different geomorphic units. The geomorphic units developed on various litho-stratigraphic units are presented in Table 2.2. The ground water prospects of different geomorphic units are interpreted as follows:

- *Alluvial Plain:* It is level or gently sloping and slightly undulating land surface produced by extensive deposition of alluvium found near the bank of Brahmani river. The ground water potential is good to excellent which can be tapped through dug well.

- *Weathered Pediplain*: These units are characterized by the presence of relatively thicker weathered material. Depending upon the depth of weathered materials, these are broadly classified as shallow (up to 5m), moderate (5-20m) and deep (>20m). This hydro-geomorphic units are mostly developed upon Bonai Granite and rarely over the metasediments of Darjing group. Most of the area under this unit are agricultural land. Depending upon the thickness of the weathered zone, the ground water potential is moderate to good and important for construction of dug well and dug-cum-bore well.
- *Pediment:* It is gently sloping rocky surface with or without a thin veneer of soil cover. Part of Bonai and Gurundia blocks come under this unit. The area under this unit is generally considered to be the poor ground water potential zone. The presence of fractures represented by lineaments over pediment indicate some ground water potentiality.
- *Intermontane Valley:* These are almost flat valleys surrounded by hills all around and mostly observed in Koira and Gurundia blocks. Owing to their position, these units are highly favourable loci for ground water occurrence and important for dug well.
- *Inselbergs:* These are isolated hill made up of quartizite of Deogarh Group with limited areal extension surrounded by plain land all around, observed in Bonai block. Ground water potential is very poor in these units.
- *Structural Hills:* These are group of curvilinear folded hill ranges. Compositionally these hills consist of Banded Iron Formation (BIF) in Koira block and metasediments in Gurundia block. They act as runoff zone with poor recharge condition.
- *Residual Hills*: Residual hills of Quartzite are found in the central part of the area. They act as runoff zone and ground water potential is very poor.
- *Denudational Hills*: These are massive hill ranges interspersed with intermontane valley. They also act as runoff.
- *Lineament*: The lineament of the study area unfolds the fact that fractures control the movement and storage of ground water in the area. Lineaments of NE-SW, N-S, NW-SE and E-W trend are observed in the area. However, the NE-SW trending lineament are dominant over the study area. The 'ground truthing' studies reveal that better yields are found from the area in the vicinity of NE-SW trending lineament. (Sahu and Sahoo, 2006) It is also marked that the areas of intersection points of lineaments in pediplains, intermontane valleys, pediments and alluvial plains area to be considered during selection of well sites because such locations have good ground water potentialities.
- *Interpretation of Resistivity data*: On the basis of resistivity survey, 4 or 5 geo-electrical sub-surface layers set-up is found in the study area. These layers are top soil, highly weathered zone, semi-weathered zone, fractured zone and bedrock. In has also been marked that in some cases the semi-weathered and fractured zones are not distinguished clearly from each other because of similarity in resistivity values. The correlation of lithology with resistivity values is presented in the Table 2.3.

Table 2.2: Hydro Geomorphic units vis-a-vis Lithostratigraphy of the study area

Map Unit	Geomorphic Unit	Litho-Stratigraphic Unit	Description
AP_8	Alluvial Plain	Alluvium (Sand, Silt and Clays)	A level or gently sloping, slightly undulating land surface produced by extensive deposition of alluvium
SH_5	Structural Hill	Darjing Group (Quartzite, Phyllite and Schist)	Liner to arcuate hills showing definite trend line.
IV_5	Intermontane Valley	Darjing Group (Quartzite, Phyllite and Schist)	Linear to curvilinear valleys occurring within the hills The depression generally filled with colluval deposits
$BPPS_5$	Shallow Weathered Buried Pediplain	Darjing Group (Quartzite, Phyllite and Schist)	Flat terrain with shallow overburden. Extensive occur-ence of buried pediment forms this unit
DH_4	Denudational Hill	Bonai Granite	Relict hills which have undergone the process of denudation
RH_4	Residual Hill	Bonai Granite	Isolated hill, surrounded by plains on all sides
P_4	Pediment	Bonai Granite	Broad, gently sloping rock floor, erosional surface of low relief
BP_4	Buried Pediment	Bonai Granite	Gently sloping rock floor covered with thick unconsolidated sediments
$BPPD_4$	Deeply Weathered Buried Pediplain	Bonai Granite	Flat terrain with 15-20 m thick overburden
SH_3	Structural Hill	Iron Ore Group (BHQ, BHJ, Phyllite, Quartzite, Lava, Conglomerate)	Linear to arcuate hills showing define trend lines
DH_3	Denudational Hill	Iron Ore Group (BHQ, BHJ, Phyllite, Quartzite, Lava, Conglomerate)	Relict hills which have undergone the process of denudation generally expressing themselves as barren, rocky and steep sided
IV_3	Intermontane Valley	Iron Ore Group (BHQ, BHJ, Phyllite, Quartzite, Lava, Conglomerate)	A linear or curvilinear depression valley within the hills, filled with colluvial deposits of IOG sediments
$BPPS_3$	Shallow Weathered Buried Pediplain	Iron Ore Group (BHQ, BHJ, Phyllite, Quartzite, Lava, Conglomerate)	A flat, slightly undulating land surface with shallow overburden.
SH_2	Structural Hill	Deogarh Group (Quartzite and Schist)	Linear to arcuate hills showing definite trend lines
SH_2	Structural Hill	Deogarh Group (Quartzite and Schist)	Linear to arcuate hills showing definite trend lines
P_2	Pediment	Deogarh Group (Quartzite and schist with BIF)	Gently sloping rock floor, erosional surface of low relief covered with thin veneer of detritus

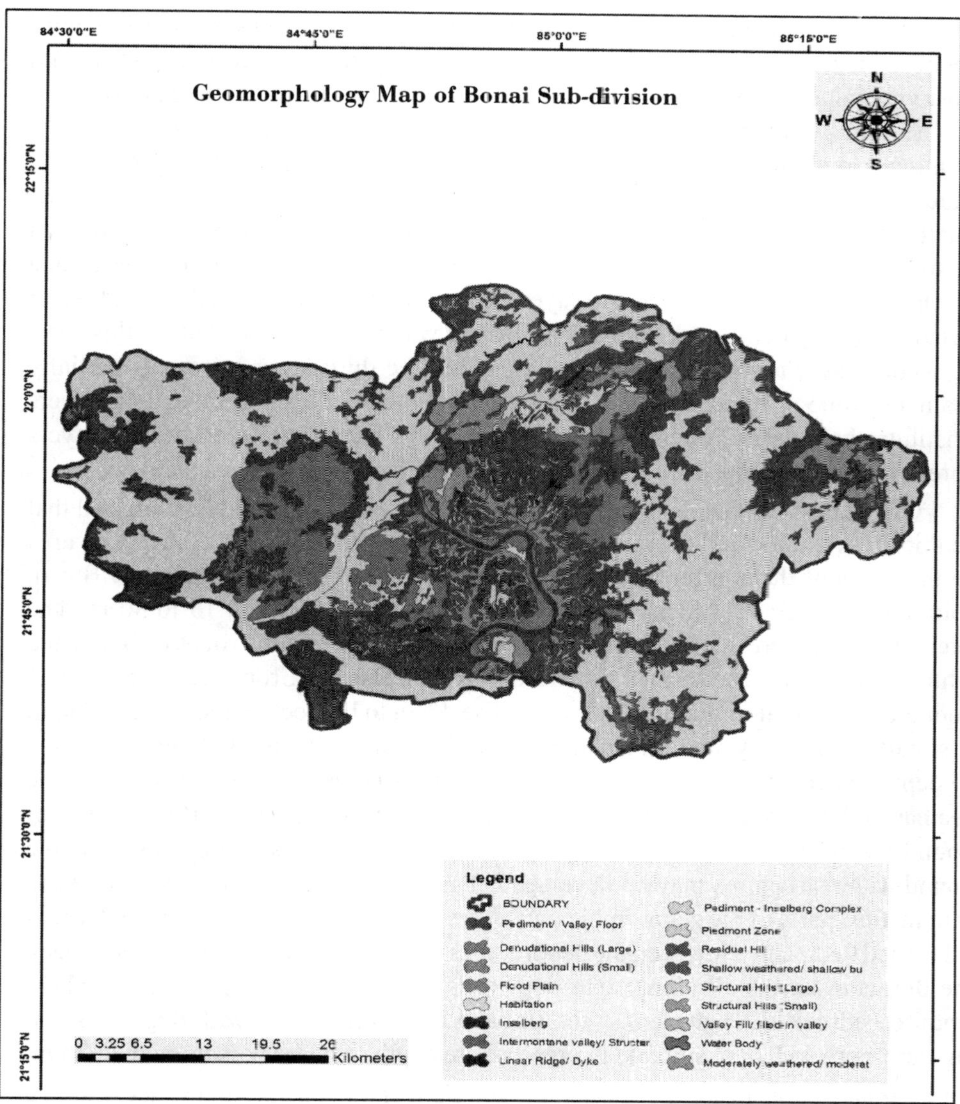

Fig. 2.2: **Geomorphology map of the study area**

Table 2.3: Cor-relation of lithology with resistivity values

Resistivity range (ohm – m)	Probable Lithology
9-188	Top soil (clayey sands, sandy loams, lateritic soils)
55-155	Highly weathered zone
156-384	Semi-weathered zone
385-500>	Fractured zone
500	Massive bedrock

The top soil layer of variable nature has resistivity value between 9 to 188 ohm-m whose maximum thickness is 4.5 m. The highly weathered layer in identified with resistivity value ranging from 55 to 155 ohm-m having a maximum thickness of 19.5 m. The semi-weathered zone is indicated by resistivety value 156 to 384 ohm-m having a maximum thickness of 25m. The fractured zone is indicated by resistivity value 385 to 500 ohm-m. The hard rock layer shows very high resistivity value, usually greater than 500 ohm-m indicating devoid of water. However, the prominent fracture zones are restricted within a depth of 60 to 70m below the ground level. In a four layered case, the 2nd and 3rd layers are interpreted as potential ground water horizons from which a good amount of ground water can be extracted. In this case, the second layer represents weathered zone and the third layer represents partially weathered zone or fractured zone. In a five layered case, the 2nd, 3rd and 4th layers constitute the aquifer system. In this case the 2nd layer, 3rd layer and 4th layers represent weather zone, semi-weathered zone and fractured zone respectively.

On the basis of geophysical investigation and results obtained it is inferred that the thickness of the aquifer varies from place to place. In most part of the study area the thickness of the aquifer materials is more than 30m. In small patches of Bonai, Koira and Lahunipada block, the thickness of aquifer is between 15 to 30 m. The potential aquifers are confined to weathered and fractured granitic rocks of Bonai and Lahunipada blocks. The aquifer systems of IOG and Darjing Group are relatively less productive than that of the Bonai Granite. The depth to bedrock in more than 30 m in most part of the study area. In small patches of Bonai, Koira and Lahunipada block, the depth to bedrock ranges from 15 to 30m. VES studies in the area reveal that the area has high potentiality for exploitation of ground water through different kinds of ground water structures. Depending upon the depth to massive bedrock, suitable ground water structures may be developed. The depth to bedrock ranges from 30 to 70 m in most parts of the geomorphic units like: Alluvial Plains, Intermontane Valleys and Buried Pediplain. However, the depth to massive bedrock is 15 to 30 m in pediment. The dug-cum-bore well along with dug wells may be constructed in areas where depth to bedrock lies between 15 to 30m and bore wells along with dug wells and dug-cum-bore wells are suitable in areas where depth to bedrock is more than 30 m.

- *Ground water Resource Estimation and Budgeting:* The ground water resource estimation, draft estimation and budgeting (block-wise) for the year 2015 are presented in tabular form (Table 2.4 to 2.9).

Ground Water Potential

The study reveals that the net annual utilisable ground water resource of Bonai, Gurundia, Koira and Lahunipada blocks are: 3,524.23 HM, 3,935.13 HM, 3,557.37 HM and 5,245.66 HM respectively. These findings are in accordance with the findings of Paul and Sahu (2000) who reported that the groundwater potential in the state is high. The maximum annual utilizable ground water resource is in Lahunipada block and minimum is in Bonai block. The net ground water draft of Bonai, Gurundia, Koira and Lahunipada blocks are: 252.70 HM, 301..00 HM. 114.10 HM and 227.50 HM respectively. The maximum ground water draft is in Gurundia block and minimum is in Koira block.

Table 2.4: Groundwater resource estimation and budgeting (Bonai block)

Resource	
1. Gross Groundwater Resource	5034.62 HM
2. Net Utilisable Resource (70% of Gross)	3524.23 HM
DRAFT (Based on well census)	
1. Gross Groundwater Draft (Annual)	361.00 HM
2. Net Groundwater Draft (70% of Gross)	252.70 HM
Groundwater Balance	3271.53 HM
Stage of Development	7.17%
Category	White/Safe
Allocation	
1. Domestic and drinking (10% of balance)	327.15 HM
2. Available for irrigation	2944.38 HM

Table 2.5: Groundwater resource estimation and budgeting (Gurundia Block)

Resource	
1. Gross Groundwater Resource	5621.62 HM
2. Net Utilisable Resource (70% of Gross)	3935.13 HM
DRAFT (Based on well census)	
1. Gross Groundwater Draft (Annual)	430.00m HM
2. Net Groundwater Draft (70% of Gross)	301.00 HM
Groundwater Balance	3634.13 HM
Stage of Development	7.65 %
Category	White/Safe
Allocation	
1. Domestic and drinking (10% of balance)	363.41
2. Available for irrigation	3270.72 HM

Table 2.6: Groundwater resource estimation and budgeting (Koira Block)

Resource	
1. Gross Groundwater Resource	5081.97 HM
2. Net Utilizable Resource (70% of Gross)	3557.37 HM
DRAFT (Based on well census)	
1. Gross Groundwater draft (Annual)	163.00 HM
2. Net Groundwater Draft (70% of Gross)	114.10 HM
Groundwater Balance	3443.27 HM
Stage of Development Category	3.20%
Allocation	White/Safe
1. Domestic and drinking (10% of balance)	344.32 HM
2. Available for irrigation	3098.95 HM

Table 2.7: Groundwater resource estimation and budgeting (Lahunipada Block)

Resource	
1. Grouses Ground water Resource	7493.81 HM
2. Net Utilisable Resource (70% of Gross)	5245.66 HM
DRAFT (Based on well census)	
1. Gross GW Draft (Annual)	325.00 HM
2. Net GW Draft (70% of Gross)	227.50 HM
Groundwater Balance	5018.16 HM
Stage of Development Category	4.34%
Allocation	White/Safe
1. Domestic and drinking (10% of balance)	501.81 HM
2. Available for irrigation	4516.35 HM

The groundwater balance as on December 201 of Bonai, Gurundia, Koira and Lahunipada blocks are: 3,271.53 HM, 3,634.13 HM, 3,443:27 HM and 5,018.16 HM respectively. The total ground water balance of the study area is 15367.09 HM out of which 13830.39 HM can be utilised for additional irrigation purpose. The stage of ground water development of Bonai. Gurundia. Koira and Lahunipada blocks are only 7.17 per cent, 7.65 per cent, 3.20 per cent and 4.34 per cent respectively. All the blocks come under White/Safe categories. The ground water development in the study area is abysmally low which need further development through suitable ground water structure to combat drought.

Prospects for Ground Water Development

As the present level of ground water development in the study area is low (5%) and the total irrigated area from all sources is also very less. The development of balance ground water resources will certainly provide irrigational facility round the year. In the study area, the ground water can be developed through dug wells, dug-cum-bore wells and bore wells. But deep bore wells appear to be advantageous structure for ground water exploitation due to their high yields, and continuous discharge throughout the year and utilisation of deeper storage ground water. In low lying area, the ground water development is feasible through dug wells with depth range 8-10 m. The recommended diameter of the well is 4 to 6 m. Each dug well can have command area of 0.75 to 1 ha. In case of moderately elevated area, ground water can be developed through dug wells and dug-cum-bore wells. In the high land areas, the suitable structures for ground water development are bore wells having a depth range or 50-70 m, since the potential fracture zones are restricted within a depth of 70m. Each bore well can have command area up to 8 ha.

The intensity and spacing of different ground water structures has been worked out basing on the utilisable ground water potential available for each block of the study area. In the Precambrian crystalline areas, optimum spacing between two adjacent wells should be 150 m to 380m and intensity should be 3 to 4 per sq.km., and 11 to 40 per sq.km., for standard dug well with pump set and Tenda respectively. Table 2.8 shows the feasibility of groundwater structures in different geomorphic Units in the study area[13].

Irrigation Potential

The balance ground water resources that can be safely used for irrigation purpose in the area has been estimated to be 13,830 HM. This quantity of ground water can safely sustain installation of 13,830 numbers of additional standard dug wells with pump sets in addition to the existing ground water structures.

Table 2.8: Feasibility of groundwater structures in different geomorphic units

Sl. No.	Geomorphic Units	Type of Structures	Depth Range (m)	Diameter (m)	Yields (lps)	Command Area (Hect)
1.	Low lying Areas	Dug well	8-10	4-6	< 5	0.75-1
2.	Moderately elevated areas	Dug well	10 - 15	4.5 - 6	< 3	0.5-0.75
		Dug-cum-bore well	10-15 (DW)+ 30m (BW)	4.5-6 (DW) 100mm (BW)	Upto 5	1 to 1.5
3.	High land areas	Bore well	50 - 100	150mm	< 10	Upto 8

It has been estimated that a standard dug well with pump set can irrigate an average area of 1.25 ha., for Kharif crops and 0.75 ha., for Rabi crops. Therefore, a total additional area of 17287 ha and 10372 ha., can be irrigated during Kharif and Rabi season respectively. With the ground water development in the Bonai area the cultivable wastelands can be managed scientifically. Table 2.9 shows the block-wise existing groundwater structures and further feasible groundwater structure and additional irrigation potential in the study area.

Table 2.9: Groundwater structure and additional irrigation potential (hect.)

Name of the Block	Existing Groundwater Structure			Further Feasible Groundwater Structure Dug wells with Pump sets	Additional Irrigation Potential (hect.)		
	Dug well with Tenda	Dug well with Pump Sets	Bore wells		Kharif	Rabi	Total
Bonai	613	155	11	2944	3680.00	2208.00	5888
Gurundia	549	263	01	3271	4088.75	2453.25	6542
Koira	287	77	—	3099	3873.75	2324.25	6198
Lahunipada	602	138	03	4516	5645.00	3387.00	9032
Total	2051	633	15	13830	17287.50	10372.50	27660

Groundwater Resource Development

The agriculture in the study area is mostly rainfed which bear the adverse effects of drought resulting in crop loss. Thus, there is a need of groundwater exploitation to save the crop and provide safe drinking water. From the groundwater estimation of the study area, it is evident that there exists a vast scope for its development to enhance irrigation potential, and for rural water supply. The hydrogeological condition of the study area reveals that groundwater occurs under two different systems, *i.e.*, mainly in the top saturated weathered mantle and in the shallow and deep fracture systems. The groundwater abstraction through open wells restricted up to the weathered mantle cannot meet the requirements of the inhabitants throughout the year (particularly in peak summer). The only alternative is to get water from fractured zones through suitable groundwater structures, which may be helpful for the development of the agrarian based poor socio-economic conditions of the people in the study area; because till now only dug/open wells are being utilised for domestic and agricultural purpose. The most suitable planning for the assured source of water supply round the year can be achieved by different types of groundwater structures as discussed below.

- *Dug wells:* Dug wells are most common groundwater structures in the study area as well as in Orissa (Bhuyan, 2000) and are feasible in almost all geological formations. The most favourable sites are the topographic lows, abandoned and buried stream channels and areas in the close vicinity of rivers and streams etc. In such areas, the water table during pre-monsoon vary between 7 and 13 m bgl. Therefore, the depth of the dug well should be within the range of 10-15 m bgl. In such areas centrifugal pumps of 1 to 1.5 HP may be used satisfactorily and each dug well can irrigate about 0.75 to 1 hect of land round the year. In the areas with deep water table, however submersible or eject pumps of 1 to 1.5 HP may be used. The depth of the irrigation dug well generally depends upon the depth of water table, availability of the saturated weathered residuum and crop water requirement during peak summer.
- *Dug-cum-bore wells:* Dug-cum-bore wells are very effective in high land and medium land areas to obtain better yields. A vertical bore of 150 or 100mm diameter may be drilled through the bottom of dug well to tap shallow fracture zones within a depth of 30 to 45 m bgl. The bore may be left uncased barring few meters at the top, which requires to be cased with blank pipe to avoid filling up of the bore and generally the casing rises up to one metre above the bottom of the dug well for the same reason. The depth of the dug well should be from 10 to 15 m bgl with a diameter of 4.5 m to 6m. This structure is suitable for medium and high land areas comprising of granite, schist etc. Submersible or centrifugal pump of 1 to 1.5 HP capacity may be installed in such a well. This type of structure may irrigate 1 to 1.5 hect., of land in summer.
- *Bore wells:* Bore wells are most suitable structures for tapping groundwater from deeper water bearing fractured zones. In the hard rock areas of the study area three to four water bearing fracture zones are encountered within a depth of 100m. Therefore, the maximum depth of such a well in the area should be restricted to 100m depending on the availability of the water bearing fractured zones. Such a well is suitable for areas comprising of granite, granite gneiss and mica schist etc. The diameter of each well should be 150mm for the weathered

zone and 100mm for bedrock zones and the top weathered zone may be cased by blank casing pipes (150mm) leaving the rest of the bore hole open. Submersible pumps with 2 to 5 HP capacity are generally preferred for this well. An energized bore well can irrigate up to 8 hect., of land round the year.

In addition to the above groundwater structures the following factors also need to be considered for a better and sustainable management of the groundwater resources of the study area without causing any adverse effect on natural environment.

- *Change of cropping pattern and cropping intensity:* Since the thickness of aquifers in the study area is variable and irregular, the discharge of the wells tapping such aquifers also vary widely. But the present cropping pattern is largely governed by the factors like: convention, convenience and other socio-economic aspects rather than the water availability and suitability. Wherever discharge from wells is low, farmers should be advised to switch over to crops with less duty (water requirement) like: maize, barley, gram, oilseeds and pulses. Further, conservation of groundwater would facilitate summer cultivation, thereby increasing the cropping intensity of the area.
- *Application of modern irrigation practices:* Modern irrigation methods mainly aim at conserving water and optimising the use of irrigation water. Sprinkler and drip irrigation systems are the latest technological advancement for economic use of water in water-short (water-stress) regions.

Groundwater Resource Conservation and Augmentation

Keeping in view the above facts, rainwater harvesting, groundwater conservation and augmentation are considered to be the only solution to maintain a balance between the annual recharge and discharge. Artificial recharge techniques play a major role for conservation of groundwater. (Raghunath, 1987; Karanath, 1987; Ballukraya, 2001; and Jha, 2000, Sahu 2003, Sahu 2008, Nandi *et al.* 2015). The main source of groundwater recharge is rainfall, which is mostly lost as surface runoff and hence the only alternative to replenish the groundwater is by artificial means.

Groundwater Recharge Zones

Generally artificial recharge means intentional replenishment of water into groundwater bodies. It is a means of augmenting the natural infiltrations of surface water into a groundwater reservoir at a rate that vastly exceeds that of the natural percolation. The following objectives can be achieved through artificial recharge techniques.

1. To prevent decline of the groundwater reserves and to improve groundwater levels and availability.
2. To supplement existing supplies.
3. To improve water quality in aquifers.
4. To check surface runoff during monsoon.
5. To ensure availability of groundwater at specific place and time.

The study area can be grouped into 4 natural groundwater recharge zone based on the porosity, permeability and runoff characteristics of the land. The landforms, lithology, presence of lineaments, slope factor, land use/land cover and surface water bodies available play an important role to infer these natural recharge sites.

Zone 1 – The fracture controlled small valleys filled with unconsolidated sediments, buried pediments with thick weathered zones, intermontane valleys and areas with good vegetative covers in the foothill regions are the zones of good recharge. These areas are very gently sloping and are mostly cultivated land, which help in the retention of surface water.

Zone 2 – This zone occupies the shallow weathered pediplains adjacent to the zone 1, with good concentration of lineaments. The recharge rate is good to moderate.

Zone 3 – This zone represents the higher slope area of buried pediments with scanty vegetation and structural hills traversed by fractures and fissures. The groundwater recharge rate is moderate to low.

Zone 4 – The denudational and residual hills of the study area which have only open and degraded forest cover with steep slope are runoff zones and categorized as zone 4, where the minor fractures are the only linear area through which percolation may take place.

Artificial Recharge

Considering the hydrogeological set-up, natural recharge conditions, groundwater potential, future optimal use of groundwater, soil and slope of the area, prevailing land use and cropping pattern in the study area proposed artificial recharge structures have been proposed. Suitable sites for specific water harvesting structures/artificial recharge structures such as: percolation tank, check dam, gully plugs have been demarcated. Besides these, sites for agriculture-related measures which will aid artificial recharge have also been shown in the map. The construction of artificial recharge structures will not only augment groundwater resources, but also will help in solving geo-environmental problems like land degradation by soil erosion and loss of soil moisture.

Percolation Tank

Percolation tanks are shallow tanks constructed at appropriate places in natural or diverted stream courses and provided with a waste weir to allow excess water to continue its course. The ideal site for construction of percolation tanks are gently slope, terrain of light soils, weathered materials of moderate thickness and fractures zones. However, these tanks need scraping of bottoms once in a year or two depending on the rate of accumulation of fine sediments at the bottom of the tank.

Percolation tank is the most suitable structure for recharging groundwater in the hard rock areas, because in addition to artificial recharge it contributes directly to irrigation from the stored water. Percolation tanks in the study area may be selected at comparatively higher elevations with creation of embankments only on sideways and on downslope sides. The upslope sides should remain open for easy entry of surface runoff water. Within the study area such structures may be constructed around Sarsara, Jhirdapali, Talita, Kello, Kasada, Koira, Ergeda, Kuradihi etc.

Percolation-Cum-Irrigation Tank

The main purpose of this tank is percolation and to hold flow of silt. In addition, the stored water is used for cultivation in the nearby areas through field canals. This type of tank is usually created on the upstream side of first order stream having a good catchment area for sufficient entry of runoff water. Accordingly suitable sites can be selected around the villages Tikayatpali, Sarasara, Kasada, Kantasara, Khandadhar, Lahunipada, Damdhara etc.

Check dam

The purpose of check dam is to reduce runoff velocity, to minimise erosion and to allow percolation of surface water. Sites for check dams have been selected on lower order stream (up to 3rd order) with catchment area of about 40 hect., where the level of groundwater fluctuation is high and slope is moderate. Such structures can be of help around villages Ergeda, S. Balang. Sole, Malda etc.

Subsurface Bund/Artificial Dyke

Artificial subsurface dykes are feasible in hard rock areas in narrow gently sloping valleys where bedrock occurs at shallow depth and valley fills consists of about 4 to 8 m., of pervious materials. Groundwater reservoirs can be created by constructing subsurface dykes across the flow direction of groundwater. Subsurface dykes of 1 to 4 m., height are found to be effective in augmenting the groundwater resources particularly in hard rock areas underlain by fractured aquifers. By keeping the top of the dyke 1 m below the land surface, the riparian rights of the farmers downstream are not violated and water logging or salt accumulation on the upstream side of the dam is prevented (Ahnfors, 1981). The dyke can be constructed with materials like: clays, bitumen, polythene sheets besides bricks and concrete depending on localconditions. Such structures in the study area may be constructed around villages-Dharanidharpali, Kasada, Talita etc.

Contour Bunding

Contour bunding is the construction of small bunds across the slope of the land on a contour. Each contour bund acts as a barrier to the flow of water and check the runoff water, thus contributing a part to recharge of groundwater through water spreading. In the study area suitable sites are in upland and hilly regions of Koira, Gurundia and Lahunipada blocks. The upslope of the cultivated lands may be selected for contour bunding to save the cultivated areas from soil erosions and to facilitate groundwater recharge.

Gully Plugging

In the hard rock areas particularly in plateau regions formation of numerous gullies is a common phenomenon and the study area is not an exception to that. The main cause of formation of such gullies is large-scale deforestation followed by heavy

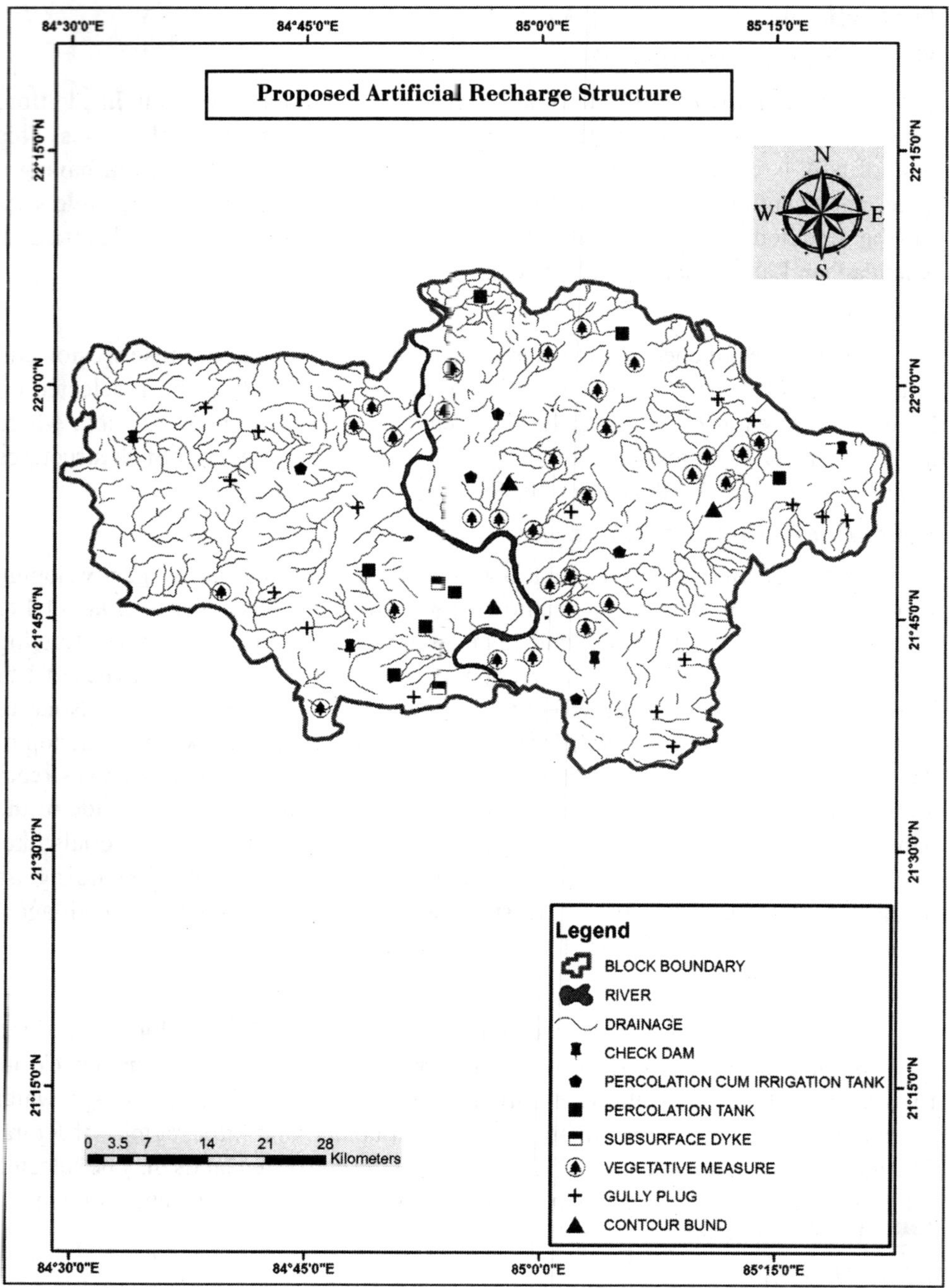

Fig. 2.3: **Proposed artificial structures in the study area**

soil erosion due to surface runoff creating waste land on both sides of the stream courses. In such a rocky area where scope for cultivation is limited, the land suitable for agriculture is being converted to waste land rapidly. In the study area there is an urgent need for plugging the gullies with the use of locally available materials particularly in the cultivated areas of Koira, Lahunipada and Gurundia blocks. By adopting such measures, the top soil can be protected as well as the rate of infiltration of water can be increased.

Agriculture-related Measure

The wasteland areas such as: land with/without scrubs, undercultivated cropped areas and open and degraded forest land are to be brought under afforestation which is also a measure of rainwater harvesting. Areas with/without scrubs are mostly located on shallow buried pediplain and less frequently on pediments. These areas because of the gentle to moderate slope are suitable for agro-horticulture and hortipasture. Suitable species of horticultural plants can be planted on these lands to check runoff and augment groundwater recharge. The scrubs lands on higher slopes may be planted with fodder and fuel wood varieties. The degraded forest land of the area around Kuliposh, Khuntgaon, Kasada, Dharidharpali, Telidihi etc., canbe brought under afforstation. These vegetative measures will check the soil erosion besides recharging the groundwater.

Hydrofracturing

The unconventional technique of hydrofracturing may be undertaken for improving the yields of bore wells in hard rock areas (Chauhan, 2000; Shulka, 2000; Umrikar, 2002 and Viswanathan, 2002). This technique has the following advantages.

1. Widening of existing fractures.
2. Removal of clogging in the fracture connectivity.
3. Creation of interconnection of fractures.
4. Extending the length of the old fractures.
5. Creation of new fractures in the aquifers.

Groundwater Resource Protection

Protection of aquifers against over-exploitation, quality deterioration or pollution from agricultural wastes and fertilizer leachates is an important aspect of groundwater management. Development should be limited to the annual recharge, otherwise it will lead to decline in water level and increase in the cost of water lifting, failure of wells and also in extreme cases land subsidence. Safe spacing norms between wells should be strictly adhered.

Comparisons of the results of the chemical analysis with the ISI (1983) standards revealed that the water is generally suitable for drinking and other domestic purposes. The tube well waters of Koira Block is, however, invariably rich in iron contents. Suitable measures need to be adopted to reduce the menace. It is a fact that use of low cost Terracotta Water Filter, developed by Regional Research Laboratory (RRL),

Bhubaneswar, Orissa, is a better solution to this iron pollution problem. The effects of opencast mining activities on ground water regime in the Koira Block have been studied. The ground water level depletion in the mining belt is due to the decrease in the groundwater recharge potential which is attributed to the excavation of iron and manganese ores and associated rocks, siltation of drainage system and deforestation. Ground water pollution potential study adopting DRASTIC Model (Aller *et al.* 1987) revealed that the ground water in the mining area is moderately susceptible to pollution. Therefore, the wastwater from the mines and the effluents from the concentration plans need to be properly managed and monitored continuously so as to save the ground water sanctuary from contamination.

Conclusions

The sustainable groundwater development of the area requires scientific management in the fields of resource location, estimation, development, conservation and augmentation and protection. The study reveals that the weathered residuum and fracture systems control the groundwater occurrence and movement. Since the stage of development of groundwater in the area is very low (6%), there is a vast scope for groundwater development through suitable structures to face drought condition. A large-scale intensive groundwater development programme need to be launched on a scientific basis. The most suitable planning for the assured source of supply round the year can be achieved by different types of site-specific groundwater structures such as: dug wells, dug-cum-bore wells and bore wells. The change in cropping pattern and adoption of modern irrigation practices like sprinkler and drip irrigation systems is the need of the hour.

Rainwater harvesting, groundwater conservation and augmentation is needed to maintain the balance between annual recharge and discharge. Artificial recharge techniques play a major role for conservation of groundwater. Considering the hydrogeological set-up, natural recharge condition, soil and slope of the area, land use pattern, future optimal use of groundwater, suitable sites for specific artificial structures like percolation tank, check dam, subsurface dyke, gully plug etc., have been demarcated. The unconventional technique of hydrofracturing may be undertaken to rejuvenate the sick wells or for improving the yields of tube wells in hard rock areas. The artificial recharge structures will also help in solving geo-environmental problem like land degradation by soil erosion, loss of moisture etc. It can be concluded that the Water Resource Management (WRM) is a highly dynamic process, covering wide spectrum of activities. These activities are highly multidisciplinary, involving earth scientists, engineers in the area of hydrology, hydraulics, water supply, irrigation and environmentalists, agriculturalists, ecologists, economists, lawyers, sociologists, politicians and end-users. Implementation of groundwater scheme can be more effective through people's participation. Hence, involvement of Non-Government Organizations (NGO's) and voluntary organizations is needed to assist in this gigantic task employing local volunteers and unemployed youths who have clear understanding of the landforms and land uses etc.

REFERENCES

Ahnfors, M. (1981). Methods to Sustain Groundwater for Longer Duration by means of Subterranean Dams, *NESCO Rept. on Inter-Regional Seminar on Groundwater in Hard Rocks,* Coimbatore, India, pp. 101-104.

Aller, L., Lehr, J.H, Petty, R. and Bennett, T. (1987). DRASTIC: A Standardized System to Evaluate Groundwater Pollution Potential using Hydrogeologic Setting. *Jour. Geol. Soc. India,* Vol. 29, pp. 23-37.

Ballukraya, P.N. (2001). Over-Exploitation of Groundwater: Consequences and Remedial Measures, *Jour. Appl. Hydrol,* Vol. XIV, No. 4, pp. 27-36.

Chadha, D.K. (2000). Groundwater Resource Potential and Scope for Development in Orissa. In *Proc. of Seminar on "Prospect of Groundwater Development and Management in Orissa"* Central Ground Water Board, Bhubaneswar, Orissa, pp. 1-9.

Chauhan, S.S. (2000). Achievements, Constraints and Remedies - Groundwater Exploration in Orissa. In: *"Proc. of Seminar on "Groundwater Resources of Orissa for 2020"*, Central Ground Water Board, Bhubaneswar, Orissa, pp. 1-11.

GEC (1997). Groundwater Estimation Committee, *Report, Ministry of the Water Resources, Government of India,* New Delhi.

ISI (Presently known as Bureau of Indian Standards) (1983). *Indian Standards Specifications for drinking water,* IS: 10500

Jha, B.M. (2000). Sustainability of Water Resources in Orissa. In: *"Proc. of Seminar on Groundwater Resources of Orissa for 2020", Central Ground Water Board*, Bhubaneswar, Orissa. pp. 13-22.

Karanth, K.R. (1987). Groundwater Assessment, Development and Management. Tata McGraw- Hill Publ. Co. Ltd., New Delhi, India pp. 720.

Mahalik, N.K. (1998). 'Precambrians' *in Geology and Mineral Resources of Orissa*. SGAT Publ. Bhubaneswar, pp. 43-81.

Nandi D. Sahu P.C., and Mondal S. (2015). Ground Water Potential Studies Using Geo-Spatial Technique A Casestudy In Karanjia Block of Odisha, India, *International Journal of Recent Scientific Research,* Vol. 6, Issue, 11, pp. 7380-7384.

Raghunath, H.M. (1987). Groundwater, Willey Eastern Ltd., (2nd Ed.) New Delhi, India, pp. 563.

Sahu, P.C. (2003). Hydrogeological Studies in the Bonai Sub-division of Sundargarhdist, Orissa, India, Ph.D Thesis (Unpublished), Sambalpur University, Burla.

Sahu, P.C. (2008). Geomorphological and Lineament Studies for targeting Ground water in Digapahandi block, Ganjamdisrict, Orissa. *Vistas in Geol. Research* U.U. Spl. Publication Geology (7), pp. 193-200.

Sahu, P.C. and Sahoo, H.K. (2006). Targetting Ground Water in Tribal Dominated Bonai Area of drought prone Sundergarh Disrict, Orissa India - A Combined Geophysical and Remote sensing Approach. *J. Hum. Ecol,* 20(2), pp. 109-115.

Shukla, N.K. (2000). Iron in Groundwater - Experiences from Rural Water Supply Sector in Orissa. In: *Proc. of Seminar on "Prospect of Groundwater Development and Management in Orissa"* CGWB, Bhubaneswar, pp. 121-123.

Umrikar, B.N. (2002). Artificial Recharge and Water Conservation Techniques in Deccan Trap Aquifers of Maharastra. *Jour. Appl. Hydrol.,* Vol. XV, No. 1, pp. 23-30.

Viswanathan, K.S. (2002). Water Resources Development - Management of Critical areas in Eritrea, Asmara. *Jour Appl. Hydrol.,* Vol. XV, No. 4, pp. 21-25.

Pages 30-71

WATER RESOURCES: MAPPING, MONITORING AND MANAGEMENT
***Edited by*: Dr. Pawan Kumar Tyagi; Dr. Avnish Chauhan & Dr. Pawan Kumar Bharti**
***Edition* : 2017**
ISBN : 978-93-5056-861-3
***Published by* : Discovery Publishing House Pvt. Ltd., New Delhi (India)**

Water Quality Assessment of Kali River in Western UP, India

Pooja Tomar

ABSTRACT

Kali river is a major tributary of Yamuna river and is lifeline of thousand peoples in western Uttar Pradesh. Kali river has been subjected to the assault of the adverse impact of industrialization and urbanization. The problem has aggravated because of uncontrolled flow of a large quantity of untreated industrial, municipal and domestic liquid waste directly drained into river, the present pollution load significantly contributed to carry a lot of toxic heavy metals merged into river water, sediments and ultimately accumulated into various living organisms.

In the present study, water samples were collected from five sampling zones of the river Kali and analysed for water quality assessment using physico-chemical parameters. Some chemical variables were found slightly high in river water samples collected from downstream sites. Correlation between various physico-chemical variables was also calculated. The present work highlighted the tremendous chemical pollution and drastic temporal and spatial change in water quality of river Kali. However, water quality was slightly restored by river ecosystem at downstream sites.

Keywords: Water quality, River ecosystem, Kali river, Western UP, Physico-chemical variables.

INTRODUCTION

The rivers provide water for industry, agriculture commercial aquaculture and domestic purposes. Unfortunately the same rivers are being polluted by indiscriminate disposal of sewage and industrial wastes as a plethora of human activities. River pollution has already acquired a serious dimension in India, with most of its fourteen

---

Aquatic Biodiversity and Conservation Laboratory, Department of Zoology and Environmental Sciences, Gurukula Kangri University, Haridwar - 249 404, India.

rivers being grossly polluted. The situations are more or less same in small rivers and associated tributaries. The available natural freshwater resources today are threatened by hazards of pollution; particularly rivers are greatly polluted due to release of untreated effluents and waste materials from agriculture concerns and industries located around rivers. Rivers are the most important water resources in the world in general and India in particular great civilization developed along the bank of rivers and even today most of the development has taken place in the cities or in the location near the rivers (Bharti and Malik, 2005).

The poor living conditions of people in settlements around rivers, non-availability of treatment from urban areas and negligence of industries for treatment of effluents before release in natural water bodies are the major reason for pollution of Indian rivers (Chavan and Wagh, 2005). The river water quality is deteriorated not only by increasing domestic and industrial waste water discharges but also due to excessive abstraction of water from river mainly for irrigation rendered then dry or with meager flow in non-monsoon periods followed by increasing waste water (Sastry *et al.* 1972, Bhalla and Bharti, 2014). On the banks of river Kali, several towns, major cities and industries are situated, which have very less or no proper management of sewage drains and effluents are being discharged directly or indirectly into the river which is deteriorating the water quality of river Kali day-by-day.

The river western Kali is polluted at several points the main pollutants come from the discharge of domestic and industrial waste the industrial units of U.P., are supplied with the water from small perennial streams from foothills of Shivalik Himalaya. Although there are several large cities all along the bank of Kali river and serve as water source to supply water to these cities and towns. The rivers has been indiscriminately polluted and misused over the years, despite of its extra ordinary resilience and recuperative capacities severely polluted. Due to increase of population and industrialization, the water quality of river Kali has been degraded from domestic sewage and industrial effluents that contains large number of chemicals. Kali River and its main tributaries Yamuna together have several types of industrial manufacturing units along with their banks. These industries both extract large volumes of water from the river for their manufacturing process, and also discharge their industrial effluents often with nominal or no treatment directly to the river. The increase in industrialization and chemical based agriculture within the catchments of the Kali river east in western U.P., is identified as being responsible for considerable Pollution in the river. Muzaffarnagar town is developing very fast in term of business and small scale industries, its situated on the eastern bank of river Kali and all the waste water of the town is directly discharged into the river through three major drains (Tomar, 2011). At present, the water quality of river Kali is degrading day-by-day therefore, regular monitoring is essential for the maintenance of ecological balance and assessment of self-purification capacity. Hence, the monitoring and assessment programme of Kali River was executed by evaluating physico-chemical characteristics of surface water of Kali River at western Uttar Pradesh, India.

Study Area

The river Kali in western Uttar Pradesh is a small perennial river having a basin area of about 750 Km., and lies between altitude 29° 33" N to 29° 21" N and longitude 77° 43" to 77° 39"E in the Muzffarnagar district of Uttar Pradesh (Fig. 3.1; satellite view). The climate in this region is moderate subtropical monsoonal. The average annual rainfall in the area is about 1000 mm, a major part of which is receiving during the monsoon period.

The following sampling locations have been selected for the study:

- Sampling Zone - A: Rohana.
- Sampling Zone - B: Muzaffarnagar City.
- Sampling Zone - C: Sujru.
- Sampling Zone - D: Bagrajpur Industrial Area.
- Sampling Zone - E: Mandawali.

Three samples (A1, A2, A3; B1, B2, B3; C1, C2, C3; D1, D2, D3 and E1, E2, E3) were taken from each sampling station in every season *i.e.,* summer, Monsoon, winter.

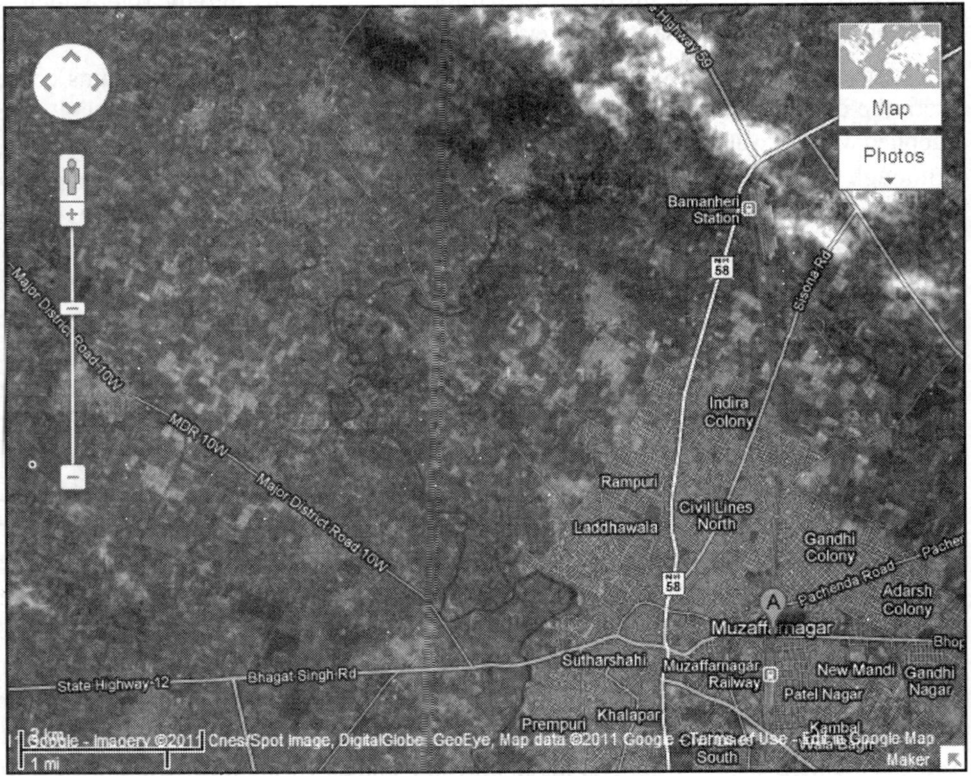

Fig. 3.1: **Satellite image of Muzaffarnagar city showing the Kali river catchment area (Left from city)**

Material and Methods

Water samples were collected in BOD bottles and polypropylene bottles for laboratory experiments. Some parameters were determined immediately on sampling sites, for rest parameters samples were preserved and stored in refrigerator at 4°C.

All chemicals and reagents used were of analytical reagent grade (Merck). Double distilled water was used throughout the study. All glassware and plastic ware were soaked in 10 per cent HNO3 for 24 h. The washing was completed with double distilled water rinse.

The sampling was done during 2008-10 in morning period from the each selected sampling zones. The water samples were taken in BOD bottles and polypropylene bottles for physical and chemical analysis. Following materials were used in sampling process: Sampling bottles, Pipettes, Reagents and Glassware, Chemical bottles, Bag, Polythene bag, Plastic cane, Thermometer, pH meter.

The samples of Kali water were analyzed using standard methods (Wetzel, 1975; Trivedi and Goel, 1984; APHA, 1998).

Results and Discussion

In highly populated and pre-dominantly rural catchments, the river Kali is heavily utilized as water resources for domestic, agricultural and industrial uses. The waste from different industries are discharged it two different sampling sites of river Kali. The present study was undertaken to determine the Temporal and spatial variation in water quality of river Kali at Muzaffarnagar district in different seasons for the years 2008-10 indicated existing pollution load in river water.

Sampling Zone A (Rohana)

Temperature (°C)

The temperature of water at sampling zone A (Rohana) was observed maximum (38.7°C) during summer season and minimum (15.5°C) in winter season. At this zone, A zone consists of A_1, A_2, A_3. At A_1, the temperature reported maximum (32.8°C) during summer and minimum (15.5°C) in winter season. At A_2 point, the temperature recorded maximum (38.7°C) in summer and minimum (18.6°C) in winter seasons and at A_3 point, the temperature was observed maximum (34.9°C) and minimum (17.8°C) in winter season. The average value of temperature at point A_1, A_2 and A_3 was reported as 24.70 ± 8.71, 31.16 ± 10.95 and 26.33 ± 8.55 respectively.

pH

pH of river water at sampling Zone A, was reported maximum (8.15) during monsoon season and minimum (7.62) in winter season. At this zone, A_1 point, showed the maximum (7.82) and minimum (7.65) during summer and winter respectively. At A_2 point, the maximum pH was observed (8.15) during monsoon and minimum (7.84) in winter season and at A_3 point, the pH was reported maximum (8.00) and minimum (7.85) during monsoon and winter respectively. The average of value of pH at point A_1, A_2 and A_3 was reported as 7.70 ± 0.11, 8.03 ± 0.17 and 7.94 ± 0.08 respectively.

Turbidity (N.T.U.)

In this Zone, the turbidity was reported maximum (1364.51 N.T.U.) in summer and minimum (580.23 N.T.U.) in winter season. The Turbidity of water at point A_1 was observed maximum (42.00 N.T.U.) in monsoon and minimum (26.51 N.T.U.) in winter season. The average mean value of turbidity at this point A_1 was reported as lowest (35.34 ± 7.97 N.T.U). At point A_2, the turbidity was found maximum (72.00 N.T.U.) in monsoon season and minimum (47.5 N.T.U.) in winter. The average mean value of turbidity at this point A_2 was reported as highest (63.17 ± 13.60 N.T.U) and at point A_3, the Turbidity was observed maximum (53.57 N.T.U.) and minimum (37.71 N.T.U.) during monsoon and winter respectively. The average mean value of turbidity at this point A_3 was reported as 45.93 ± 7.94 N.T.U.

Total Dissolved Solids (mg/l)

The concentration of total dissolved solids at zone A was recorded maximum (1268.51 mg/l) in summer and minimum (341.72 mg/l) during winter season. In this zone, at point A_1, the maximum (403.15 mg/l) concentration of TDS was recorded in summer and minimum (341.72 mg/l) in winter season. The average mean value of TDS at pint A_1 was recorded as 374.96 ± 31.02 mg/l. At point A_2, the TDS concentration was recorded maximum (1268.51 mg/l) and minimum (1208.50 mg/l) in summer and winter respectively. The average mean value of TDS at point A_2 was recorded as 1247.34 ± 33.68 mg/l. At point zone A_3, the maximum concentration (868.51 mg/l) of total dissolved solids were observed during summer and minimum concentration (732 mg/l) recorded during winter season. The average mean value of TDS was observed as 813.18 ± 71.45mg/l.

Dissolved Oxygen (mg/l)

At zone A, DO was observed maximum (7.82 mg/l) during monsoon season and minimum (6.12 mg/l) in winter season. In this zone, the A_1 point showed the maximum concentration (7.21 mg/l) of DO during monsoon and minimum (6.12 mg/l) in winter season. The average mean value of DO concentration was recorded as 6.72 ± 0.55 mg/l at point A_1. At point A_2, the DO concentration was recorded maximum (7.82 mg/l) and minimum (6.65 mg/l) in monsoon and winter season respectively. The average mean value of DO concentration at point A_2 was recorded as 7.07 ± 0.65 mg/l. At point A_3, the DO level was observed maximum (6.89 mg/l) during monsoon and minimum (6.21 mg/l) during summer. The average DO concentration level was observed at point A_3 as 6.52 ± 0.34 mg/l.

Free CO_2 (mg/l)

The Free carbon dioxide was observed maximum (2.50 mg/l) in summer and minimum (0.90 mg/l) in monsoon season at zone A. In this zone A, the point A_1, indicated the concentration of CO_2 as 2.01 mg/l (maximum) during summer and 0.09 mg/l (minimum) during winter. The average mean value of free CO_2 level was reported as 1.31 ± 0.34 at point A_1. At point A_2, a little bid difference was found in CO_2

concentration in surface water. In this A_2 point, the maximum concentration (2.50 mg/l) of CO_2 was observed during summer and minimum (1.05 mg/l) in monsoon season. The average mean value of CO_2 at point A_2 was recorded as 1.6 ± 0.54 mg/l. At point A_3, the concentration of Free CO_2 was maximum (1.90 mg/l) and minimum (0.98 mg/l) during summer and winter respectively. The average mean value of Free CO_2 was observed as 1.30 ± 0.001 mg/l at point A_3.

Hardness (mg/l)

The hardness of river water was analysed seasonally. The hardness of river water was observed maximum (381.50 mg/l) in summer season and minimum (311.00 mg/l) in winter season at zone A. In this zone A, the point A_1 showed the maximum (326.75 mg/l) hardness during summer and minimum (311.00 mg/l) during winter season. The average mean concentration of hardness was observed as 320.67 ± 8.46 mg/l at point A_1. At point A_2, the hardness was reported maximum (381.50 mg/l) during summer and minimum (322.75 mg/l) in winter. The average mean value of hardness was reported as 348.75 ± 29.95 mg/l at point A_2. At point A_3, the value of hardness was observed maximum (341.41 mg/l) during monsoon and minimum (244.75 mg/l) in winter season. The average value of hardness was observed as 334.18 ± 8.801mg/l at point A_3.

Total Alkalinity (mg/l)

The alkalinity was found maximum (315.12 mg/l) during monsoon season and minimum (244.75 mg/l) during winter season at zone A. In this zone, at point A_1, the maximum alkalinity (276.00 mg/l) was observed during monsoon season and minimum (257.25 mg/l) in winter season. The average mean value of alkalinity was reported as 269.42 ± 10.55 mg/l at point A_1. At point A_2, the alkalinity was reported maximum (315.12 mg/l) in monsoon and minimum (280.76 mg/l) during winter season. The average mean value of alkalinity was found as 300.29 ± 17.66 mg/l at point A_2. Similarly, at point A_3, the alkalinity was found maximum (255.60 mg/l) in summer and minimum (244.75 mg/l) during winter season. The average value of alkalinity was reported as 250.04 ± 5.43 mg/l at point A_3.

Biological Oxygen Demand (mg/l)

At zone A, the BOD was estimated as maximum (52.81 mg/l) during monsoon season and minimum (28.75 mg/l) in winter season. In this zone, at point A_1, the maximum concentration of BOD (45.41 mg/l) was observed during monsoon season and minimum (34.51 mg/l) during winter season. The average mean value of BOD values were reported as 41.36 ± 5 96 mg/l at point zone A_1. At point A_2, the BOD level was reported maximum (52.81 mg/l) in monsoon season and minimum (35.91 mg/l) during winter season. The average value of BOD at point zone A_2 was reported as 45.88 ± 8.85 mg/l and at point A_3, the BOD level was reported maximum (47.25 mg/l) in monsoon and minimum (28.75 mg/l) during winter season and indicated the average mean value of BOD as 38.54 ± 9.29 mg/l at point A_3.

Chemical Oxygen Demand (mg/l)

The concentration of COD was reported maximum (71.02 mg/l) in monsoon and minimum (55.82 mg/l) during winter at zone A. In this zone, at point A_1, the COD level was reported as maximum (62.12 mg/l) in monsoon season and minimum (55.82 mg/l) during winter season and showed the average mean value of COD as 61.15 ± 4.80 mg/l. At point A_2, the BOD concentration was observed maximum (71.02 mg/l) during monsoon season and minimum (61.82 mg/l) during winter season. The average mean value of COD was reported as 67.02 ± 4.71 mg/l at point A_2. Similarly, at point A_3, the maximum COD value (64.69 mg/l) was observed during monsoon and minimum (59.21 mg/l) in winter season. The average value of COD was found 61.97 ± 2.74 mg/l at point A_3 in zone A.

Chloride (mg/l)

The chloride concentration was generally found maximum (42.81 mg/l) in monsoon season and minimum (23.16 mg/l) during winter season at zone A. In this zone A, at point A_1, the chloride was observed maximum (36.95 mg/l) in monsoon season and minimum (23.16 mg/l) during winter season and constituted the average mean value of chloride ion as 30.94 ± 7.05 mg/l. At point A_2, the maximum concentration of chloride ion was reported (42.81 mg/l) in monsoon and minimum (29.75 mg/l) during winter season. The average mean value of chloride ion was reported as 36.69 ± 6.57 mg/l at point A_2. Similarly, at point A_3, the chloride ion showed maximum (36.48 mg/l) level in monsoon and minimum (27.92 mg/l) during winter season and reported the average mean value of chloride ion as 32.86 ± 4.43 mg/l at point A_3.

Calcium (mg/l)

The calcium ion concentration was generally found maximum (43.76 mg/l) in monsoon season and minimum (22.81 mg/l) during winter season at zone A. In this zone A, at point A_1, the calcium ion was observed maximum (33.12 mg/l) in monsoon season and minimum (25.16 mg/l) during winter season and constituted the average mean value of chloride ion as 29.58 ± 4.08 mg/l. At point A_2, the maximum concentration of calcium ion was reported (43.76 mg/l) in monsoon and minimum (28.91 mg/l) during winter season. The average mean value of calcium ion was reported as 37.36 ± 7.63 mg/l at point A_2. Similarly, at point A_3, the calcium ion showed maximum (39.82 mg/l) level in monsoon and minimum (12.91 mg/l) during winter season and reported the average mean value of calcium ion as 31.68 ± 8.53 mg/l at point A_3.

Magnesium (mg/l)

The magnesium ion concentration was generally found maximum (35.93 mg/l) in monsoon season and minimum (12.91 mg/l) during winter season at zone A. In this zone A, at point A_1, the magnesium ion was observed maximum (21.59 mg/l) in monsoon season and minimum (16.81 mg/l) during winter season and constituted the average mean value of magnesium ion as 19.39 ± 2.41 mg/l. At point A_2, the maximum concentration of magnesium ion was reported (35.93 mg/l) in monsoon and minimum (22.81 mg/l) during winter season. The average mean value of magnesium ion was reported as 28.85 ± 6.62 mg/l at point A_2. Similarly, at point A_3, the magnesium ion showed maximum (31.23 mg/l) level in monsoon and minimum (12.91 mg/l) during winter season and reported the average mean value of magnesium ion as 22.92 ± 9.28 mg/l at point A_3.

Phosphates (mg/l)

The phosphate concentration was generally found maximum (1.96 mg/l) in winter season and minimum (0.48 mg/l) during monsoon season at zone A. In this zone A, at point A_1, the phosphate ion was observed maximum (1.39 mg/l) in winter season and minimum (0.48 mg/l) during monsoon season and constituted the average mean value of phosphate ion as 0.94 ± 0.45 mg/l. At point A_2, the maximum concentration of phosphate ion was reported (1.96 mg/l) in winter and minimum (1.75 mg/l) during monsoon season. The average mean value of phosphate ion was reported as 1.87 ± 0.14 mg/l at point A_2. Similarly, at point A_3, the phosphate ion showed maximum (1.68 mg/l) level in winter and minimum (0.69 mg/l) during monsoon season and reported the average mean value of phosphate ion as 1.1 ± 0.52 mg/l at point A_3.

Nitrates (mg/l)

The Nitrates concentration was generally found maximum (6.36 mg/l) in summer season and minimum (2.62 mg/l) during winter season at zone A. In this zone A, at point A_1, the nitrate was observed maximum (3.51 mg/l) in monsoon season and minimum (2.62 mg/l) during winter season and constituted the average mean value of nitrates ion as 2.99 ± 0.46 mg/l. At point A_2, the maximum concentration of nitrates ion was reported (6.36 mg/l) in summer and minimum (5.12 mg/l) during monsoon season. The average mean value of nitrate ion was reported as 5.74 ± 0.62 mg/l at point A_2. Similarly, at point A_3, the nitrate ion showed maximum (3.65 mg/l) level in monsoon and minimum (3.11 mg/l) during winter season and reported the average mean value of nitrate ion as 3.31 ± 0.29 mg/l at point A_3.

Sampling Zone B (Muzaffarnagar City)

Temperature (°C)

The temperature of water at sampling zone B was observed maximum (32.43°C) during summer season and minimum (18.71°C) in winter season. At this zone, B zone consists of B_1, B_2 and B3. At B_1, the temperature reported maximum (31.45°C) during summer and minimum (21.75°C) in winter season. At B_2 point, the temperature recorded maximum (32.43°C) in summer and minimum (19.73°C) in winter seasons and at B_3 point, the temperature was observed maximum (31.25°C) and minimum (18.71°C) in winter season. The average value of temperature at point B_1, B_2 and B_3 was reported as 27.12 ± 4.93, 27.30 ± 6.69 and 26.13 ± 6.58.

pH

pH of river water at sampling Zone B, was reported maximum (8.65) during summer season and minimum (7.75) in winter season. At this zone, B_1 point, showed the pH maximum (8.00) and minimum (7.75) during monsoon and winter respectively.

At B_2 point, the maximum pH was observed (8.65) during summer and minimum (7.81) in winter season and at B_3 point, the pH was reported maximum (7.95) and minimum (7.83) during monsoon and winter respectively. The average of value of pH at point B_1, B_2 and B_3 was reported as 7.86 ± 0.13, 8.18 ± 0.43 and 7.88 ± 0.06.

Turbidity (N.T.U.)

In this Zone-B, the turbidity was reported maximum (79.26 N.T.U.) in monsoon and minimum (39.00 N.T.U.) in winter season. The Turbidity of water at point B_1 was observed maximum (53.00 N.T.U.) in monsoon and minimum (39.00 N.T.U.) in winter season. The average mean value of turbidity at this point B_1 was reported as lowest (45.36 ± 7.09 N.T.U). At point B_2, the turbidity was found maximum (79.26 N.T.U.) in monsoon season and minimum (67.06 N.T.U.) in winter season. The average mean value of turbidity at this point B_2 was reported as highest (72.94 ± 6.11 N.T.U) and at point B_3, the Turbidity was observed maximum (78.00 N.T.U.) and minimum (57.00 N.T.U.) during monsoon and winter respectively. The average mean value of turbidity at this point B_3 was reported as 68.06 = 10.54 N.T.U.

Total Dissolved Solids (mg/l)

The concentration of total dissolved solids at zone B, was recorded maximum (929.55 mg/l) in summer and minimum (378.00 mg/l) during winter season. In this zone, at point B_1, the maximum (765.81 mg/l) concentration of TDS was recorded in summer and minimum (521.23 mg/l) in winter season. The average mean value of TDS at pint B_1 was recorded as 609.77 ± 135.55 mg/l. At point B_2, the TDS concentration was recorded maximum (929.55mg/l) and minimum (674.16 mg/l) in summer and monsoon respectively. The average mean value of TDS at point B_2 was recorded as 812.07 ± 128.91 mg/l. At point zone B_3, the maximum concentration (658.23 mg/l) of total dissolved solids were observed during summer and minimum concentration (378.00 mg/l) recorded during winter season. The average mean value of TDS was observed as 509.24 ± 140.95 mg/l.

Dissolved Oxygen (mg/l)

At zone B, DO was observed maximum (6.92 mg/l) during monsoon season and minimum (4.12 mg/l) in summer season. In this zone, the B_1 point showed the maximum concentration (5.67 mg/l) of DO during monsoon and minimum (4.12 mg/l) in summer season. The average mean value of DO concentration was recorded as 4.91 ± 0.77 mg/l at point B_1. At point B_2, the DO concentration was recorded maximum (6.92 mg/l) and minimum (5.83 mg/l) in monsoon and summer season respectively. The average mean value of DO concentration at point B_2 was recorded as 6.20 ± 0.62 mg/l. At point B_3, the DO level was observed maximum (6.36 mg/l) during monsoon and minimum (5.21 mg/l) during summer. The average DO concentration level was observed at point B_3 as 5.62 ± 0.64 mg/l.

Free CO_2 (mg/l)

The Free carbon dioxide was observed maximum (3.02 mg/l) in summer and minimum (1.12 mg/l) in winter season at zone B. In this zone B, the point B_1, indicated the concentration of CO_2 as 2.35 mg/l (maximum) during summer and 1.32 mg/l (minimum) during winter. The average mean value of free CO_2 level was reported as 1.78 ± 0.52 at point B_1. At point B_2, a little bid difference was found in CO_2 concentration in surface water. In this B_2 point, the maximum concentration (3.02 mg/l) of CO_2 was observed during summer and minimum (1.63 mg/l) in winter season. The average mean value of CO_2 at point B_2 was recorded as 2.38 ± 0.72 mg/l. At point B_3, the concentration of Free CO_2 was maximum (2.92 mg/l) and minimum (1.12 mg/l) during summer and winter respectively. The average mean value of Free CO_2 was observed as 2.01 ± 0.50 mg/l at point B_3.

Hardness (mg/l)

The hardness of river water was analysed seasonally. The hardness of river water was observed maximum (384.16 mg/l) in monsoon season and minimum (319.78 mg/l) in winter season at zone B. In this zone B, the point B_1 showed the maximum (332.52 mg/l) hardness during summer and minimum (319.78 mg/l) during winter season. The average mean concentration of hardness was observed as 326.48 ± 6.40 mg/l at point B_1. At point B_2, the hardness was reported maximum (384.16 mg/l) during monsoon and minimum (356.26 mg/l) in winter season. The average mean value of hardness was reported as 371.89 ± 14.25 mg/l at point B_2. At point B_3, the value of hardness was observed maximum (347.38 mg/l) during summer and minimum (3321.25 mg/l) in winter season. The average value of hardness was observed as 338.72 ± 7.79 mg/l at point B_3.

Total Alkalinity (mg/l)

The alkalinity was found maximum (351.27 mg/l) during monsoon season and minimum (257.00 mg/l) during winter season at zone B. In this zone, at point B_1, the maximum alkalinity (285.64 mg/l) was observed during summer season and minimum (259.00 mg/l) in winter season. The average mean value of alkalinity was reported as 274.63 ± 13.91 mg/l at point B_1. At point B_2, the alkalinity was reported maximum (351.27 mg/l) in monsoon and minimum (286.92 mg/l) during winter season. The average mean value of alkalinity was found as 321.89 ± 32.54 mg/l at point B_2. Similarly, at point B_3, the alkalinity was found maximum (295.00 mg/l) in monsoon and minimum (257.00 mg/l) during winter season. The average value of alkalinity was reported as 280.33 ± 20.43 mg/l at point B_3.

Biological Oxygen Demand (mg/l)

At zone B, the BOD was estimated as maximum (28.23 mg/l) during monsoon season and minimum (12.52 mg/l) in winter season. In this zone, at point B_1, the maximum concentration of BOD (21.81 mg/l) was observed during monsoon season and minimum (12.62 mg/l) during winter season. The average mean value of BOD values were reported as 17.09 ± 4.59 mg/l at point zone B_1. At point B_2, the BOD level was reported maximum (28.23 mg/l) in monsoon season and minimum (15.72 mg/l) during winter season. The average value of BOD at point zone B_2 was reported as 20.70 ± 6.63 mg/l and at point B_3 the BOD level was reported maximum (20.72

mg/l) in monsoon and minimum (12.52 mg/l) during winter season and indicated the average mean value of BOD as 15.96 ± 4.25 mg/l at point B_3.

Chemical Oxygen Demand (mg/l)

The concentration of COD was reported maximum (68.95 mg/l) in monsoon and minimum (29.97 mg/l) during winter at zone B. In this zone, at point B_1, the COD level was reported as maximum (68.95 mg/l) in monsoon season and minimum (34.81 mg/l) during winter season and showed the average mean value of COD as 52.16 ± 17.08 mg/l. At point B_2, the COD concentration was observed maximum (62.72mg/l) during monsoon season and minimum (29.97 mg/l) during winter season. The average mean value of COD was reported as 47.07 ± 16.42 mg/l at point B_2. Similarly, at point B_3, the maximum COD value (65.90 mg/l) was observed during monsoon and minimum (32.15 mg/l) in winter season. The average value of COD was found 49.59 ± 16.90 mg/l at point B_3 in zone B.

Chloride (mg/l)

The chloride concentration was generally found maximum (151.21 mg/l) in monsoon season and minimum (128.65 mg/l) during winter season at zone B. In this zone B, at point B_1, the chloride was observed maximum (146.32 mg/l) in monsoon season and minimum (128.81 mg/l) during winter season and constituted the average mean value of chloride ion as 136.86 ± 8.84 mg/l. At point B_2, the maximum concentration of chloride ion was reported (151.21 mg/l) in monsoon and minimum (1132.81 mg/l) during winter season. The average mean value of chloride ion was reported as 142.17 ± 9.20 mg/l at point B_2. Similarly, at point B_3, the chloride ion showed maximum (147.05 mg/l) level in monsoon and minimum (128.65 mg/l) during winter season and reported the average mean value of chloride ion as 137.92 ± 9.20 mg/l at point B_3.

Calcium (mg/l)

The calcium ion concentration was generally found maximum (43.76 mg/l) in monsoon season and minimum (22.81 mg/l) during winter season at zone B. In this zone B, at point B_1, the calcium ion was observed maximum (33.12 mg/l) in monsoon season and minimum (25.16 mg/l) during winter season and constituted the average mean value of chloride ion as 29.58 ± 4.08 mg/l. At point B_2, the maximum concentration of calcium ion was reported (43.76 mg/l) in monsoon and minimum (28.91 mg/l) during winter season. The average mean value of calcium ion was reported as 37.36 ± 7.63 mg/l at point B_2. Similarly, at point B_3, the calcium ion showed maximum (39.82 mg/l) level in monsoon and minimum (12.91 mg/l) during winter season and reported the average mean value of calcium ion as 31.68 ± 8.53 mg/l at point B_3.

Magnesium (mg/l)

The magnesium ion concentration was generally found maximum (32.17 mg/l) in monsoon season and minimum (126.95 mg/l) during winter season at zone B. In this zone B, at point B_1, the magnesium ion was observed maximum (29.65 mg/l) in monsoon season and minimum (19.82 mg/l) during winter season and constituted the average mean value of magnesium ion as 24.28 ± 4.98 mg/l. At point B_2, the maximum concentration of magnesium ion was reported (32.17 mg/l) in monsoon and minimum (22.38 mg/l) during winter season. The average mean value of magnesium ion was reported as 26.96 ± 4.92 mg/l at point B_2. Similarly, at point B_3, the magnesium ion showed maximum (27.46 mg/l) level in monsoon and minimum (18.51 mg/l) during winter season and reported the average mean value of magnesium ion as 22.60 ± 4.52 mg/l at point B_3.

Phosphates (mg/l)

The phosphate concentration was generally found maximum (2.95 mg/l) in winter season and minimum (0.82 mg/l) during monsoon season at zone B. In this zone B, at point B_1, the phosphate ion was observed maximum (1.72 mg/l) in summer season and minimum (0.82 mg/l) during monsoon season and constituted the average mean value of phosphate ion as 1.22 ± 0.46 mg/l. At point B_2, the maximum concentration of phosphate ion was reported (2.95 mg/l) in summer and minimum (2.15 mg/l) during monsoon season. The average mean value of phosphate ion was reported as 2.55 ± 0.40 mg/l at point B_2. Similarly, at point B_3, the phosphate ion showed maximum (1.82 mg/l) level in summer and minimum (1.39 mg/l) during monsoon season and reported the average mean value of phosphate ion as 1.58 ± 0.22 mg/l at point B_3.

Nitrates (mg/l)

The Nitrates concentration was generally found maximum (3.56 mg/l) in monsoon season and minimum (2.79 mg/l) during summer season at zone B. In this zone B, at point B_1, the nitrate was observed maximum (3.21 mg/l) in monsoon season and minimum (2.79 mg/l) during summer season and constituted the average mean value of nitrates ion as 2.96 ± 0.22 mg/l. At point B_2, the maximum concentration of nitrates ion was reported (3.56 mg/l) in monsoon and minimum (3.32 mg/l) during winter season. The average mean value of nitrate ion was reported as 3.43 ± 0.12 mg/l at point B_2. Similarly, at point B_3, the nitrate ion showed maximum (3.42 mg/l) level in monsoon and minimum (3.12 mg/l) during winter season and reported the average mean value of nitrate ion as 3.28 ± 17.91 mg/l at point B_3.

Sampling Zone C (Sujru)

Temperature (°C)

The temperature of water at sampling zone C (Sujru) was observed maximum (35.32°C) during summer season and minimum (16.46°C) in winter season. At this zone, C zone consists of C_1, C_2 and C_3. At C_1, the temperature reported maximum (34.20°C) during summer and minimum (16.46°C) in winter season. At C_2 point, the temperature recorded maximum (35.32°C) in summer and minimum (17.52°C) in winter seasons and at C_3 point, the temperature was observed maximum (33.12°C) and minimum (17.23°C) in winter season. The average value of temperature at point C_1, C_2 and C_3 was reported as 25.72 ± 8.89, 27.07 ± 8.97 and 25.29 ± 7.95.

pH

pH of river water at sampling Zone C, was reported maximum (8.62) during monsoon season and minimum (7.46) in winter season. At this zone, C_1 point, showed the pH maximum (8.62) and minimum (7.76) during monsoon and winter respectively. At C_2 point, the maximum pH was observed (8.00) during monsoon and minimum (7.55) in summer season and at C_3 point, the pH was reported maximum (7.82) and minimum (7.46) during monsoon and winter respectively. The average of value of pH at point C_1, C_2 and C_3 was reported as 8.10 ± 0.46, 7.77 ± 0.22 and 7.62 ± 0.18 respectively.

Turbidity (N.T.U.)

In this Zone-C, the turbidity was reported maximum (62.75 N.T.U.) in monsoon and minimum (29.57 N.T.U.) in winter season. The Turbidity of water at point C_1 was observed maximum (43.86 N.T.U.) in monsoon and minimum (29.57 N.T.U.) in winter season. The average mean value of turbidity at this point C_1 was reported as lowest (36.25 ± 7.19 N.T.U). At point C_2, the turbidity was found maximum (62.75 N.T.U.) in monsoon season and minimum (38.95 N.T.U.) in winter season. The average mean value of turbidity at this point C_2 was reported as highest (51.57 ± 11.96 N.T.U) and at point C_3, the Turbidity was observed maximum (51.32 N.T.U.) and minimum (44.91 N.T.U.) during monsoon and winter respectively. The average mean value of turbidity at this point C_3 was reported as 47.91 ± 3.22 N.T.U.

Total Dissolved Solids (mg/l)

The concentration of total dissolved solids at zone C was recorded maximum (205.50 mg/l) in monsoon and minimum (146.39 mg/l) during winter season. In this zone, at point C_1, the maximum (195.65 mg/l) concentration of TDS was recorded in monsoon and minimum (153.28 mg/l) in winter season. The average mean value of TDS at pint C_1 was recorded as 170.68 ± 22.17 mg/l. At point C_2, the TDS concentration was recorded maximum (205.50 mg/l) and minimum (175.39 mg/l) in monsoon and summer respectively. The average mean value of TDS at point C_2 was recorded as 181.57 ± 21.52 mg/l. At point zone C_3, the maximum concentration (187.00 mg/l) of total dissolved solids were observed during monsoon and minimum concentration (146.39 mg/l) recorded during winter season. The average mean value of TDS was observed as 167.26 ± 20.33 mg/l.

Dissolved Oxygen (mg/l)

At zone C, DO was observed maximum (8.12 mg/l) during monsoon season and minimum (6.35 mg/l) in summer season. In this zone, the C_1 point showed the maximum concentration (8.34 mg/l) of DO during monsoon and minimum (6.35 mg/l) in summer season. The average mean value of DO concentration was recorded as 7.36 ± 0.99 mg/l at point C_1. At point C_2, the DO concentration was recorded maximum (8.80 mg/l) and minimum (7.07 mg/l) in monsoon and summer season respectively. The average mean value of DO concentration at point C_2 was recorded as 7.77 ± 0.91 mg/l. At point C_3, the DO level was observed maximum (8.12 mg/l) during monsoon and minimum (7.21 mg/l) during summer. The average DO concentration level was observed at point C_3 as 7.55 ± 0.49 mg/l.

Free CO_2 (mg/l)

The Free carbon dioxide was observed maximum (4.03 mg/l) in summer and minimum (1.02 mg/l) in winter season at zone C. In this zone C, the point C_1, indicated the concentration of CO_2 as 3.85 mg/l (maximum) during summer and 1.01 mg/l (minimum) during winter. The average mean value of free CO_2 level was reported as 2.45 ± 1.55 at point C_1. At point C_2, the CO_2 concentration in surface water reported as maximum concentration (4.03 mg/l) of CO_2 was observed during summer and minimum (1.02 mg/l) in winter season. The average mean value of CO_2 at point B_2 was recorded as 2.36 ± 1.32 mg/l. At point C_3, the concentration of Free CO_2 was maximum (3.03 mg/l) and minimum (0.93 mg/l) during summer and winter respectively. The average mean value of Free CO_2 was observed as 1.67 ± 0.59 mg/l at point C_3.

Hardness (mg/l)

The hardness of river water was analysed seasonally. The hardness of river water was observed maximum (241.62 mg/l) in monsoon season and minimum (196.25 mg/l) in winter season at zone C. In this zone C, the point C_1 showed the maximum (235.62 mg/l) hardness during monsoon and minimum (196.25mg/l) during winter season. The average mean concentration of hardness was observed as 215.87 ± 19.68 mg/l at point C_1. At point C_2, the hardness was reported maximum (241.62 mg/l) during monsoon and minimum (203.25 mg/l) in winter season. The average mean value of hardness was reported as 222.35 ± 19.18 mg/l at point C_2. At point C_3, the value of hardness was observed maximum (231.82 mg/l) during summer and minimum (207.91 mg/l) in winter season. The average value of hardness was observed as 221.79 ± 12.41 mg/l at point C_3

Total Alkalinity (mg/l)

The alkalinity was found maximum (309.00 mg/l) during summer season and minimum (235.62 mg/l) during winter season at zone C. In this zone, at point C_1, the maximum alkalinity (309.00 mg/l) was observed during summer season and minimum (282.50 mg/l) in winter season. The average mean value of alkalinity was reported as 295.05 ± 13.30 mg/l at point C_1. At point C_2, the alkalinity was reported maximum (278.12 mg/l) in monsoon and minimum (248.15 mg/l) during winter season. The average mean value of alkalinity was found as 267.09 ± 16.48 mg/l at point C_2. Similarly, at point C_3, the alkalinity was found maximum (269.82 mg/l) in summer and minimum (235.62 mg/l) during winter season. The average value of alkalinity was reported as 256.23 ± 18.15 mg/l at point C_3.

Biological Oxygen Demand (mg/l)

At zone C, the BOD was estimated as maximum (16.32 mg/l) during monsoon season and minimum (8.13 mg/l) in winter season. In this zone, at point C_1, the maximum concentration of BOD (15.82 mg/l) was observed during monsoon season and minimum (9.36 mg/l) during winter season. The average means value of BOD values were reported as 12.51 ± 3.23 mg/l at point zone C_1. At point C_2, the BOD level was reported maximum (16.32 mg/l) in monsoon season and minimum (10.61 mg/l) during winter season. The average value of BOD at point zone C_2 was reported as 13.15 ± 2.90 mg/l and at point C_3, the BOD level was reported maximum (13.82 mg/l) in monsoon and minimum (8.13 mg/l) during winter season and indicated the average mean value of BOD as 11.19 ± 2.87 mg/l at point C_3.

Chemical Oxygen Demand (mg/l)

The concentration of COD was reported maximum (53.21 mg/l) in monsoon and minimum (30.78 mg/l) during winter at zone C. In this zone, at point C_1, the COD level was reported as maximum (47.61 mg/l) in monsoon season and minimum (31.92 mg/l) during winter season and showed the average mean value of COD as 41.12 ± 8.19 mg/l. At point C_2, the COD concentration was observed maximum (53.21 mg/l) during monsoon season and minimum (33.82 mg/l) during winter season. The average mean value of COD was reported as 45.08 ± 10.07 mg/l at point C_2. Similarly, at point C_3, the maximum COD value (49.16 mg/l) was observed during monsoon and minimum (30.78 mg/l) in winter season. The average value of COD was found 41.85 ± 9.75 mg/l at point C_3 in zone C.

Chloride (mg/l)

The chloride concentration was generally found maximum (5381.00 mg/l) in monsoon season and minimum (22.51 mg/l) during winter season at zone C. In this zone C, at point C_1, the chloride was observed maximum (5381.00 mg/l) in monsoon season and minimum (36.12 mg/l) during winter season and constituted the average mean value of chloride ion as 1821.99 ± 3082.19 mg/l. At point C_2, the maximum concentration of chloride ion was reported (59.50 mg/l) in monsoon and minimum (49.98 mg/l) during winter season. The average mean value of chloride ion was reported as 55.6 ± 4.99 mg/l at point C_2. Similarly, at point C_3, the chloride ion showed maximum (32.82 mg/l) level in monsoon and minimum (22.51 mg/l) during winter season and reported the average mean value of chloride ion as 28.40 ± 5.31 mg/l at point C_3.

Calcium (mg/l)

The calcium ion concentration was generally found maximum (58.92 mg/l) in monsoon season and minimum (31.32 mg/l) during winter season at zone C. In this zone C, at point C_1, the calcium ion was observed maximum (58.09 mg/l) in monsoon season and minimum (38.02 mg/l) during winter season and constituted the average mean value of chloride ion as 46.73 ± 10.29 mg/l. At point C_2, the maximum concentration of calcium ion was reported (58.92 mg/l) in monsoon and minimum (38.76 mg/l) during winter season. The average mean value of calcium ion was reported as 48.98 ± 10.08 mg/l at point C_2. Similarly, at point C_3, the calcium ion showed maximum (53.61 mg/l) level in monsoon and minimum (31.32 mg/l) during winter season and reported the average mean value of calcium ion as 41.18 ± 11.36 mg/l at point C_3.

Magnesium (mg/l)

The magnesium ion concentration was generally found maximum (28.59 mg/l) in monsoon season and minimum (11.75 mg/l) during winter season at zone C. In this zone C, at point C_1, the magnesium ion was observed maximum (23.51 mg/l) in monsoon season and minimum (13.62 mg/l) during winter season and constituted the average mean value of magnesium ion as 18.57 ± 4.94 mg/l. At point C_2, the maximum concentration of magnesium ion was reported (28.59 mg/l) in monsoon and minimum (16.85 mg/l) during winter season. The average mean value of magnesium ion was reported as 22.23 ± 5.93 mg/l at point C_2. Similarly, at point C_3, the magnesium ion showed maximum (21.69 mg/l) level in monsoon and minimum (11.75 mg/l) during winter season and reported the average mean value of magnesium ion as 16.59 ± 4.97 mg/l at point C_3.

Phosphates (mg/l)

The phosphate concentration was generally found maximum (1.17 mg/l) in summer season and minimum (0.34 mg/l) during monsoon season at zone C. In this zone C, at point C_1, the phosphate ion was observed maximum (0.95 mg/l) in summer season and minimum (0.34 mg/l) during monsoon season and constituted the average mean value of phosphate ion as 0.71 ± 0.32 mg/l. At point C_2, the maximum concentration of phosphate ion was reported (1.17 mg/l) in summer and minimum (0.77 mg/l) during monsoon season. The average mean value of phosphate ion was reported as 0.95 ± 0.20 mg/l at point C_2. Similarly, at point C_3, the phosphate ion showed maximum (0.86 mg/l) level in summer and minimum (0.56 mg/l) during monsoon season and reported the average mean value of phosphate ion as 0.71 ± 0.15 mg/l at point C_3.

Nitrates (mg/l)

The Nitrates concentration was generally found maximum (2.91 mg/l) in monsoon season and minimum (0.81 mg/l) during winter season at zone C. In this zone C, at point C_1, the nitrate was observed maximum (2.91 mg/l) in monsoon season and minimum (1.26 mg/l) during winter season and constituted the average mean value of nitrates ion as 1.85 ± 0.92 mg/l. At point C_2, the maximum concentration of nitrates ion was reported (2.55 mg/l) in monsoon and minimum (1.37 mg/l) during winter season. The average mean value of nitrate ion was reported as 2.08 ± 0.62 mg/l at point C_2. Similarly, at point C_3, the nitrate ion showed maximum (1.68 mg/l) level in monsoon and minimum (0.81 mg/l) during winter season and reported the average mean value of nitrate ion as 1.15 ± 0.46 mg/l at point C_3.

Sampling Zone D (Bagrajpur Industrial area)

Temperature (°C)

The temperature of water at sampling zone D (Bagrajpur Industrial area) was observed maximum (36.48°C) during summer season and minimum (116.75°C) in winter season. At this zone, D zone consists of D_1, D_2 and D_3. At D_1, the temperature reported maximum (36.32°C) during summer and minimum (18.28°C) in winter season. At D_2 point, the temperature recorded maximum (36.38°C) in summer and minimum (17.65°C) in winter seasons and at D_3 point, the temperature was observed maximum (34.82°C) and minimum (16.75°C) in winter season. The average value of temperature at point D_1, D_2 and D_3 was reported as 27.64 ± 9.04, 27.36 ± 9.43 and 26.27 ± 9.07.

pH

pH of river water at sampling Zone D, was reported maximum (7.32) during monsoon season and minimum (5.73) in winter season. At this zone, D_1 point, showed the pH maximum (6.85) and minimum (5.52) during monsoon and summer respectively. At D_2 point, the maximum pH was observed (7.32) during monsoon and minimum (6.07) in summer season and at D_3 point, the pH was reported maximum (6.72) and minimum (5.73) during monsoon and winter respectively. The average of value of pH at point D_1, D2 and D_3 was reported as 6.21 ± 0.56, 6.50 ± 0.71 and 6.12 ± 0.53.

Turbidity (N.T.U.)

In this Zone-D, the turbidity was reported maximum (185.65 N.T.U.) in monsoon and minimum (128.56 N.T.U.) in winter season. The Turbidity of water at point D1 was observed maximum (168.53 N.T.U.) in monsoon and minimum (133.39 N.T.U.) in winter season. The average mean value of turbidity at this point D_1 was reported as lowest (152.96 ± 17.91 N.T.U). At point D_2, the turbidity was found maximum (185.65 N.T.U.) in monsoon season and minimum (143.69 N.T.U.) in winter season. The average mean value of turbidity at this point D_2 was reported as highest (166.09 ± 21.12 N.T.U) and at point D_3, the Turbidity was observed maximum (142.51 N.T.U.) and minimum (128.56 N.T.U.) during monsoon and winter respectively. The average mean value of turbidity at this point D_3 was reported as 134.91 ± 7.06 N.T.U.

Total Dissolved Solids (mg/l)

The concentration of total dissolved solids at zone D was recorded maximum (1465.82 mg/l) in summer and minimum (1292.65 mg/l) during winter season. In this zone, at point D_1, the maximum (1425 59 mg/l) concentration of TDS was recorded in summer and minimum (1292.65 mg/l) in winter season. The average mean value of TDS at pint D_1 was recorded as 1354.69 ± 67.16 mg/l. At point D_2, the TDS concentration was recorded maximum (1465.82 mg/l) and minimum (1328.25 mg/l) summer and winter respectively. The average mean value of TDS at point D_2 was recorded as 1406.94 ± 70.89 mg/l. At point zone D_3, the maximum concentration (1365.87 mg/l) of total dissolved solids were observed during summer and minimum concentration (1295.89 mg/l) recorded during winter season. The average mean value of TDS was observed as 1327.83 ± 35.39 mg/l at pint D_3.

Dissolved Oxygen (mg/l)

At zone D, DO was observed maximum (6.31 mg/l) during monsoon season and minimum (1.45 mg/l) in summer season. In this zone, the D_1 point showed the maximum concentration (5.96 mg/l) of DO during monsoon and minimum (1.45 mg/l) in summer season. The average mean value of DO concentration was recorded as 4.08 ± 2.35 mg/l at point D_1. At point D_2, the DO concentration was recorded maximum (6.23 mg/l) and minimum (4.38 mg/l) in monsoon and summer season respectively. The average mean value of DO concentration at point D_2 was recorded as 5.05 ± 1.02 mg/l. At point D_3, the DO level was observed maximum (6.31 mg/l) during monsoon and minimum (4 34 mg/l) during summer. The average DO concentration level was observed at point D_3 as 5.06 ± 1.09 mg/l.

Free CO_2 (mg/l)

The Free carbon dioxide was observed maximum (4.1 mg/l) in summer and minimum (1.9 mg/l) in monsoon season at zone D. In this zone D, the point D_1, indicated the concentration of CO_2 as 4.1 mg/l (maximum) during summer and 3.09 mg/l (minimum) during winter. The average mean value of free CO_2 level was reported 3.56 ± 0.51 at point D_1. At point D_2, the CO_2 concentration in surface water reported as maximum concentration (3.8 mg/l) of CO_2 was observed during winter and minimum (3.07 mg/l) in summer season. The average mean value of CO_2 at point D_2 was recorded as 3.36 ± 0.39 mg/l. At point D_3, the concentration of Free CO_2 was maximum (2.5 mg/l) and minimum (1.9 mg/l) during winter and monsoon respectively. The average mean value of Free CO_2 was observed as 2.16 ± 0.31 mg/l at point D_3.

Hardness (mg/l)

The hardness of river water was analysed seasonally. The hardness of river water was observed maximum (698.51 mg/l) in monsoon season and minimum (386.72 mg/l) in winter season at zone D. In this zone D, the point D_1 showed the maximum (698.51mg/l) hardness during monsoon and minimum (665.00 mg/l) during winter season. The average mean concentration of hardness was observed as 683.14 ± 16.93 mg/l at point D_1. At point D_2, the hardness was reported maximum (470.79 mg/l) during monsoon and minimum (452.61 mg/l) in winter season. The average mean value of hardness was reported as 464.42 ± 10.24 mg/l at point D_2. At point D_3, the value of hardness was observed maximum (451.39 mg/l) during summer and minimum (386.72 mg/l) in winter season. The average value of hardness was observed as 423.23 ± 33.13 mg/l at point C_3.

Total Alkalinity (mg/l)

The alkalinity was found maximum (412.75 mg/l) during summer season and minimum (332.75 mg/l) during winter season at zone D. In this zone, at point D_1, the maximum alkalinity (372.00 mg/l) was observed during summer season and minimum (338.65 mg/l) in winter season. The average mean value of alkalinity was reported as 353.12 ± 17.10 mg/l at point D_1. At point D_2, the alkalinity was reported maximum (412.75 mg/l) in monsoon and minimum (376.75 mg/l) during winter season. The average mean value of alkalinity was found as 396.00 ± 18.13 mg/l at point D_2. Similarly, at point D_3, the alkalinity was found maximum (359.62 mg/l) in summer and minimum (332.75 mg/l) during winter season. The average value of alkalinity was reported as 347.96 ± 13.78 mg/l at point D_3.

Biological Oxygen Demand (mg/l)

At zone D, the BOD was estimated as maximum (74.83 mg/l) during summer season and minimum (44.53 mg/l) in winter season. In this zone, at point D_1, the maximum concentration of BOD (68.32 mg/l) was observed during summer season and minimum (49.89 mg/l) during winter season. The average means value of BOD values were reported as 58.18 ± 9.35 mg/l at point zone D_1. At point D_2, the BOD level was reported maximum (74.83 mg/l) in winter season and minimum (54.66 mg/l) during winter season. The average value of BOD at point zone D_2 was reported as 64.06 ± 10.15 mg/l and at point D_3, the BOD level was reported maximum (65.25 mg/l) in summer and minimum (44.53 mg/l) during winter season and indicated the average mean value of BOD as 55.68 ± 10.45 mg/l at point D_3.

Chemical Oxygen Demand (mg/l)

The concentration of COD was reported maximum (246.82 mg/l) in monsoon and minimum (117.32 mg/l) during winter at zone D. In this zone, at point D_1, the COD level was reported as maximum (234.21 mg/l) in monsoon season and minimum (49.89 mg/l) during winter season and showed the average mean value of COD as 178.15 ± 58.59 mg/l. At point D_2, the COD concentration was observed maximum (246.82 mg/l) during monsoon season and minimum (172.62 mg/l) during winter season. The average mean value of COD was reported as 204.98 ± 37.99 mg/l at point D_2. Similarly, at point D_3, the maximum COD value (231.53 mg/l) was observed during monsoon and minimum (163.92 mg/l) in winter season. The average value of COD was found 188.92 ± 37.08 mg/l at point D_3 in zone D.

Chloride (mg/l)

The chloride concentration was generally found maximum (248.91 mg/l) in monsoon season and minimum (158.39 mg/l) during winter season at zone D. In this zone D, at point D_1, the chloride was observed maximum (172.58 mg/l) in summer season and minimum (158.39 mg/l) during winter season and constituted the average mean value of chloride ion as 165.61 ± 7.09 mg/l. At point D_2, the maximum concentration of chloride ion was reported (248.91 mg/l) in monsoon and minimum (229.56 mg/l) during winter season. The average mean value of chloride ion was reported as 240.09 ± 9.79 mg/l at point D_2. Similarly, at point D_3, the chloride ion showed maximum (212.00 mg/l) level in monsoon and minimum (168.27 mg/l) during winter season and reported the average mean value of chloride ion as 194.36 ± 23.06 mg/l at point $D_{3.}$

Calcium (mg/l)

The calcium ion concentration was generally found maximum (243.86 mg/l) in summer season and minimum (145.82 mg/l) during winter season at zone D. In this zone D, at point D_1, the calcium ion was observed maximum (162.91 mg/l) in monsoon season and minimum (127.63 mg/l) during winter season and constituted the average mean value of chloride ion as 146.2 ± 17.71 mg/l. At point D_2, the maximum concentration of calcium ion was reported (243.86 mg/l) in monsoon and minimum (207.68 mg/l) during summer season. The average mean value of calcium ion was reported as 220.83 ± 20.01 mg/l at point D_2. Similarly, at point D_3, the calcium ion showed maximum (186.21 mg/l) level in monsoon and minimum (145.82 mg/l) during summer season and reported the average mean value of calcium ion as 162.04 ± 21.34 mg/l at point D_3.

Magnesium (mg/l)

The magnesium ion concentration was generally found maximum (166.29 mg/l) in monsoon season and minimum (63.98 mg/l) during winter season at zone D. In this zone D, at point D_1, the magnesium ion was observed maximum (111.18 mg/l) in monsoon season and minimum (96.87 mg/l) during winter season and constituted the average mean value of magnesium ion as 103.67 ± 7.18 mg/l. At point D_2, the maximum concentration of magnesium ion was reported (166.29 mg/l) in monsoon and minimum (153.81 mg/l) during winter season. The average mean value of magnesium ion was reported as 159.54 ± 6.30 mg/l at point D_2. Similarly, at point D_3, the magnesium ion showed maximum (78.80 mg/l) level in monsoon and minimum (63.98 mg/l) during winter season and reported the average mean value of magnesium ion as 72.9 ± 7.86 mg/l at point D_3.

Phosphates (mg/l)

The phosphate concentration was generally found maximum (4.11 mg/l) in summer season and minimum (1.88 mg/l) during winter season at zone D. In this zone D, at point D_1, the phosphate ion was observed maximum (4.11 mg/l) in summer season and minimum (3.08 mg/l) during winter season and constituted the average mean value of phosphate ion as 3.61 ± 0.51 mg/l. At point D_2, the maximum concentration of phosphate ion was reported (3.72 mg/l) in summer and minimum (2.52 mg/l) during winter season. The average mean value of phosphate ion was reported as 3.03 ± 0.61 mg/l at point D_2. Similarly, at point D_3, the phosphate ion showed maximum (2.53 mg/l) level in summer and minimum (1.88 mg/l) during monsoon season and reported the average mean value of phosphate ion as 2.19 ± 0.32 mg/l at point D_3.

Nitrates (mg/l)

The Nitrates concentration was generally found maximum (5.31 mg/l) in summer season and minimum (3.67 mg/l) during winter season at zone D. In this zone, at point D_1, the nitrate was observed maximum (3.93 mg/l) in monsoon season and minimum (3.67 mg/l) during winter season and constituted the average mean value of nitrates ion as 3.82 ± 0.13 mg/l. At point D_2, the maximum concentration of nitrates ion was reported (5.31 mg/l) in summer and minimum (5.21 mg/l) during winter season. The average mean value of nitrate ion was reported as 5.26 ± 0.05 mg/l at point D_2. Similarly, at point D_3, the nitrate ion showed maximum (4.19 mg/l) level in monsoon and minimum (4.08 mg/l) during winter season and reported the average mean value of nitrate ion as 4.15 ± 0.06 mg/l at point D_3.

Sampling Zone E (Mandawali)

Temperature (°C)

The temperature of water at sampling zone E (Mandawali) was observed maximum (34.26°C) during summer season and minimum (16.63°C) in winter season. At this zone, E zone consists of E_1, E_2 and E_3. At E_1, the temperature reported maximum

(32.93°C) during summer and minimum (16.63°C) in winter season. At E_2 point, the temperature recorded maximum (34.26°C) in summer and minimum (17.55°C) in winter seasons and at E_3 point, the temperature was observed maximum (33.16°C) and minimum (17.08°C) in summer and winter season respectively. The average value of temperature at point E_1, E_2 and E_3 was reported as 25.38 ± 8.21, 27.14 ± 8.62 and 25.92 ± 8.16 respectively.

pH

pH of river water at sampling Zone E, was reported maximum (8.78) during monsoon season and minimum (7.66) in winter season. At this zone, E_1 point, showed the pH maximum (8.87) and minimum (7.66) during monsoon and winter season respectively. At E_2 point, the maximum pH was observed (8.87) during monsoon and minimum (7.79) in winter season and at E_3 point, the pH was reported maximum (8.58) and minimum (8.00) during monsoon and winter respectively. The average of value of pH at point E_1, E_2 and E_3 was reported as 8.13 ± 0.65, 8.19 ± 0.59 and 8.27 ± 0.29 respectively.

Turbidity (N.T.U.)

In this Zone-E, the turbidity was reported maximum (50.17 N.T.U.) in monsoon and minimum (18.76 N.T.U.) in winter season. The Turbidity of water at point E_1 was observed maximum (45.62 N.T.U.) in monsoon and minimum (23.18 N.T.U.) in winter season. The average mean value of turbidity at this point E_1 was reported as lowest (32.48 ± 11.70 N.T.U). At point E_2, the turbidity was found maximum (235.68 N.T.U.) in monsoon season and minimum (123.76 N.T.U.) in winter season. The average mean value of turbidity at this point E_2 was reported as 28.47 ± 12.04 N.T.U and at point E_3, the Turbidity was observed maximum (50.17 N.T.U.) and minimum (21.35 N.T.U.) during monsoon and winter respectively. The average mean value of turbidity at this point E_3 was reported as 1688.29 ± 2882.75 N.T.U.

Total Dissolved Solids (mg/l)

The concentration of total dissolved solids at zone E was recorded maximum (200.11 mg/l) in monsoon and minimum (134.28 mg/l) during winter season. In this zone, at point E_1, the maximum (186.92 mg/l) concentration of TDS was recorded in monsoon and minimum (134.28 mg/l) in winter season. The average mean value of TDS at pint E_1 was recorded as 157.49 ± 26.86 mg/l. At point E_2, the TDS concentration was recorded maximum (200.11 mg/l) and minimum (141.62 mg/l) monsoon and winter respectively. The average mean value of TDS at point E2 was recorded as 166.53 ± 30.19 mg/l. At point zone E_3 the maximum concentration (195.87 mg/l) of total dissolved solids were observed during monsoon and minimum concentration (137.37 mg/l) recorded during winter season. The average mean value of TDS was observed as 162.28 ± 30.20 mg/l at pint E_3.

Dissolved Oxygen (mg/l)

At zone D, DO was observed maximum (7.31 mg/l) during monsoon season and minimum (5.95 mg/l) in summer season. In this zone, the E_1 point showed the maximum concentration (7.00 mg/l) of DO during monsoon and minimum (6.18 mg/l) in winter season. The average mean value of DO concentration was recorded as 6.48 ± 0.45 mg/l at point E_1. At point E_2, the DO concentration was recorded maximum (7.31 mg/l) and minimum (6.28 mg/l) in monsoon and winter season respectively. The average mean value of DO concentration at point E_2 was recorded as 6.64 ± 0.58 mg/l. At point E_3, the DO level was observed maximum (7.23 mg/l) during monsoon and minimum (5.95 mg/l) during summer. The average DO concentration level was observed at point E_3 as 6.39 ± 0.72 mg/l.

Free CO_2 (mg/l)

The Free carbon dioxide was observed maximum (4.04 mg/l) in summer and minimum (1.01 mg/l) in monsoon season at zone E. In this zone E, the point E_1, indicated the concentration of CO_2 as 3.03 mg/l (maximum) during monsoon and 2.04 mg/l (minimum) during winter. The average mean value of free CO_2 level was reported 2.46 ± 1.84 at point E_1. At point E_2, the CO_2 concentration in surface water reported as maximum concentration (4.04 mg/l) of CO_2 was observed during summer and minimum (1.02 mg/l) in winter season. The average mean value of CO_2 at point E_2 was recorded as 2.32 ± 1.34 mg/l. At point E_3, the concentration of Free CO_2 was maximum (3.63 mg/l) and minimum (1.01 mg/l) during summer and winter respectively. The average mean value of Free CO_2 was observed as 2.22 ± 1.16 mg/l at point E_3.

Hardness (mg/l)

The hardness of river water was analyzed seasonally. The hardness of river water was observed maximum (253.11 mg/l) in monsoon season and minimum (193.21 mg/l) in winter season at zone E. In this zone E, the point E_1 showed the maximum (244.65 mg/l) hardness during monsoon and minimum (198.85 mg/l) during winter season. The average mean concentration of hardness was observed as 223.10 ± 23.02 mg/l at point E_1. At point E_2, the hardness was reported maximum (253.11 mg/l) during monsoon and minimum (201.62 mg/l) in winter season. The average mean value of hardness was reported as 228.99 ± 25.89 mg/l at point E_2. At point E_3, the value of hardness was observed maximum (250.65 mg/l) during monsoon and minimum (193.21 mg/l) in winter season. The average value of hardness was observed as 223.72 ± 28.89 mg/l at point E_3.

Total Alkalinity (mg/l)

The alkalinity was found maximum (312.81 mg/l) during monsoon season and minimum (271.57 mg/l) during winter season at zone E. In this zone, at point E_1, the maximum alkalinity (312.81 mg/l) was observed during monsoon season and minimum (271.57 mg/l) in winter season. The average mean value of alkalinity was reported as 290.003 ± 20.96 mg/l at point E_1. At point E_2, the alkalinity was reported maximum (253.11 mg/l) in monsoon and minimum (201.62 mg/l) during winter season. The average mean value of alkalinity was found as 288.08 ± 21.55 mg/l at point E_2. Similarly, at point E_3, the alkalinity was found maximum (311.25 mg/l) in monsoon and minimum (270.00 mg/l) during winter season. The average value of alkalinity was reported as 288.64 ± 20.91 mg/l at point E_3.

Biological Oxygen Demand (mg/l)

In zone E, the BOD was estimated as maximum (24.00 mg/l) during monsoon season and minimum (14.59 mg/l) in winter season. In this zone, at point E_1, the maximum concentration of BOD (21.32 mg/l) was observed during monsoon season and minimum (14.59 mg/l) during winter season. The average means value of BOD values were reported as 17.52 ± 3.45 mg/l at point zone E_1. At point E_2, the BOD level was reported maximum (23.21 mg/l) in monsoon season and minimum (14.84 mg/l) during winter season. The average value of BOD at point zone E_2 was reported as 18.33 ± 4.35 mg/l and at point E_3, the BOD level was reported maximum (24.00 mg/l) in monsoon and minimum (14.62 mg/l) during winter season and indicated the average mean value of BOD as 18.56 ± 4.87 mg/l at point E_3.

Chemical Oxygen Demand (mg/l)

The concentration of COD was reported maximum (57.13 mg/l) in monsoon and minimum (31.91 mg/l) during winter at zone E. In this zone, at point E_1, the COD level was reported as maximum (57.13 mg/l) in monsoon season and minimum (33.75 mg/l) during winter season and showed the average mean value of COD as 46.3 ± 11.78 mg/l. At point E_2, the COD concentration was observed maximum (56.92 mg/l) during monsoon season and minimum (32.81 mg/l) during winter season. The average mean value of COD was reported as 46.02 ± 12.22 mg/l at point E_2. Similarly, at point E_3, the maximum COD value (51.61 mg/l) was observed during monsoon and minimum (31.91 mg/l) in winter season. The average value of COD was found 43.57 ± 10.33 mg/l at point E_3 in zone E.

Chloride (mg/l)

The chloride concentration was generally found maximum (63.00 mg/l) in monsoon season and minimum (31.32 mg/l) during winter season at zone E. In this zone E, at point E_1, the chloride was observed maximum (57.88 mg/l) in monsoon season and minimum (37.39 mg/l) during winter season and constituted the average mean value of chloride ion as 48.99 ± 10.51 mg/l. At point E_2, the maximum concentration of chloride ion was reported (63.00 mg/l) in monsoon and minimum (38.16 mg/l) during winter season. The average mean value of chloride ion was reported as 51.92 ± 12.64 mg/l at point E_2. Similarly, at point E_3, the chloride ion showed maximum (54.59 mg/l) level in monsoon and minimum (31.32 mg/l) during winter season and reported the average mean value of chloride ion as 46.23 ± 12.94 mg/l at point E_3.

Calcium (mg/l)

The calcium ion concentration was generally found maximum (66.00 mg/l) in monsoon season and minimum (29.52 mg/l) during winter season at zone E. In this zone E, at point E_1, the calcium ion was observed maximum (63.81 mg/l) in monsoon season and minimum (32.91 mg/l) during winter season and constituted the average mean value of chloride ion as 47.31 ± 15.56 mg/l. At point E_2, the maximum concentration of calcium ion was reported (66.00 mg/l) in monsoon and minimum (35.82 mg/l) during summer season. The average mean value of calcium ion was reported as 50.11 ± 15.15 mg/l at point E_2. Similarly, at point E_3, the calcium ion showed maximum (52.18 mg/l) level in monsoon and minimum (29.52 mg/l) during winter season and reported the average mean value of calcium ion as 41.11 ± 11.34 mg/l at point E_3.

Magnesium (mg/l)

The magnesium ion concentration was generally found maximum (32.68 mg/l) in monsoon season and minimum (17.00 mg/l) during winter season at zone E. In this zone E, at point E_1, the magnesium ion was observed maximum (31.00 mg/l) in monsoon season and minimum (17.00 mg/l) during winter season and constituted the average mean value of magnesium ion as 23.02 ± 7.20 mg/l. At point E_2, the maximum concentration of magnesium ion was reported (32.68 mg/l) in monsoon and minimum (20.00 mg/l) during winter season. The average mean value of magnesium ion was reported as 25.20 ± 6.64 mg/l at point E_2. Similarly, at point E_3, the magnesium ion showed maximum (32.00 mg/l) level in monsoon and minimum (18.17 mg/l) during winter season and reported the average mean value of magnesium ion as 24.23 ± 7.07 mg/l at point E_3.

Phosphates (mg/l)

The phosphate concentration was generally found maximum (1.12 mg/l) in summer season and minimum (0.68 mg/l) during monsoon season at zone E. In this zone E, at point E_1, the phosphate ion was observed maximum (1.09 mg/l) in summer season and minimum (0.68 mg/l) during monsoon season and constituted the average mean value of phosphate ion as 0.91 ± 0.21 mg/l. At point E_2, the maximum concentration of phosphate ion was reported (1.12 mg/l) in summer and minimum (0.87 mg/l) during monsoon season. The average mean value of phosphate ion was reported as 1.00 ± 0.12 mg/l at point E_2. Similarly, at point E_3, the phosphate ion showed maximum (1.11 mg/l) level in summer and minimum (0.87 mg/l) during monsoon season and reported the average mean value of phosphate ion as 0.97 ± 0.13 mg/l at point E_3.

Nitrates (mg/l)

The Nitrates concentration was generally found maximum (3.23 mg/l) in monsoon season and minimum (1.29 mg/l) during winter season at zone E. In this zone, at point E_1, the nitrate was observed maximum (3.00 mg/l) in monsoon season and minimum (1.30 mg/l) during winter season and constituted the average mean value of nitrates ion as 2.00 ± 0.88 mg/l. At point E_2, the maximum concentration of nitrates ion was reported (3.23 mg/l) in summer and minimum (1.42 mg/l) during winter season. The average mean value of nitrate ion was reported as 2.14 ± 0.96 mg/l at point E_2. Similarly, at point E_3, the nitrate ion showed maximum (2.84 mg/l) level in monsoon and minimum (1.29 mg/l) during winter season and reported the average mean value of nitrate ion as 1.87 ± 0.84 mg/l at point E_3.

Temperature plays a vital role in chemical, biological processes and also for the life of aquatic organisms in the stream environment. Microorganisms affecting the breakdown of organic matter in stream are profoundly influenced by temperature changes, then lower temperature. The rate of oxidation of organic matter was as much as greater during summer than winter. The higher value in temperature was due to the addition of sugar industry and paper mill effluents along with municipal waste at few zones. The finding was similar to that observed by Palharya *et al.* (1993) for the river ecosystem. They reported that the sensitivity of many organisms of toxic wastes is also influenced by change in water temperature is very important of aquatic life flora and fauna and was moderate (15.04°C to 21.89°C) throughout the season at river Ravi. Prasad and Patil (2008) and Kumar and Dua (2009) reported similar trends as observed for river Ravi. Bharti (2012a) also indicated the similar trend for surface water temperature of a small river in the lower Himalaya.

pH determination is an important factor for realizing the nature and extent of pollution. An increase in value of pH by one unit means a tenfold decrease in H+ ion concentration (*i.e.,* in the intensity of acidic nature). It means that a small change in pH is a considerable change in H+ ion concentration. Many important chemical and biological processes only take place at a certain pH values or within a narrow range. pH is the indicator of acidic and alkaline condition of water status. The pH of water body indicates degree of deterioration of the water quality (Singh and Bharti, 2015, Bharti, 2012a, Bharti, 2013). BIS have recommended 6.5-8.5 range of pH for the use of water for various purposes. Below 5.00 or above 8.80 are definitely detrimental to aquatic life. The literature cited suggests that the industrialization and urbanization are modifying the pH of natural water by effluents. The pH values of river Kali during the present study period was found both acidic and alkaline in nature. The similar findings have been observed by the David (1956) in river Bandra. Khadse *et al.* (2008) have reported higher pH at some sites that could be due to bicarbonates and carbonates of calcium and magnesium in water. The main source of such chemicals may be because of urban runoff or industrial waste water. Bharti (2012b) also indicated the similar trend for surface water pH of a Sahastradhara river in the Shivalik Himalaya.

In term of TDSs, this situation is comparable to the findings as observed by the Singh *et al.* (2005) in river Gomti due to the addition of waste effluents in the river at Lucknow. Khadse *et al.* (2008) reported similar findings due to waste effluents being discharged into the river Kanhan. Bharti *et al.* (2012a) also indicated the similar trend for TDSs in surface water of a river in Meghalaya.

Dissolved oxygen (DO) is the utmost need for all the aquatic organisms. Oxygen is sparingly soluble in water and its solubility is low at higher temperature .The oxygen is likely to be due to depletion of dissolved oxygen that depends upon the biodegradability of the organic matter in the ecosystem. The molecular diffusion from air and production of oxygen due to photo synthetic activity of the phytoplankton, try to replenish oxygen in the stream. When the rate of de oxygenation is more than the rate of re-oxygenation, the oxygen budget of the river water reduces. The reduced dissolved oxygen level can be detrimental to the aquatic life. Inhabiting there in, the minimum concentration of dissolved oxygen should be 5.0 mg/l at 20°C or 57 per cent dissolved oxygen saturation for healthy condition of aquatic life (Gupta and Bharti, 2016, Bharti *et al.* 2012a). According to the Manivasakam, (1980), the dissolved oxygen in the water is essential for aquatic life. Deficiency of dissolved oxygen gives bad odor to water due to anaerobic decomposition of organic wastes.

The change in DO is due to the mixing of sugar industry effluents, municipal, domestic wastes with Kali river. Bhaskaran *et al.* (1963) reported oxygen relationship between BOD and DO contents in river Gomti. A similar observation has been reported by Verma *et al.* (1984) that BOD and DO have significant relationship and directly indicate organic pollutant load in surface water system in river Kali (east). The quality of the water in terms of DO content is always of primary importance because of waste discharge point in water (Bharti, 2012b). The DO is required for aerobic oxidation of the wastes by Mukherjee *et al.* (1993) in Ganga river. DO may be a potential indicator of river quality in assessing urban impacts on river ecosystem (Kannel *et al.* 2007). The similar trends have been reported for Hindon river by Suthar *et al.* (2009), the worst condition of DO of river being between 3.10 to 4.03 mg/l at Ghaziabad. Bharti (2014) found a maximum value of DO in the surface water of Sahastradhara river at Dehradun.

The hardness of water is caused by multivalent metallic cations calcium and magnesium that are most abundant in natural water. Water with <50 mg/l hardness is considered soft, >150 mg/l moderately hard and >300 mg/l very hard. A relationship between carbonate hardness and organic pollution has been reported by Parkash and Rawat (1981). Laiman and Dixit (1989) observed an increase in the total hardness up to about 350 mg/l in Ganga and Bhagirathi river waters due to the mixing of industrial effluents. According to Sinha, (1988) the river water with hardness ranged from 20 mg/l to 150 mg/l may be considered as moderately hard while that of the effluent water with range of 150 mg/l to 300 mg/l as hard. Similar observations (as observed in the present study) have been reported by Chandra *et al.* (1996) who reported higher value of hardness in river Ramganga and Sabarmati due to mixing of sewage, industrial and domestic effluents in to the river. Bharti *et al.* (2012c) also indicated the similar trend for hardness of surface water of a small river in southern Bhutan.

Alkalinity is a measure of its capacity to neutralize acids. The determination of alkalinity aids in understanding of the buffering capacity and interpretation of the treatment process. The major portion of alkalinity in natural water is caused by bicarbonates and carbonates. Hydro-oxide alkalinity is seen only if industries discharge their waste in to a stream of water or in case of high algal activity in it. The total alkalinity was lower in monsoon months probably due to the dilution of the concentration of nutrients during monsoon and to rise in water level. It is quite clear from the data obtained from Kali water samples that total alkalinity is frequently increased by the addition of industrial and domestic waste of drain inputs and attains maximum value of total alkalinity. The similar trend has been reported by Ramesh *et al.* (1992), for the river Damodar in Bihar, the alkalinity being much higher. Bharti (2012a) also indicated the similar trend for surface water alkalinity of a Sahastradhara river at Dehradun (Uttarakhand), India.

The biochemical oxygen demand (BOD) is one of the most important tests for determining the strength of the polluting water, sewage industrial wastes, effluents etc. BOD is defined as the quantity of oxygen required by the bacteria in stabilizing the decomposable organic matter under aerobic conditions. The effect of BOD depends on other factors and it is not always safe to accept any definite oxygen limit without considering other hazards. BOD value increase after mixing of waste discharge is usually due decomposition of organic degradable matter in the river water that indicates the organic pollution load into the water. A higher increase in the BOD value due to the mixing of industrial and domestic wastes has been observed by the Agarwal (1990).

A trend of decrease in BOD in downstream site was observed, which further indicated the self-purification capacity of this river as also observed by Suthar *et al.* (2009) in Hindon river at Ghaziabad. According to the Royal commission (1972) of sewage disposal water having BOD more than 5 mg/l is unsafe for domestic use. Similar trends have been studied by Paythkin and Krivoshein (1980) and Golterman *et al.* (1983). It was concluded that increase flow rate, temperature and sedimentation load reduced BOD. Bhutiani and Khanna, (2007) have reported a similar pattern for river Suswa. Bharti (2012a) also indicated the similar trend for BOD in surface water of a small river in the lower Himalaya. BOD standard for in land surface water in India is 2, 3 and 4 different purposes. In river Kali BOD exceeded to a great extent due to mixing of waste effluents at different sampling sites.

The chemical oxygen demand (COD) is the measurement of oxygen required for the oxidation of organic matter in the sample. It is especially useful when the BOD cannot be determined on account of the presence of toxic substances. The use of river water with high value of COD may cause health hazards to both humans and domestic animals as suggested by Bermejo *et al.* (1981). The observation made by workers like: Sinha *et al.* (1989), Gautam *et al.* (1989), Saxena, (1994) have indicated that the measurement of COD is of great importance for water having unfavorable conditions for the growth of microorganisms such as: presence of toxic chemical.

Similar finding have been reported by Motwani *et al.* (1956) who also observed the similar pattern of COD, BOD and DO distribution in river Sone in Bihar due to addition of Rohtash Industrial area wastes. Similar findings were reported by Alam *et al.* (2007) for the river Surma and by Khadse *et al.* (2008) for the river Kanhan. Mukherjee *et al.* (1993) have reported that about 47 per cent COD comes from industrial sources in Indian River system. In present study in Kali river, the COD was higher due to discharge of Industrial wastes.

High chloride content indicates heavy pollution. It is observed that chloride is positively correlated with calcium hardness, salinity, alkalinity, Sulphate and nitrates. The chloride content remains more in summer followed by winter and monsoon season. Earlier high values of chloride have been reported by Murthy *et al.* (1994) and Singh and Mahaveer (1997) in Tungabhadra and Ganga river water because of the mixing with domestic waste-effluents. The present finding is similar to that of Murthy *et al.*

(1994) and Singh and Mahaveer (1997) in Tungabhadra and Ganga river water because of the mixing of domestic sewage with water. Higher concentration of chloride content indicates heavy pollution (Bhalla and Bharti, 2014).

The phosphate like nitrogen is also an essential nutrient for living organisms. Effect of phosphate has been widely reported by various workers (Rounse and Nelso, 1966). The phosphates are gradually hydrolyzed in water to the stable form the kind of matter as decomposed and biologically to release phosphate into the river body (Harmer, 1977). Phosphate concentration decreased due to the dilution of river water. The present trend was similar to that as reported by Bhadra *et al.* (2005) in North Bangal Terai River Kaljani - A tributary of river Torsa. It was observed that phosphate contamination is due to the disposal of detergent contaminated sewage and direct washing of cloths in to the river. The higher values at different sampling points were due to mixing of waste effluent and agriculture runoff.

The presence of nutrient in all the living matter explains the intimate association of environmental chemistry in the biological system. The biological system transformation of nitrogen in aquatic ecosystem appears to the qualitatively similar in many respects to those occurring in the soil ecosystem. Urea and uric acid have been shown responsible for the aquatic nitrate for fresh water phytoplankton (Syrett, 1962 and Guillard, 1963). During the present investigation period (mean value of three seasons *i.e.,* winter, summer and monsoon), nitrate concentration was observed in the range of 1.85 mg/l to 3.82 mg/l with a minimum value at Zone C and Maximum value at Zone D. The similar findings have been observed by Mitchell *et al.* (2001) for the river Logger and by Suthar *et al.* (2009) on water quality assessment for the river Hindon at Ghaziabad.

Waste material reacts with each other as a result the river water is being polluted and many toxic substances which ultimately make the water pollution and also severely affect the productivity of the aquatic ecosystem. Increasing quantity of toxic substances in water resources is currently an area of greater concern especially since a large number of industries are discharging their metal containing effluents in to fresh water without any adequate treatment (Canter, 1996; Bharti, 2012b; Bharti, 2012c). It was observed that the main cause of river Kali pollution mainly due to the addition of various industrial wastes (Sugar, Distillery, Chemical, Rubber, Paints, Paper, Dairies and City Municipal wastes), which finally merge into the river throughout its course. Among various industrial wastes, the distillery and paper effluents were the main polluting sources, because of their higher BOD, COD and TDS and low pH and low DO concentration (Bharti, 2007b).

Conclusion

It has been concluded that the Kali river water quality in terms of various physico-chemical variables is moderately polluted, which needs a strong conservation strategy to combat and minimize the pollution load. The river pollution is mainly of organic type, due to the indiscriminate discharge of quantities of untreated wastewater from

Table 3.1: Seasonal variation in physico-chemical variables of river Kali at sampling Zone-A

Parameters/ Sampling Points	Summer	Monsoon	Winter	Mean ± S.D.
Temperature (°C)				
A1	32.8 23.5 – 76.7	25.8 17.5 – 33.8	15.5 12.8 – 19.5	24.70 ± 8.71
A2	38.7 25.8 – 38.9	36.2 26.6 – 39.3	18.6 14.7 – 24.9	31.16 ±10.95
A3	34.9 23.8 – 36.9	26.3 19.6 – 33.9	17.8 12.6 -21.9	26.33 ± 8.55
pH				
A1	7.82 7.81 – 7.92	7.62 7.51 – 7.80	7.65 7.81 – 7.96	7.70 ± 0.11
A2	8.10 8.21 - 8.61	8.15 8.12 – 8.42	7.84 7.81 – 7.96	8.03 ± 0.17
A3	7.98 7.91 – 8.31	8.00 7.76 – 8.20	7.85 7.81 – 7.93	7.94 ± 0.08
Turbidity (NTU)				
A1	37.51 31.25-47.00	42.00 33.71-55.00	26.51 24.00-29.00	35.34 ± 7.97
A2	70.00 57.00-88.00	72.00 55.00-93.00	47.5 44.00-52.00	63.17 ± 13.60
A3	46.51 43.58-53.52	53.57 44.12-57.81	37.71 38.00-41.00	45.93 ± 7.94
TDS (mg/l)				
A1	403.15 371.00-436.00	380.00 351.00-420.00	341.72 331.00-362.00	374.96 ± 31.02
A2	1268.51 1210.00-1356.00	1265 1151.00-1380.00	1208.5 1130.00-1290.00	1247.34 ± 33.68
A3	868.51 820.00-921.00	838.51 762.00-900.6	732.51 681.00-790.00	813.18 ± 71.45
DO (mg/l)				
A1	6.12 5.32-6.93	7.21 7.30-7.80	6.84 6.40-7.31	6.72 ± 0.55
A2	6.65 5.89-6.54	7.82 7.11-7.91	6.74 6.51-7.89	7.07 ± 0.65
A3	6.21 5.46-6.45	6.89 5.26-6.72	6.46 6.29-6.51	6.52 ± 0.34
Free CO_2 (mg/l)				
A1	2.01 2.00-2.03	0.90 0.021-0.93	1.02 1.00-1.08	1.31 ± 0.34
A2	2.50 2.41-2.57	1.05 1.02-1.09	1.25 1.21-1.29	1.6 ± 0.54
A3	1.90 1.88-1.93	1.022 1.011-1.032	0.98 0.95-0.99	1.30 ± 0.001
Hardness (mg/l)				
A1	326.75 321.00-337.00	324.25 318.00-332.00	311.00 295.00-381.00	320.67 ± 8.46
A2	381.50 372.00-342.00	342 332.00-347.00	322.75 311.00-331.00	348.75 ± 29.95
A3	341.41 331.00-342.00	336.75 335.00-346.00	324.38 311.00-229.00	334.18 ± 8.801

Contd...

Total alkalinity (mg/l)				
A1	275.00 262.00-285.00	276.00 272.00-284.00	257.25 252.00-264.00	269.42 ± 10.55
A2	305.00 287.00-315.00	315.12 325.00-365.00	280.76 316.00-334.00	300.29 ± 17.66
A3	249.76 221.00 – 256.71	255.60 212.86-276.00	244.75 241.00-253.00	250.04 ± 5.43
BOD (mg/l)				
A1	44.15 32.42-53.51	45.41 36.72-54.21	34.51 32.20-35.21	41.36 ± 5.96
A2	48.91 29.71-54.62	52.81 35.81-55.61	35.91 27.82-36.52	45.88 ± 8.85
A3	39.61 23.81-41.25	47.25 31.82-48.26	28.75 24.60-29.82	38.54 ± 9.29
COD (mg/l)				
A1	62.51 51.00-71.91	65.12 52.00-69.71	55.82 48.00-58.00	61.15 ± 4.80
A2	68.21 50.81-70.00	71.02 54.38-74.29	61.82 51.23-62.91	67.02 ± 4.71
A3	62.00 43.26-63.91	64.69 50.26-65.81	59.21 35.68-61.91	61.97 ± 2.74
Chloride (mg/l)				
A1	32.76 25.32-36.86	36.91 28.26-38.21	23.16 22.81-26.58	30.94 ± 7.05
A2	37.51 31.51-41.52	42.81 33.18-43.61	29.75 26.85-31.87	36.69 ± 6.57
A3	34.19 33.51-41.52	36.48 34.18-38.89	27.92 23.52-29.31	32.86 ± 4.43
Calcium (mg/l)				
A1	30.36 27.32-34.22	33.21 30.15-34.57	25.16 25.00-28.26	29.58 ± 4.08
A2	39.42 31.61-41.21	43.76 39.18-44.26	28.91 25.61-29.81	37.36 ± 7.63
A3	32.41 29.58-33.61	39.82 33.26-41.81	22.81 20.82-23.93	31.68 ± 8.53
Magnesium (mg/l)				
A1	19.78 18.12-21.62	21.59 18.37-23.61	16.81 15.61-17.36	19.39 ± 2.41
A2	27.81 26.81-29.52	35.93 29.51-36.81	22.81 19.61-23.25	28.85 ± 6.62
A3	24.61 18.91-25.00	31.23 23.65-32.68	12.91 11.78-14.68	22.92 ± 9.28
Phosphates (mg/l)				
A1	1.39 1.21-1.59	0.48 0.42-0.71	0.96 0.80-1.14	0.94 ± 0.45
A2	1.96 1.51-2.19	1.71 1.50-178	1.95 1.82-2.36	1.87 ± 0.14
A3	1.68 1.52-1.83	0.69 0.52-0.91	0.93 0.80-1.22	1.1± 0.52
Nitrates (mg/l)				
A1	2.85 2.82-2.91	3.51 2.79-3.65	2.62 2.60-2.72	2.99 ± 0.46
A2	6.36 5.92-7.65	5.12 4.72-5.95	5.74 5.69-5.79	5.74 ± 0.62
A3	3.18 3.15-3.22	3.65 3.25-3.92	3.11 3.11-3.28	3.31 ± 0.29

Table 3.2: Seasonal variation in physico-chemical variables of river Kali at sampling Zone-B

Parameters/ Sampling points	Summer	Monsoon	Winter	Mean ± S.D.
Temperature (°C)				
B1	31.45 31.40-35.82	28.15 27.68-32.65	21.75 17.26-23.75	27.12 ± 4.93
B2	32.43 29.54-32.96	29.75 26.25-31.65	19.73 16.26-21.31	27.30 ± 6.69
B3	31.25 29.95-32.30	28.42 26.87-31.23	18.71 17.34-20.85	26.13 ± 6.58
pH				
B1	7.82 7.76-7.91	8.00 7.65-8.31	7.75 7.21-8.61	7.86 ± 0.13
B2	8.65 7.65-8.90	8.07 7.82-8.25	7.81 7.91-8.19	8.18 ± 0.43
B3	7.86 7.75-8.18	7.95 7.72-8.16	7.83 7.66-8.15	7.88 ± 0.06
Turbidity (NTU)				
B1	44.07 36.01-47.00	53.00 37.00-61.00	39.00 35.01-44.00	45.36 ± 7.09
B2	72.51 63.00-85.00	79.26 59.00-88.00	67.06 60.88-75.00	72.94 ± 6.11
B3	69.17 56.00-72.00	78.00 54.00-93.00	57.00 43.50-67.00	68.06 ± 10.54
TDS (mg/l)				
B1	765.81 745.00-782.00	521.23 491.00-546.00	542.26 483.00-615.00	609.77 ± 135.55
B2	929.55 861.00-965.00	674.16 625.00-748.00	832.5 685.00-856.00	812.07 ± 128.91
B3	658.23 592.00-681.00	491.50 454.00-526.00	378.00 332.00-439.00	509.24 ± 140.95
DO (mg/l)				
B1	4.12 3.58-4.32	5.67 4.82-6.21	4.95 4.69-5.32	4.91 ± 0.77
B2	5.83 4.53-6.02	6.92 5.61-7.51	5.86 4.63-6.21	6.20 ± 0.62
B3	5.21 3.49-5.94	6.36 5.32-7.21	5.28 4.35-5.86	5.62 ± 0.64
Free CO_2 (mg/l)				
B1	2.35 0.96-2.83	1.68 0.65-1.92	1.32 1.06-1.63	1.78 ± 0.52
B2	3.02 2.01-3.15	2.50 0.98-2.08	1.63 0.75-1.96	2.38 ± 0.72
B3	2.92 0.85-2.96	2.00 1.64-2.05	1.12 1.09-1.18	2.01 ± 0.50
Hardness (mg/l)				
B1	332.52 318.00-341.00	327.15 310.75-336.27	319.78 312.06-322.00	326.48 ± 6.40
B2	375.26 364.00-395.00	384.16 365.00-391.00	356.26 345.21-365.00	371.89 ± 14.25
B3	347.38 332.46-349.91	332.25 311.75-341.00	336.53 334.00-344.00	338.72 ± 7.79

Contd...

Total alkalinity (mg/l)				
B1	285.64 264.51-293.00	279.25 267.60-288.00	259.00 242.25-268.27	274.63 ± 13.91
B2	327.50 275.00-327.90	351.27 295.00-363.00	286.92 275.00-312.07	321.89 ± 32.54
B3	289.00 269.50-292.00	295.00 286.00-306.00	257.00 249.75-276.00	280.33 ± 20.43
BOD (mg/l)				
B1	16.86 11.73-17.69	21.81 16.21-22.09	12.62 10.61-14.21	17.09 ± 4.59
B2	18.16 16.23-19.43	28.23 23.65-29.84	15.72 13.29-18.91	20.70 ± 6.63
B3	14.65 10.32-15.01	20.72 17.38-21.56	12.52 10.85-14.05	15.96 ± 4.25
COD (mg/l)				
B1	52.71 48.07-61.81	68.95 55.78-71.67	34.81 28.21-39.83	52.16 ± 17.08
B2	48.52 46.54-49.21	62.72 60.71-66.78	29.97 27.65-31.81	47.07 ± 16.42
B3	50.72 46.81-53.71	65.90 63.17-68.53	32.15 29.81-35.09	49.59 ± 16.90
Chloride (mg/l)				
B1	135.45 123.31-138.58	146.32 134.21-149.32	128.81 124.00-132.61	136.86 ± 8.84
B2	142.48 136.25-147.21	151.21 142.10-156.00	132.81 127.78-137.32	142.17 ± 9.20
B3	138.06 131.55-147.86	147.05 138.00-149.61	128.65 124.00-132.00	137.92 ± 9.20
Calcium (mg/l)				
B1	137.31 132.51-142.98	142.32 138.50-144.00	126.95 124.00-129.00	135.53 ± 7.84
B2	144.68 142.10-148.15	152.60 142.8-155.61	136.64 132.76-141.32	144.64 ± 7.98
B3	135.84 131.78-141.91	140.00 136.00-143.50	132.43 127.87-137.91	136.09 ± 3.79
Magnesium (mg/l)				
B1	23.37 21.50-27.81	29.65 25.32-31.68	19.82 17.26-21.78	24.28 ± 4.98
B2	26.34 24.00-28.31	32.17 29.31-34.67	22.38 19.71-24.47	26.96 ± 4.92
B3	21.84 17.59-23.50	27.46 21.81-29.54	18.51 16.21-19.35	22.60 ± 4.52
Phosphates (mg/l)				
B1	1.72 1.45-1.81	0.82 0.54-0.95	1.12 0.84-1.27	1.22 ± 0.46
B2	2.95 2.84-3.02	2.15 1.86-2.43	2.56 1.41-2.64	2.55 ± 0.40
B3	1.82 1.57-2.05	1.39 1.22-1.57	1.52 1.38-1.82	1.58 ± 0.22
Nitrates (mg/l)				
B1	2.79 2.72-2.95	3.21 3.06-3.47	2.88 2.65-2.95	2.96 ± 0.22
B2	3.41 3.34-3.47	3.56 3.38-4.12	3.32 3.21-3.43	3.43 ± 0.12
B3	3.31 3.19-3.38	3.42 3.21-4.12	3.12 3.00-3.29	3.28 ± 17.91

Table 3.3: Seasonal variation in physico-chemical variables of river Kali sampling Zone-C

Parameters/ Sampling Points	Summer	Monsoon	Winter	Mean ± S.D.
Temperature (°C)				
C1	34.20 25.10-37.40	26.50 19.21-33.95	16.46 13.81-22.59	25.72 ± 8.89
C2	35.32 26.12 – 37.10	28.37 17.00- 34.50	17.52 14.00-22.40	27.07 ± 8.97
C3	33.12 25.13-36.82	25.53 18.76-33.58	17.23 13.58-23.35	25.29 ± 7.95
pH				
C1	7.92 7.76-8.00	8.62 8.12-8.87	7.76 7.63-8.50	8.10± 0.46
C2	7.55 7.46-7.85	8.00 7.64-8.27	7.76 7.26-7.86	7.77 ± 0.22
C3	7.59 7.51-7.95	7.82 7.74-8.07	7.46 7.31-7.76	7.62 ± 0.18
Turbidity (NTU)				
C1	35.32 27.55-46.00	43.86 31.00-55.00	29.57 25.81-36.16	36.25 ± 7.19
C2	53.00 44.58-62.00	62.75 51.00-75.81	38.95 37.00-48.51	51.57 ± 11.96
C3	47.50 43.00-52.00	51.32 42.90-61.54	44.91 37.81-49.48	47.91± 3.22
TDS (mg/l)				
C1	163.12 138.91-185.35	195.65 176.91-205.00	153.28 138.46-176.31	170.68 ± 22.17
C2	175.39 163.78-207.12	205.50 185.32-216.52	163.81 158.52-183.92	181.57 ± 21.52
C3	168.39 152.71-200.00	187.00 168.12-198.91	146.39 138.56-159.82	167.26 ± 20.33
DO (mg/l)				
C1	6.35 6.31-7.15	8.34 7.65-8.42	7.39 7.32-7.84	7.36 ± 0.99
C2	7.07 7.00-7.46	8.80 7.25-8.87	7.45 7.00-7.52	7.77 ± 0.91
C3	7.21 7.18-7.41	8.12 7.86-854	7.31 7.22-7.40	7.55 ± 0.49
Free CO_2 (mg/l)				
C1	3.85 3.74-3.91	2.50 2.41-2.55	1.01 0.95-1.06	2.45 ± 1.55
C2	4.03 3.88-4.06	2.02 1.89-2.05	1.02 0.99-1.07	2.36 ± 1.32
C3	3.03 2.95-3.10	1.04 0.91-1.09	0.93 0.88-0.98	1.67 ± 0.59
Hardness (mg/l)				
C1	215.75 110.75-223.00	235.62 210.71-255.91	196.25 178.00-209.15	215.87 ± 19.68
C2	222.17 198.65-232.78	241.62 218.25-251.51	203.25 182.72-217.81	222.35 ± 19.18
C3	225.65 176.78-237.18	231.82 215.62-239.25	207.91 186.71-216.32	221.79 ± 12.41

Contd...

Total alkalinity (mg/l)				
C1	309.00 292.561-313.58	293.65 272.16-303.92	282.50 273.25-295.00	295.05 ± 13.30
C2	275.00 265.81-287.51	278.12 271.21-285.53	248.15 231.75-262.78	267.09 ± 16.48
C3	269.82 261.52-285.00	263.25 251.39-273.12	235.62 227.50-256.82	256.23 ± 18.15
BOD (mg/l)				
C1	12.35 10.51-14.32	15.82 13.86-16.59	9.36 8.71-10.92	12.51± 3.23
C2	12.53 11.62-14.34	16.32 13.62-16.92	10.61 9.36-11.23	13.15 ± 2.90
C3	11.62 10.05-11.86	13.82 12.33-13.91	8.13 8.00-8.27	11.19 ± 2.87
COD (mg/l)				
C1	43.82 39.51-47.26	47.61 40.28-52.24	31.92 27.39-33.58	41.12 ± 8.19
C2	48.21 41.95-52.69	53.21 46.29-55.87	33.82 29.46-36.97	45.08 ± 10.07
C3	45.62 41.39-49.53	49.16 42.69-54.36	30.78 27.56-35.65	41.85 ± 9.75
Chloride (mg/l)				
C1	48.87 43.15-52.20	53.81 46.31-61.32	36.12 31.82-42.50	1821.99 ± 3082.19
C2	57.32 53.67-62.86	59.50 56.75-65.81	49.98 40.78-56.52	55.6 ± 4.99
C3	29.88 22.51-35.89	32.82 29.21-37.65	22.51 19.58-27.52	28.40 ± 5.31
Calcium (mg/l)				
C1	44.07 39.24-47.85	58.09 51.64-62.23	38.02 32.51-41.31	46.73 ± 10.29
C2	49.25 43.64-53.26	58.92 55.34-64.36	38.76 34.52-44.69	48.98 ± 10 08
C3	38.61 35.06-41.56	53.61 48.39-55.67	31.32 28.39-33.68	41.18 ± 11.36
Magnesium (mg/l)				
C1	18.59 16.29-20.67	23.51 19.51-28.34	13.62 10.53-16.74	18.57 ± 4.94
C2	21.26 17.84-23.24	28.59 24.36-33.41	16.85 14.09-19.12	22.23 ± 5.93
C3	16.32 14.35-18.36	21.69 19.37-23.18	11.75 10.39-14.68	16.59 ± 4.97
Phosphates (mg/l)				
C1	0.95 0.64-1.06	0.34 0.29-0.74	0.84 0.75-0.93	0.71± 0.32
C2	1.17 1.08-1.37	0.77 0.62-0.89	0.91 0.88-0.93	0.95 ± 0.20
C3	0.86 0.81-0.92	0.56 0.52-0.64	0.72 0.67-0.78	0.71 ± 0.15
Nitrates (mg/l)				
C1	1.38 1.26-1.49	2.91 2.84-3.00	1.26 0.95-1.31	1.85 ± 0.92
C2	2.31 1.75-2.36	2.55 2.28-2.66	1.37 1.19-1.42	2.08 ± 0.62
C3	0.97 0.82-0.98	1.68 1.55-1.72	0.81 0.75-0.86	1.15 ± 0.46

Table 4: Seasonal variation in physico-chemical variables of river Kali at sampling Zone-D

Parameters/ Sampling Points	Summer	Monsoon	Winter	Mean ± S.D.
Temperature (°C)				
D1	36.32 33.05-36.48	28.31 27.22-28.69	18.28 17.37-18.66	27.64 ± 9.04
D2	36.48 33.36-37.41	27.95 27.45-28.19	17.65 17.34-18.08	27.36 ± 9.43
D3	34.82 33.49-34.96	27.23 26.95-27.86	16.75 16.34-17.24	26.27 ± 9.07
pH				
D1	5.82 5.42-5.91	6.85 6.72-6.89	5.95 5.76-5.95	6.21± 0.56
D2	6.07 5.98-6.10	7.32 7.16-7.36	6.12 6.06-6.17	6.50 ± 0.71
D3	5.91 5.75-5.98	6.72 6.67-6.78	5.73 5.71-5.79	6.12 ± 0.53
Turbidity (NTU)				
D1	156.95 146.81-167.82	168.53 152.00-179.87	133.39 116.89-147.86	152.96 ± 17.91
D2	168.92 151.32-173.81	185.65 159.53-192.81	143.69 132.81-159.11	166.09 ± 21.12
D3	133.65 125.85-141.71	142.51 133.61-159.11	128.56 125.73-135.62	134.9067 ± 7.06
TDS (mg/l)				
D1	1425.59 1278.66-1446.00	1375.82 1327.67-1388.95	1292.65 1243.81-1312.68	1364.69 ± 67.16
D2	1465.82 1372.81-1474.00	1426.75 1408.11-1435.80	1328.25 1285.11-1345.87	1406.94 ± 70.89
D3	1365.87 1326.80-1372.61	1321.72 1268.95-1336.82	1295.89 1259.71-1309.11	1327.83 ± 35.39
DO (mg/l)				
D1	4.83 3.85-7.44	5.96 4.36-7.52	1.45 3.85-4.95	4.08 ± 2.35
D2	4.55 3.78-664	6.23 4.32-6.82	4.38 410-5.62	5.05 ± 1.02
D3	4.53 3.88-6.85	6.31 5.59-6.92	4.34 4.21-4.86	5.06 ± 1.09
Free CO_2 (mg/l)				
D1	4.1 3.05-4.3	3.5 3.00-3.6	3.09 2.89-3.3	3.56 ± 0.51
D2	3.07 3.00-3.2	3.2 3.1-3.3	3.8 3.2-4.00	3.36 ± 0.39
D3	2.08 2.00-2.1	1.9 1.3-2.05	2.5 2.1-2.9	2.16 ± 0.31
Hardness (mg/l)				
D1	685.92 662.00-708.10	698.51 684.00-716.58	665.00 659.12-694.81	683.14 ± 16.93
D2	469.86 458.45-476.11	470.79 458.91-484.26	452.61 432.10-476.89	464.42 ± 10.24
D3	431.59 428.11-44.11	451.39 439.59-460.72	386.72 365.21-391.82	423.23 ± 33.13

Contd...

Total alkalinity (mg/l)				
D1	372.00 361.10-386.50	348.72 348.12-365.81	338.65 331.58-348.62	353.12 ± 17.10
D2	412.75 395.65-421.91	398.50 387.21-411.26	376.75 368.52-395.13	396 ± 18.13
D3	359.62 351.81-368.91	351.50 349.00-362.00	332.75 329.62-342.81	347.96 ± 13.78
BOD (mg/l)				
D1	68.32 52.41-79.62	56.32 49.81-63.80	49.89 42.61-57.42	58.18 ± 9.35
D2	74.83 66.82-78.53	62.68 51.23-68.11	54.66 46.83-59.84	64.06 ± 10.15
D3	65.25 60.57-68.12	57.25 51.27-59.71	44.53 42.11-49.32	55.68 ± 10.45
COD (mg/l)				
D1	182.91 162.85-186.32	234.21 195.13-243.31	117.32 109.73-121.52	178.15 ± 58.59
D2	195.5 181.62-200.13	246.82 225.61-263.81	172.62 152.81-182.61	204.98 ± 37.99
D3	171.32 125.67-182.59	231.53 228.50-246.11	163.92 152.81-174.00	188.92 ± 37.08
Chloride (mg/l)				
D1	172.58 167.21-182.51	165.87 158.26-168.92	158.39 149.82-162.61	165.61± 7.09
D2	241.82 225.68-246.31	248.91 229.84-254.11	229.56 218.50-231.00	240.09 ± 9.79
D3	212.00 196.13-219.00	202.82 185.32-212.39	168.27 182.16-191.89	194.35 ± 23.06
Calcium (mg/l)				
D1	148.06 142.84-151.31	162.91 158.36-164.00	127.63 124.00-129.34	146.2 ± 17.71
D2	207.68 195.64-212.36	243.86 238.39-248.68	210.95 204.96-213.78	220.83 ± 20.01
D3	145.82 139.66-149.34	186.21 151.19-158.35	154.09 182.98-191.32	162.04 ± 21.34
Magnesium (mg/l)				
D1	102.95 89.28-98.65	111.18 100.21-119.28	96.87 95.67-112.91	103.67 ± 7.18
D2	158.53 153.29-162.87	166.29 163.25-168.39	153.81 150.78-159.78	159.54 ± 5.30
D3	75.92 73.45-79.15	78.80 71.36-76.95	63.98 58.36-69.48	72.9 ± 7.86
Phosphates (mg/l)				
D1	4.11 4.01-5.34	3.63 3.56-3.95	3.08 3.00-3.22	3.61± 0.51
D2	3.72 3.68-3.79	2.85 2.80-2.89	2.52 2.45-2.57	3.03 ± 0.61
D3	2.53 2.50-2.58	2.18 2.14-2.26	1.88 1.82-1.93	2.19 ± 0.32
Nitrates (mg/l)				
D1	3.86 3.84-3.95	3.93 3.90-4.00	3.67 3.64-3.78	3.82 ± 0.13
D2	5.31 5.29-5.36	5.27 5.22-5.39	5.21 5.16-5.36	5.26 ± 0.05
D3	4.17 4.10-4.24	4.19 4.15-.29	4.08 4.00-4.15	4.15 ± 0.06

Table 3.5: Seasonal variation in physico-chemical variables of river Kali at sampling Zone-E

Parameters/ Sampling Points	Summer	Monsoon	Winter	Mean ± S.D.
Temperature (°C)				
E1	32.93 28.45-34.52	26.58 23.89-28.63	16.63 14.36-19.57	25.38 ± 8.21
E2	34.26 33.12-36.28	29.62 25.47-31.68	17.55 16.38-18.00	27.14 ± 8.62
E3	33.16 30.65-36.75	27.51 25.38-29.71	17.08 15.00-17.84	25.92 ± 8.16
pH				
E1	7.86 7.80-7.88	8.87 8.46-8.93	7.66 7.52-7.78	8.13 ± 0.65
E2	7.93 7.87-8.00	8.87 8.59-8.89	7.79 7.75-7.85	8.19 ± 0.59
E3	8.23 8.00-8.35	8.58 8.52-8.78	8.00 7.51-8.37	8.27 ± 0.29
Turbidity (NTU)				
E1	28.65 24.68-31.84	45.62 41.78-49.32	23.18 20.46-25.75	32.48 ± 11.70
E2	24.71 22.65-28.41	41.95 37.00-42.00	18.76 17.65-19.21	28.47 ± 12.04
E3	26.52 22.39-28.54	50.17 48.22-52.74	21.35 20.78-22.68	1688.29 ± 2882.75
TDS (mg/l)				
E1	151.27 145.39-157.54	186.92 182.14-189.35	134.28 131.98-138.49	157.49 ± 26.86
E2	157.87 154.88-169.74	200.11 192.74-212.37	141.62 136.33-148.12	166.53 ± 30.19
E3	153.59 149.69-157.36	195.87 191.75-200.00	137.37 135.67-141.91	162.28 ± 30.20
DO (mg/l)				
E1	6.26 6.00-6.69	7.00 6.78-7.12	6.18 6.00-6.54	6.48 ± 0.45
E2	6.34 6.03-6.45	7.31 7.00-7.65	6.28 6.14-6.36	6.64 ± 0.58
E3	5.95 5.89-6.12	7.23 7.00-7.29	6.00 5.59-6.10	6.39 ± 0.72
Free CO_2 (mg/l)				
E1	3.03 2.89-3.08	2.31 2.26-2.35	2.04 1.99-2.07	2.46 ± 1.84
E2	4.04 3.85-4.09	1.90 1.85-1.93	1.02 0.79-1.06	2.32 ± 1.34
E3	3.63 3.56-3.69	2.02 1.99-2.07	1.01 0.93-1.03	2.22 ± 1.16
Hardness (mg/l)				
E1	225.81 220.65-228.25	244.65 239.89-245.35	198.85 195.36-200.62	223.10 ± 23.02
E2	232.25 230.14 -235.9	253.11 249.89-257.13	201.62 198.15-209.34	228.99 ± 25.89
E3	227.31 223.57-234.11	250.65 247.69-254.89	193.21 190.47-200.45	223.72 ± 28.89

Contd...

Total alkalinity (mg/l)				
E1	285.63 281.54-289.13	312.81 300.00-321.65	271.57 268.15-278.35	290.003 ± 20.96
E2	288.11 281.59-291.39	309.62 300.00-310.96	266.51 262.98-278.98	288.08 ± 21.55
E3	284.68 281.95-296.14	311.25 304.69-318.37	270.00 263.87-273.91	288.64 ± 20.91
BOD (mg/l)				
E1	16.65 16.00-16.75	21.32 18.69-22.69	14.59 14.51-14.68	17.52 ± 3.45
E2	16.95 16.57-17.64	23.21 18.64-25.38	14.84 14.45-15.58	18.33 ± 4.35
E3	17.06 16.89-17.45	24.00 22.69-24.54	14.62 14.34-14.95	18.56 ± 4.87
COD (mg/l)				
E1	48.02 44.78-48.45	57.13 56.59-57.26	33.75 31.59-34.78	46.3 ± 11.78
E2	48.32 47.25-48.86	56.92 54.39-57.36	32.81 29.39-33.96	46.02 ± 12.22
E3	47.18 42.63-47.68	51.61 48.78-53.25	31.91 27.32-35.48	43.57 ± 10.33
Chloride (mg/l)				
E1	51.69 50.00-52.00	57.88 56.36-58.78	37.39 36.44-37.86	48.99 ± 10.51
E2	54.61 51.36-55.98	63.00 62.78-63.45	38.16 37.96-38.75	51.92 ± 12.64
E3	52.77 51.48-53.61	54.59 53.41-55.64	31.32 29.45-35.74	46.23 ± 12.94
Calcium (mg/l)				
E1	45.21 44.25-46.87	63.81 62.48-64.36	32.91 30.00-34.16	47.31± 15.56
E2	48.51 47.59-48.95	66.00 65.45-66.15	35.82 34.85-36.14	50.11 ± 15.15
E3	41.62 38.31-42.95	52.18 50.00-52.65	29.52 28.25-31.45	41.11 ± 11.34
Magnesium (mg/l)				
E1	21.07 20.45-21.23	31.00 30.00-32.18	17.00 16.45-17.28	23.02 ± 7.20
E2	22.93 21.54-23.65	32.68 30.48-33.24	20.00 19.61-21.34	25.20 ± 6.64
E3	22.53 21.59-23.75	32.00 31.59-32.42	18.17 17.89-18.56	24.23 ± 7.07
Phosphates (mg/l)				
E1	1.09 0.98-1.14	0.68 0.64-0.78	0.95 0.84-0.98	0.91± 0.21
E2	1.12 1.10-1.14	0.87 0.81-0.89	1.02 0.92-1.09	1.00 ± 0.12
E3	1.11 1.06-1.19	0.92 0.87-0.99	0.87 0.82-0.91	0.97 ± 0.13
Nitrates (mg/l)				
E1	1.68 1.57-1.72	3.00 2.78-3.12	1.32 1.00-1.39	2.00 ± 0.88
E2	1.76 1.71-1.79	3.23 3.00-3.31	1.42 1.25-1.52	2.14 ± 0.96
E3	1.49 1.41-1.56	2.84 2.28-2.96	1.29 1.00-1.37	1.87 ± 0.84

the towns situated on the river bank. The river Kali is receiving a huge chemical load, which can cause environmental and biological hazards among human beings, livestock and various trophic levels of the local ecosystem. High contamination in river water was observed as reflected by disposal of huge industrial effluents along with the river catchment area. It is recommended to adopt some pollution control techniques to combat the pollution.

REFERENCES

Agarwal, G.D. (1990). Water Quality in some Himalayan Rivers. In Proc. Symp. Recent Trends in Limonology, Society of Bio Sciences, Muzaffarnagar (India): 411-417.

Alam, J.B., Hossain, A., Khan, S.K., Banik, E.K., Islam, M.R. Muyen, Z. (2007). Deterioration of Water Quality of Surma River, *Environmental Monitoring and Assessment.* 134, 233-242. doi 10, 1007/s 10661-007-96127.

APHA (1998). Standard Methods for the Examination of Water and Waste Water 20th ed. Washington D.C. APHA-AWWA-WPCF pp. 1875.

Bermejo, M.F., Alvarez, D.A. and Sandino, De. C. (1981). Water Quality of the Sar and Sarela Rivers (Spain). Acta. Quin. Anal. Fae. Quim. *Compostelana,* 5:16.

Bhadra, B., Chakroborty, R., Das, S. and Nanda, A.K. (2005). Investigation of some Basic Water Quality Parameters of the North Bangal Terai River Kalijani - A tributary of River Torsa and Comparison there of with the Main Stream. *J. Environ. Biol.* 26(2): 277-286.

Bhalla, R. and Bharti, P.K. (2014). River Ecosystem Dynamics, Ancient Publishing House, Delhi, pp. 244 (ISBN: 978-93-84866-02-0).

Bharti, P.K. and Kaoud, H.A.H. (2013). Aquatic Toxicology and Pollution, Ancient Publishing House, Delhi, pp. 186 (ISBN: 978-93-8138-592-0).

Bharti, P.K. (2007a). Effect of Textile Industrial Effluents on Ground Water and Soil Quality in Panipat Region (Haryana), *Thesis submitted to Gurukula Kangri University, Haridwar,* pp. 191.

Bharti, P.K. (2007b). Why are Indian Standards not strict?, *Current Science,* 93(9): 1202.

Bharti, P.K. and Malik, D.S. (2005). Significance of Rivers in Vedic Literature, *Gurukula Shodha Bharti,* Vol. 4, pp. 217-221.

Bharti, P.K. and Niyogi, U.K. (2015). Assessment of Pollution in a Freshwater Lake at Fisher Island, Larsemann Hills over east Antarctica. *Science International,* 3(1): 25-30.

Bharti, P.K.; Malik, D.S.; Kumar, P. and Bharti, U. (2012a). Heavy Metal in Water and Sediment of Ichchhamati River in East Khasi Hills, Meghalaya, In: 'Advances in Aquatic Ecology, Vol. 6' (Eds. V.B. Sakhare and P.R.D. Escalante), Daya Publishing House, New Delhi, (ISBN 978-81-7035-782-7) pp. 88-94.

Bharti, U.; Bharti, P.K.; Malik, D.S.; Kumar, P.; Singh, G. and Singh, V. (2012b). Assessment of Heavy Metal in Water and Sediment of Hatmawdon River near Bangladesh Border in District East Khasi Hills, Meghalaya, In: 'Advances in Aquatic Ecology, Vol. 6' (Eds. V.B. Sakhare and P.R.D. Escalante), Daya Publishing House, New Delhi, (ISBN 978-81-7035-782-7) pp. 95-101.

Bharti, U.; Bharti, P.K.; Malik, D.S.; Kumar, P. and Singh, G. (2012c). Water Quality Status of Kirung Ri River at Nganglam, Pemagatshel (Bhutan), In: 'Advances in Aquatic Ecology, Vol. 6' (Eds. V.B. Sakhare and P.R.D. Escalante), Daya Publishing House, New Delhi, (ISBN 978-81-7035-782-7) pp. 50-56.

Bharti, Pawan K. (2012a). Hill-Stream Ecology, *Biotech Books,* Delhi, pp. 246 (ISBN: 978-81-7622-241-9).

Bharti, Pawan K. (2012b). Solid Waste and River Ecology, *Lambert Academic Publishing GmbH and Co. KG, Saarbrucken,* Germany, pp. 65 (ISBN: 978-3-659-12852-3).

Bharti, Pawan K. (2012c). Heavy Metals in Environment, *Lambert Academic Publishing GmbH and Co. KG, Saarbrucken,* Germany, pp. 70 (ISBN: 978-3-659-15133-0).

Bharti, Pawan K. (2013). Aquatic Environment and Toxicology, Discovery Publishing House, Delhi pp. 284 (ISBN: 978-93-5056-236-9).

Bharti, Pawan K. (2014). Water Quality Characteristics of Sahastradhara Hill Stream, Dehradun (Uttarakhand), India. *International Journal of Higher Education and Research,* 4(1): 15-27.

Bharti, Pawan K. and Singh, V. (2013). Heavy Metals Distribution in Sediment and Water of Phrinkaruh River in East Khasi hills, Meghalaya. *International Journal of Higher Education and Research,* 2(1): 55-63.

Bharti, Pawan K.; Tyagi, P.K. and Singh, V. (2014). Assessment of Heavy Metals in the Water of Sahastradhara Hill Stream at Dehradun, India. *International Journal of Environment.* 3(3): 164-172.

Bhaskaran, T.R. Chakroaborty, R.N. and Trivedi, R.C. (1983). Studies on the River Pollution: Pollution on Purification of Gomti River near Lucknow, *Journal of the Institution of Engineers.* India, 45 (6): 39-50.

Bhutiani, R., and Khanna, D.R. (2007). Ecological Study of River Suswa: Modeling DO and BOD. *Environmental Monitoring and Assessment,* 125: 183-195. doi 10, 1007/s10661-006-9251-4.

Canter, L.W. (1996). Environmental Impact Assessment, Mathematical Ecological Modeling. McGraw Hill Publishers. NewYork, pp. 680.

Chandra, R., Bahadur, Y. and Sharma, B.K. (1996). Monitoring the Quality of River Ramgana Water at Berely. *Poll. Res.,* 15 (1): 33-35.

Chavan, T.P. and Wagh, S.B. (2005). Physico-chemical Characteristics of Industrial Effluent near Sukhna River at Mide area. Chikalthana, Aurangabad, *J. of Industrial Pollution Control,* 21 (1): 23-26.

David, A. (1956). Studies on the Pollution of Bhadra River Fisheries al Bhadravathi, Mysure state with Industries Effluents. Proceedings of the National Institute of Science of India, 22 B (3), 132-160.

ECIL (2004). Methods Manual, Atomic Absorption Spectrophotometer, AAS 4129, *Electronic Corporation of India Limited,* Hyderabad-500062, pp. 85.

Gautam, A., Singh, H.R. and Sati, O.P. (1989). Seasonal Variation in Certain Oxidation Reduction Characteristics of River Bhagirathi. *Proc. Indian Natl. Sci. Acad.* 55: 111.

Goltermann, H.L., Sly, R.G. and Thomas, R.C. (1983). Study of the Relationship between Water Quality and Sediments. Pub. Unesco. pp. 541.

Guillard, R.R.L. (1963). Symp. Marine Micro Biol. (C.H. Oppenh Eimered.) Thomas, Spring Field. I, II. pp. 87.

Gupta, Sandeep and Bharti, P.K. (2016). Water Resources Management: Monitoring and Assessment, Discovery Publishing House, Delhi, pp. 202 (ISBN: 978-93-5056-799-9).

Hammer, M.J. (1977). Water and Waste – Water Technology. John, Wiley and Sons, Inc, Newyork. pp. 503.

Kannel, P.R., Lee, S., Lee, Y., Kannel, S.R. and Khan, S.P. (2007). Application of Water Quality Indices and Dissolved Oxygen as Indicator for River Classification and Urban Impact Assessment. *Environmental Monitoring and Assessment,* 132, 93-110. doi: 10. 1007/s10661-0061-9505-1.

Khadse, G.K., Patni, P.M., Kelker, P.S. and Devetta, S., (2008). Qualitative Evaluation of Kanhan River and its Tributaries Flowing over Central Indian Plateau, *Environmental Monitoring and Assessment,* 147: 83-93 doi 10. 1007/s 10661-077-0100 - x.

Kumar, A., and Dua, A. (2009). Water Quality Monitoring of River Ravi in Indian Region. *Poll. Res.* (28)2: 263-269.

Laiman and Dixit, A.M. (1989). Change in Water Quality by Industrial Water Disposal, *Ind. J. Env. Health,* 31:73.

Lakshminarayana and R.K. Someshekar (2001). Ecology of Polluted Water edited by Arvind Kunar Vol. I, Chapter II,. APH Pub. Corp. New Delhi. pp. 51-60.

Malik, D.S. and Bharti, P.K. (2005). Primary Production Efficiency of Sahastradhara Hill-stream, Dehradun, *Env. Cons. J.* 6 (3): 117-121.

Manivasakam, N. (1980). Physico-chemical Examination of Water, Sewage and Industrial Effluents, Pragati Prakashan, Meerut India. pp. 245.

Mitchell, A.W., and Furnas, M.J. (2001). River Logger - A New Total to Monitor Riverine Suspended Particle Fluxes, *Water Science and Technology,* 43(9): 115-120.

Motwani, M.P., Banerjee, S. and Karam Chandani, S.J. (1956). Some Observation on the Pollution of the River Sone by the Factory Effluents of the Rothas Industries at Dalmya Nagar (Bihar). *Ind. J. Fish.* 3(2): 334-376.

Mukherjee, D., Chattopadhyay, M., and Lahiri, S.C. (1993). Water Quality of River Ganga (The Ganges) and some of its Physico-chemical Properties. *The Environmentalist,* 13(3), 199-210. doi: 10.1007/BFOI901382.

Murthy, G.V.R., Mohan, S.V., Haris Chandra, P., and Karthikeyan, J. (1994). A Pre-liminary Study on Water Quality of River Tunnyabhadra at Kurnool town. *Indian J. Prot.,* 14 (8): 604-607.

Nelson M. S., Roline R.A, Thullen J.S, Sartoris J.J., Boutwell J.E. (2000). Invertebrate Assemblage and Trace Element Bioaccumulation Associated with Constructed Wetland, Wetlands 20: 406-415.

Palharya, J.P., Siriah, V.K. and Malviya Shabha (1993). Environmental Impact of Sewage and Effluent Disposal on the River System. Ashish Publishing House, pp. 791.

Paythkin, K.D. and Yu. S. Krivoshein (1980). Microbiology (Trans: AK Senova and V. Libovskaya). Mir Publishers, Moscow. 133-135.

Prakash, C. and Rawat, D.C., (1981). Agra Water Quality. Ind. Assoe. *Water Poll. Control.* 8: 18.

Prasad, N.R., and Patil, J.M., (2008). A Study of Physico-chemical Parameters of Krisha River Water Particularly in Western Maharastra. *Rasayan. J. Chem.* (4): 943-958.

Ramesh, M., Manavalaramanujam, R. and Kumar, S.K. (1992): Effect of Water Hardness and the Toxicity a of Malathion on Hematological Parameters of the Fresh Water Fish, Cyprious Ecotoxical. *Environ Monit. Assess.,* 2(1): 31-34.

Rounsefell, G.A. and Nelso, W.R. (1966). Effect of Phosphate on Various Workers. U.S. Fish Wild Service, Spec. Science Report Fisheries No. 535.

Sastry, C.A., Khare, G.K. and Rao, A.V. (1972). Water Pollution Problems in Madhya Pradesh. *Indian J. Env. Hlth.* Vol. 4 297-309.

Saxena, M.M. (1994). Environmental Analysis: Water, Soil and Air. Agro Botanical Publishers, pp. 180.

Sharma, S. and Bharti, P.K. (2015). Limnology and Aquatic Science, Discovery Publishing House, Delhi, pp. 195 (ISBN: 978-93-5056-735-7).

Singh V.K., Singh, P. and Mohan, D. (2005). Status of Heavy Metals in Water and Bed Sediments of River Gomti – A Tributary of the River Ganga, India. *Environmental Monitoring and Assessment,* 105: 43-67, doi: 1007/s10661-005-2816-9.

Singh, H.P, and Mahaveer, L.R. (1997). Pre-liminary Observation on Heavy Metal in Water and Sediments in Stretch of River Ganga and some of its Tributaries. *J. Envirum. Bio.,* 18: 49-53.

Singh, K. and Bharti, P.K. (2015). Limnology of Sahastradhara River at Dehradun (Uttarakhand), India, In: Limnology and Aquatic Science (Eds.- Sharma, S. and Bharti, P.K.), Discovery Publishing House, Delhi, pp. 157-168 (ISBN: 978-93-5056-735-7).

Sinha, A.K. (1988). Effect of Waste Disposal on Water Quality of River Damodar in Bihar: Physico-chemical Characteristics In: Ecology and Pollution of Indian River (Ed. R.K. Trivedi), Ashish Publication House, New Delhi, pp. 219-246.

Sinha, A.K., Srivastava, R.K., Pandey, D.P. and Modak, D.P. (1989). Water Quality Characteristics of Ganga River from Kare Manikpura to Phaphamau - A Case Study. *Indian J. Environ. Pro.* 9: 845.

Suthar, S.; Sharma, J.; Chabukdhara, M. and Nema, A. K. (2009). Water Quality Assessment of River Hindon at Ghaziabad, India: Impact of Industrial and Urban Wastewater. *Environ. Monit. Assess.,* DOI 10.1007/s 10661-009-0930-9.

Syrett, P.S. (1962). In: Physiology and Biochemistry of Algae (R.A. Lewen ed.) Acadamic Press. Newyork. pp. 320.

Tomar, P. (2011). Accumulation of Heavy Metals in Water, Sediment and Biotic Community of River Kali at Muzaffarnagar (U.P.), Thesis submitted to Gurukula Kangri University, Haridwar, pp. 177.

Trivedi R.K and Goel P.K. (1984). Chemical and Biological Methods for Water Pollution Studies, Karad, Environmental Publications, pp. 1-251.

Verma, S.R., Sharma, P., Tyagi, A., Rani, S., Gupta, A.K. and Delela, R.C. (1984). Pollution and Saprobic Status of Eastern Kalinadi, *Limnologica (Barlin),* 15 (1): 69-133.

Wetzel R.G. (1975). Limnology. W.B. Sounders Co-Philadelphia, pp. 743.

Yeragi, S.G. and Shaikh, N. (2003). Studies on Primary Productivity of Tansa River. *J. Natcon* 15(1): 125-130.

(Bharti and Khoud, 2013; Bharti, 2013).

Pages 72-91

WATER RESOURCES: MAPPING, MONITORING AND MANAGEMENT
***Edited by*: Dr. Pawan Kumar Tyagi; Dr. Avnish Chauhan & Dr. Pawan Kumar Bharti**
***Edition* : 2017**
ISBN : 978-93-5056-861-3
***Published by*: Discovery Publishing House Pvt. Ltd., New Delhi (India)**

Indian Summer Monsoon (ISM)
Variability and Predictability

Pulak Kumar Patra

ABSTRACT

Indian Summer Monsoon (ISM) or the South-West monsoon brings more than 80 per cent India's annual rainfall and is a key factor in country's economic activities especially the agriculture. The inherent variability of the monsoon rainfall and its prediction is a great challenge. Understanding the pattern and trend of spatio-temporal variation of rainfall is the key to monsoon forecasting in India. With climate change looming ahead, the monsoon prediction is becoming more risk. The present paper discusses our current understanding of the ISM – its nature, mechanism and variability. The factors considered to be responsible for the variation in ISM are dealt in detail to account for the predictability of ISM. The present practice of monsoon forecasting and the possible effect of global warming is also dealt with.

INTRODUCTION

Most of the annual rainfall in India occurs from June to September which is referred to as the summer monsoon or southwest monsoon. The influence of Indian Summer Monsoon (ISM) on our national economy cannot be over-emphasised. More than 80 per cent of India's annual rainfall is caused by ISM and a slight deviation from the expected rainfall can have great impact on the water availability, agricultural productivity, hydroelectricity generation and many other activities. The recent drought and water scarcity that badly hit more than 300 million (1/4th of country's population) people across India is evidence to it. The main reason for this unprecedented situation is attributed to the two consecutive weak monsoons in 2014 and 15. Though ISM

Department of Environmental Studies, Visva-Bharati, Santiniketan, West Bengal - 731 235, India.

acts as a saviour to India by bringing the much needed rain year after year, there are many instances in the past when excess or paucity of rain had played havoc in our life. It is possible to minimize the adverse effect of ISM if we can properly predict its behaviour and hence be prepared to face the eventuality. ISM is characterized by both its regularity in annual appearance and variability in rainfall pattern. Understanding the pattern and trend of spatial/temporal variation of rainfall is the key to monsoon forecasting in India. With climate change looming ahead, the monsoon prediction is becoming a great challenge. The present paper discusses our current understanding of the ISM – its nature, mechanism and variability. The factors considered to be responsible for the variation in ISM are dealt in detail to account for the predictability of ISM. The present practice of monsoon forecasting and the possible effect of global warming is also dealt with.

The term 'monsoon' is customarily used in India to refer to the rainy season during the northern hemisphere summer from June to September and is traditionally defined as a seasonal reversing wind accompanied by corresponding changes in precipitation. Now the term monsoon has been broadened to include almost all of the phenomena associated with the annual weather cycle within the tropical and subtropical land regions of the earth. In fact, monsoon systems are a major feature of the general circulation of the atmosphere in subtropical latitudes of most regions of the world. Indian monsoon can be considered an integral component of the world's monsoon system.

Mechanism of Monsoon

The scientific explanation of the monsoon was first proposed by Edmund Halley in 1686 through his thermal concept. He described this circulation as a gigantic land-sea breeze and the land-sea temperature contrast as its key factor. During winter the landmass of Asia cools more rapidly than the surrounding oceans. This results in the development of a strong high pressure centre over the continent. On the other hand, the pressure over adjacent oceans is relatively low. Consequently the pressure gradient is directed from land to sea. Thus cold, dry air flows from land to the ocean. In summer the pressure and temperature conditions just get reversed and as per the pressure gradient the hot and moisture laden wind flows from sea towards land. This moist unstable wind accompanied by atmospheric turbulence or landform barrier rises up and brings the rain.

Hermann Flohn, a German climatologist proposed a new explanation for the monsoon in 1951. During the northern hemisphere summer all the wind belts are displaced towards the north and in the northern winter they shift to south following the apparent movement of the sun in its zenith. As a result, in July the mean zonal axis of the equatorial winds in its zenith coincides with 10° N. In January it coincides with 5° S. The subtropical highs are also displaced a little. Under this condition the intermediate regions between these planetary zones are encroached upon by two contrasting annual wind regimes. The monsoon thus represents the succession of these two wind regimes. Flohn's explanation thus ascribes the monsoon to the thermal response of the tropical continental atmosphere to be the annual variation of solar radiation.

It is now believed that thermally induced surface low and high pressure centres alone cannot produce the monsoon circulation. Recent theories have laid greater emphasis on the influence of Tibet Plateau and the jet streams on the origin of monsoonal circulation over the Indian sub-continent and its adjoining areas. The seasonal migration of the inter-tropical convergence zone (ITCZ) or equatorial trough is mainly responsible for the seasonal reversal of the wind. December-January-February (DJF) is the winter season for the northern hemisphere. At that time the solar radiation reaching the northern latitudes are highly oblique, *i.e.*, the temperature is quite low. From the month of March onwards the earth reverses its position and the northern hemisphere moves nearer to the sun, indicating the beginning of summer in the northern hemisphere. Consequently, the land and water masses there record an increase in their surface temperature. Since the land mass gets heated more rapidly than the water, a low pressure zone is created readily on the subcontinent. With a gradual rise in the sea surface temperature (SST), the sea surface also has a low pressure zone, but less intense than that of the continental. This thermal equator so formed facilitates the migration of the ITCZ northward of its DJF position. The highest SST in the global ocean during March-April-May is observed over the northern Indian Ocean. SST and ITCZ are highly coupled and a fluctuation in the SST has a large impact on the system due to the changes occurring in evaporation rate. The higher the SST, the larger is the convective current and that in turn facilitates the formation of clouds. In ITCZ where the trade winds converge, the moist air above the oceans is forced to rise up. As it moves up, it starts getting cooled adiabatically. After attaining a certain height when the air gets cooled to dew point, and the relative humidity reaches 100 per cent, the condensation starts and clouds are formed.

The variation in winds is associated with the movement of the ITCZ. The initiation of the south west summer monsoon is marked broadly by reversal of northeasterly winds into southwesterly winds. This distribution is strongly influenced by presence of the East African mountains.

Onset and Advancement of ISM

The northern and the central Indian sub-continent heats up considerably during the hot summers from March to June. This causes a low pressure area over the area. To fill this void, the moisture-laden winds from the Indian Ocean rush into the subcontinent. These winds, rich in moisture, are drawn towards the Himalayas. The Himalayas act like a high wall, blocking the winds from passing into central Asia, and forcing them to rise. As the clouds rise, their temperature drops and precipitation occurs.

The southwest monsoon is generally expected to begin around the beginning of June and fade away by the end of September. Monsoon arrival is very often a gradual beginning with a short period of transition from extreme heat to a more humid atmosphere with light rain. The normal date of onset of monsoon can be worked out at a location based on normal rainfall computed for five days period, commonly known as a 'pentad'. A sudden increase in normal rainfall of a particular pentad over one or two preceding pentads in May, June or July depending upon location, is considered the monsoon pentad for defining the onset of monsoon. The midday of the particular pentad is taken as the normal date of onset of monsoon. India Meteorological Department (IMD) has produced maps indicating the normal dates of onset of monsoon for the country as a whole. IMD also declares the actual onset of monsoon every year for the country.

The monsoon typically breaks over Indian territory by around May 25, when it lashes the Andaman and Nicobar islands in the Bay of Bengal. However, June 1 is regarded as the date of onset of the monsoon in India, the average date on which the monsoon strikes near the Malabar Coast of Kerala. The standard deviation of onset date is 8 days which means that if the monsoon onsets between May 24 and June 9, it is considered normal. Onset before May 24 is early onset whereas onset after June 9 is called delayed or late onset. The moisture-laden winds on reaching the southernmost point of the Indian peninsula, due to its topography, become divided into two parts, the Arabian Sea branch and the Bay of Bengal branch. The Bay of Bengal branch covers north eastern states while the southern peninsula is covered by the Arabian Sea branch.

The Arabian Sea branch extends towards a low-pressure area over the Thar desert and is roughly three times stronger than the Bay of Bengal branch. This branch of the monsoon moves northwards along the Western Ghats with precipitation on coastal areas, west of the Western Ghats. The eastern areas of the Western Ghats do not receive much rain from this monsoon as the wind does not cross the Western Ghats. By June 10, it reaches Mumbai and appears over Delhi by June 29. The Bay of Bengal branch initially tracks the Coromandel Coast, from Kanyakumari in Tamil Nadu to Odisha. It flows over the Bay of Bengal heading towards north-east India and West Bengal, picking up more moisture from the Bay of Bengal. Both the branches merge somewhere in north India by the end of June and travel together to northwest India by mid-July covering the whole country.

The winds arrive at the eastern Himalayas with large amounts of rain. Mawsynram, situated on the southern slopes of the Khasi Hills in Meghalaya, is one of the wettest places on earth. After the arrival at the eastern Himalayas, the winds turn towards the west, travelling over the Indo-Gangetic Plains, and pouring rain all along its way. The monsoon reaches extreme northwest (Rajasthan) by 15th July, taking 45 days to cover the whole India. The monsoon begins to withdraw early from Rajasthan by September 1. As India further cools during September, the southwest monsoon weakens. The withdrawal of monsoon is a far more gradual process than its onset. It withdraws from Mumbai by October 5. The monsoon usually withdraws from the whole country except the southern peninsula, by October 15. By the end of November, it leaves the country. The duration of monsoon over western Rajasthan is hardly 60 days while it is 165 days over Kerala.

Using daily rainfall data for the period 1901-70, Krishnamurthy and Shukla (2000) studied the climatology of the onset, advance, persistence and withdrawal of the summer monsoon in India by constructing daily rainfall climatology composites normalized to the climatological date of onset over Kerala. After the onset on 2 June, the monsoon covers the Western Ghats with heavy rainfall and with at least 3 mm/day over the southern and eastern parts of India by 5 June. The monsoon gradually advances across the rest of India during June, and almost all of India experiences rainfall by 1 July with considerable rainfall over central India ranging up to a maximum of 12 mm/day and continued heavy rainfall over the Western Ghats and eastern hilly areas. Monsoon fully establishes over India by the end of June and thereafter sustained monsoon conditions prevail over whole of India till beginning of withdrawal in September. However, during July and August, there may be occasions of short period say about a week, when rainfall over most part of the country is absent. This low rainfall activity is termed as 'break in monsoon', which is associated with change in established monsoon circulation. In each individual year, the pattern of rainfall persists with active and break periods.

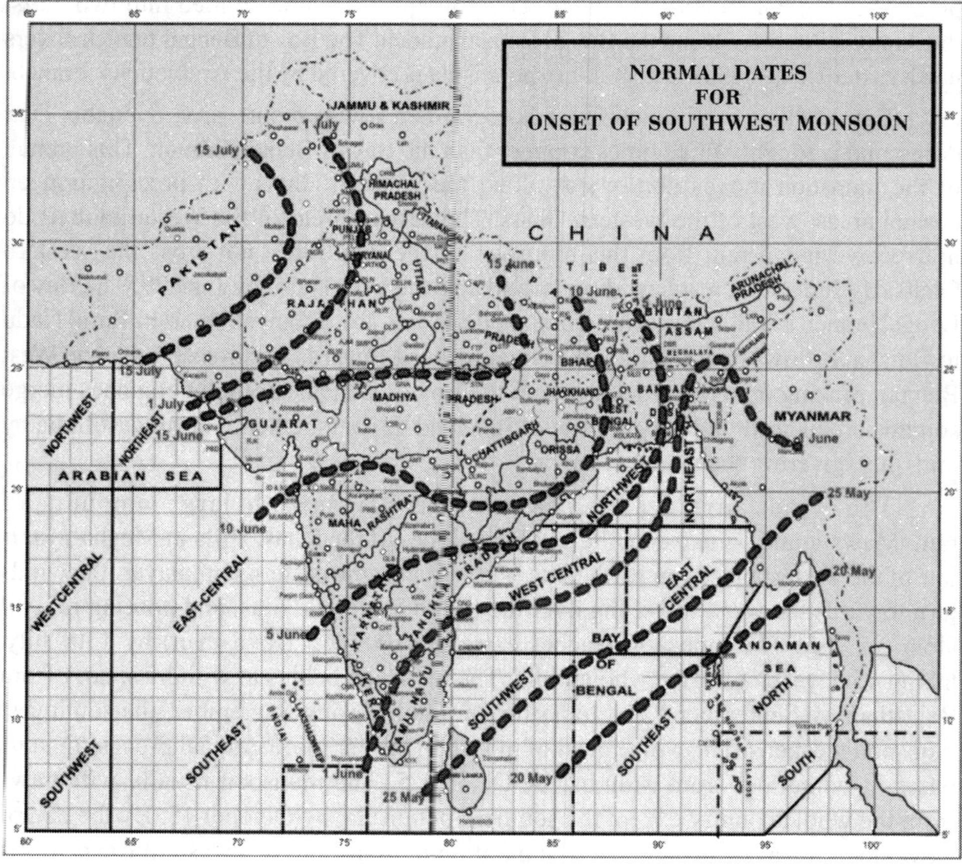

Fig. 4.1: **Normal dates for onset of ISM** (***Source*: IMD**)

Rainfall Variability

Although, ISM visits India every year without fail, its intensity, distribution and timings vary considerably both in spatial distribution and in different timescales. Thus the regular occurrence (every year from June to September) and the irregular variation (in the amount of mean rainfall) are the two remarkable features of Indian monsoon. One of the most commonly used phrases to describe the erratic nature of the monsoon of the Indian subcontinent is 'vagaries of monsoon'. There are many instances of years with flood (strong monsoon) or drought (weak monsoon) during which India as a whole receives excess or deficient seasonal rainfall, respectively. Even within a season, there is considerable variation, both in space and time, in the rainfall over India. In some years when the rain quantity is sufficient, its timing may be arbitrary. In some years, in spite of average annual rainfall, its daily distribution or the areal distribution might be substantially skewed.

- *Spatial variations:* Monsoon over India varies from more than 1000 cm in a few places in Meghalaya to less than 40 cm in Rajasthan. The coefficient of annual variation is more where the precipitation amount is less (60% in Rajasthan) and less where precipitation is more (20% in north-east and Konkan). The rainfall is a function of orography. Western Ghats and Khasi, Jaintia hills receive maximum rainfall. Deccan plateau being on leeward side of the prevailing westerly wind is a rain shadow zone and gets less rainfall. Rajasthan and parts of Gujarat receive the least rainfall. Based on rainfall data from 640 observation stations, India is meteorologically subdivided into 36 regions. The normal summer (June, July, August, September- JJAS) rainfall in these regions are presented in the Table 4.1.

The northeastern hilly regions and the Western Ghats are the areas of maximum rainfall in excess of 24 mm/day The bulk of the seasonal rainfall in the rest of India occurs in central India which receives up to about 9 mm/day. The northwest and southeast regions however receive about 3 mm/day or less. The area average of seasonal rainfall over all of India including the northeast region is 7.57 mm/day (or a total of 923 mm for the JJAS season).

The southwest region (Western Ghat region) where the onset of the monsoon is rapid, receives the maximum amount of rainfall throughout the JJAS season. The desert region in the northwest receives very little rainfall throughout the JJAS season, with peak values only around 5 mm/day. The decline in the amount of rainfall received in the above regions is also rapid during the withdrawal of the summer monsoon in September. The southeast region receives the least amount of rainfall during JJAS but receives a higher amount of rainfall from the winter monsoon during October-December.

Table 4.1: Monsoon rainfall in India

	Meteorological Sub-divisions	Rainfall (JJAS) in mm
1.	Andaman and Nicober	1693
2.	Arunachal Pradesh	1710
3.	Assam and Meghalya	1952
4.	Nagaland, Manipur, Mizoram and Tripura	1399
5.	Sub-Himalayan West Bengal and Sikkim	1926
6.	Gangetic West Bengal	1141
7.	Odisha	1169
8.	Jharkhand	1084
9.	Bihar	1024
10.	East Uttar Pradesh	910
11.	West Uttar Pradesh Plains	771
12.	Uttarakhand	1208
13.	Jammu and Kashmir	524
14.	Haryana, Chandigarh, Delhi	467
15.	Punjab	496
16.	Himachal Pradesh	774
17.	West Rajasthan	263
18.	East Rajasthan	630
19.	West Madhya Pradesh	903
20.	East Madhya Pradesh	1088
21.	Chatisgarh	1203
22.	Gujarat	910
23.	Saurashtra and Kutch	487
24.	Konkan and Goa	2800
25.	Madhya Maharashtra	701
26.	Marathwada	711
27.	Vidarbha	975
28.	Coastal Andhra Pradesh	575
29.	Telangana	767
30.	Rayalaseema	381
31.	Tamil Nadu	314
32.	Coastal Karnataka	3174
33.	North interior Karnataka	491
34.	South interior Karnataka	672
35.	Kerala	2140
36.	Laksha deep	985

Rainfall also varies in different time scales which can be expressed as intraseasonal to interannual and interdecadal.

- *Intraseasonal:* The most remarkable character of the intra-seasonal variability of rainfall over India is the occurrence of active periods with high rainfall over central India and break periods with weak or no rainfall over central India, each phase lasting for a few days. Although the onset of the southwest monsoon over Kerala has a standard deviation of 8 days with extremes being 38 days apart, the onset date is found to have no significant correlation with the subsequent seasonal rainfall over India. The nature of the intraseasonal variability of the rainfall is not different during the years of strong and weak monsoons. The variance of daily rainfall also has considerable spatial variation over India the intraseasonal variation of the Indian monsoon is found to be dominated by fluctuations on time scales of 10-20 days and 30-60 days. The active-break phases of the Indian monsoon rainfall have been associated with intraseasonal oscillations on both time scales.
- *Interannual:* Although the summer monsoon over India occurs regularly during JJAS, the year-to-year variation of the seasonal mean monsoon is quite considerable and has a major impact on India. The interannual variability of the seasonal monsoon is non-periodic, and may result from the inherent atmospheric dynamics that is nonlinear. Indian monsoon rainfall (IMR) index is the most widely used measure of the intensity of the monsoon over India and is defined as the area-weighted average of rainfall observed at well-distributed rain gauge stations all over India. A long record of the monthly mean and seasonal mean IMR index has been prepared by Parthasarathy *et al.* (1995) on the basis of observations at a network of 306 homogeneously distributed stations. Although about 2000-5000 rain gauge stations have existed all over India since the late 19th century, Parthasarathy *et al.*, carefully selected the 306 stations covering each district in the plains regions of India. Appropriate area weights have been assigned to the rainfall at each station. The long-term mean of the JJAS IMR index for the period 1871-1999 is 852 mm (about 7 mm/day), and the standard deviation for this period is 83 mm (about 0.7 mm/day) or about 10 per cent of the long-term mean. The IMR shows considerable year-to-year variation with quite a few years having substantial above normal and below-normal rainfall. Usually, years with seasonal rainfall in excess of one standard deviation above the long-term mean are referred to as flood years while those with rainfall more than one standard deviation below the mean are referred to as drought years. With this criterion, there were 18 flood years and 21 drought years during 1871-1999. There are a few instances of drought year or flood year following the other, the most notable being 1987 and 1988 which also happen to coincide with El Niño and La Niña events, respectively. Krishnamurthy and Shukla (2000) prepared a time series of IMR for the period 1901-70 based on a gridded rainfall data set generated from observations at more than 3700 stations over India. Since they included the rainfall over the hilly regions of northeast India in the

area averaged rainfall, the long term mean of their JJAS IMR is 923 mm with a standard deviation of 87 mm, both values slightly higher than those obtained by Parthasarathy *et al.* (1995). However, its time series closely resembles the time series for 1901-70 and identifies the same drought and flood years.

- *Interdecadal variability:* The variability of the Indian summer monsoon is also known to have a low-frequency component that alternates between epochs of above-normal and below-normal rainfall, each about three decades long. Several studies have provided evidence for the interdecadal variability in the monsoon and in circulation parameters. On interdecadal time scales, the monsoon rainfall is in an above-normal phase during 1880-1895 and 1932-1965 and in a below-normal phase during 1896-1931 and 1966-1990. The interdecadal IMR undergoes major transitions around 1895 and 1935.

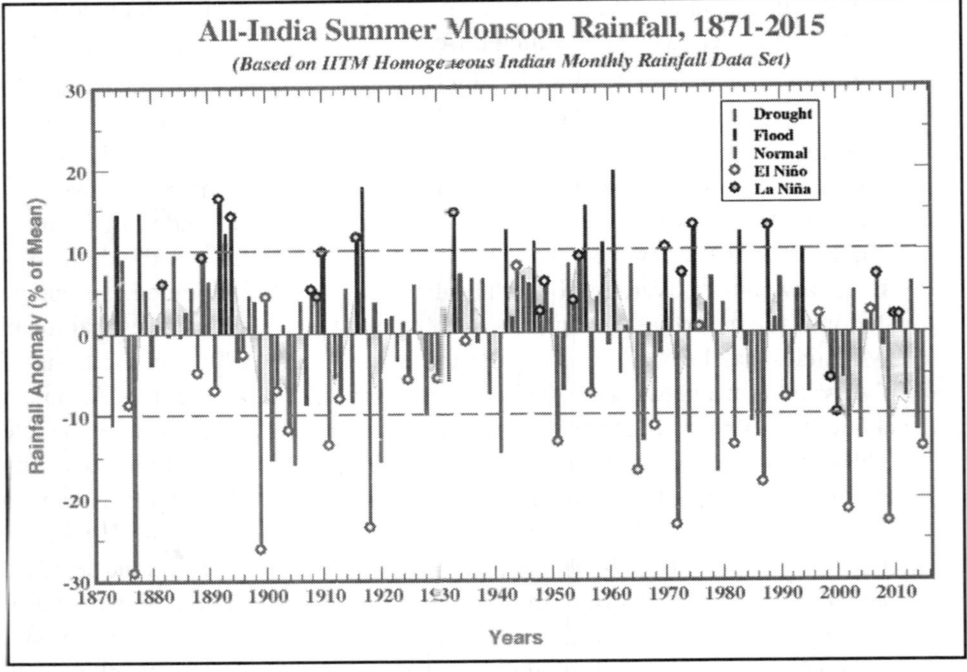

Fig. 4.2: **Interannual monsoon rainfall variation (*Source*: IITM)**

For assessing the spatial and temporal variation of rainfall in India, several studies were conducted. Parthasarathy and Dhar (1975) reported that the rainfall over India from 1931 to 1960 was increased. Kothyari and Singh (1996) reported a decreasing trend from second half of 1960s. Basistha *et al.* (2009) conducted a study on rainfall variability for Himalayan region of India and indicated that 1964 was the most probable year of change point in annual and monsoon rainfall Lal (2001) observed the random fluctuation in precipitation in India over the century with no systematic change on annual and seasonal scale. A significant rising trend of extreme rain events in India was noticed during monsoon period from 1951 to 2000 (Goswami *et al.* 2006). In

India during (1871-2005) annual and monsoon rainfall were decreased, whereas increase was noticed in pre-monsoon, post-monsoon and winter seasons (Kumar *et al.* 2009). Joshi and Pandey (2011) conducted the trend and spectral analysis of rainfall over India for a longer period (1901-2000) and reported that no significant trend was discernable during the last 10 decades. The analysis of rainfall variability was also carried out for different sub-divisions of India. Guhathakurta and Rajeevan (2008) applied linear trend analysis for observing the long-term rainfall trend in different sub-divisions of India. The statistical rainfall trend analysis on spatial and temporal scales for 45 districts of Madhya Pradesh, India was conducted and 1978 was found as most probable year of change in annual precipitation (Duhan and Pandey, 2013). Pingale *et al.* (2014) studied the spatial and temporal variation of extreme rainfall and temperature for arid and semi arid state of Rajasthan, India in 33 urban centres by using the non-parametric test called Mann-Kendall test. Khare *et al.* (2014) analysed the temporal trend of climatic parameters in Barinallah catchment over Himalayan region of India and concluded that positive insignificant rainfall trend was observed on monthly basis except October and December months. Spatio-temporal rainfall analysis over a maritime state Kerala, India was conducted for a better understanding of the rainfall variability in the state (Nair *et al.* 2014). The daily monsoon rainfall in state of Odisha was varying spatially during 1980-1999 dividing it into five homogeneous regions (Mahapatra *et al.* 2003). The summer monsoon rainfall over Odisha was studied and found that in most parts of the state the variation of seasonal rainfall was more during 1980-1999 than that of during 1901-1990 (Mahapatra and Mohanty, 2006). Patra *et al.* (2012) studied the temporal variation of monthly, seasonal, annual rainfall over Odisha in twentieth century for a longer period (1871-2006) by using both parametric and non-parametric tests and concluded that annual and monsoon rainfall was decreasing insignificantly, where as post monsoon rainfall trend was rising over the state.

Factors Responsible for Monsoon Variability

Monsoons are driven by changes in the distribution of heating, primarily by the seasonal cycle of the sun. A thermal contrast between land and sea set up a monsoon. In winter, the wind blows from the cold land over the warm sea. In summer, the warm land pulls in the wind from the ocean like a massive sea breeze. Once established, the positive feedback between the circulation and latent heat release in the rain clouds maintains the monsoon. The seasonal wind reversal is associated with the surface temperature contrast between the Indian continent and the Indian Ocean, caused by the different responses of land and sea to solar heating, during April and May. The onset of the monsoon over India involves the establishment of a low pressure region called the monsoon trough. A southeasterly wind from the southern Indian Ocean crosses the equator and gets deflected by the Earth's rotation to become a southwesterly wind flowing over India. SW monsoon wind is in fact the SE trade wind which blows from SW when the ITCZ (Intertropical convergence zone) shifts from south to north of equator. Cloudiness and rainfall are usually associated with low pressure regions such as: the monsoon trough. The day-to-day rainfall in India is caused by synoptic scale disturbances that vary in intensity, increasing from a low to a depression to a cyclone. The active and break periods are thought to be related to where the monsoon trough is over India and to the genesis and growth of the monsoon disturbances within the trough.

The interannual variability of the monsoon can be further influenced by the slowly varying forcings such as: SST, soil moisture, sea ice and snow at the surface (Charney and Shukla 1981). These global boundary forcings can modify the location and intensity of heat sources and circulation such as: Hadley and Walker circulations in the tropics. It is also known that the monsoon may have teleconnections with the climate of remote locations such as: Africa and the Atlantic Ocean. The strength of the seasonal monsoon in a particular year may depend on the relative contributions from the internal dynamics and external forcings. All these factors may function at the same time and over different time scales to intensify or reduce the seasonal progress of continental heating/cooling, land-sea pressure gradients, latent heat transport, and moisture convergence, which in turn control the strength of the monsoon circulation.

The factors responsible for year to year monsoon variability are:

- *Ocean-atmosphere coupling:* To maintain an approximate steady state climate the ocean and atmosphere move excess heat from the tropics to the heat deficit poles. The wind exerts a stress on the sea surface that induces wind driven circulations. Because of this interaction the influence of the annual cycle of the sea surface temperature (SST) is important in the seasonal movement of the convective zone. The seasonal mean SST patterns show that the warm waters are co-located with strong precipitation areas over the ocean. Warm SST occurs in the northern hemisphere mostly during June-July-August (JJA) season and mostly during (December-January-February) DJF in the southern hemisphere. During JJA, SST is greater than 28°C over the western Pacific (where ITCZ is located), Bay of Bengal and central Indian Ocean. The warm SST zone moves south in the following month with the warmest water. The organised convection is inhibited below the threshold temperature value of 28°C. Also if the SST exceeds the threshold, the convection is found to be associated more with the convergence of moist air rather than evaporation. In the land atmosphere interface heating gradients are associated with the monsoon precipitation. The monsoon rainfall in India is significantly reduced with cold SST over the Arabian Sea. Because of the interaction between atmosphere and ocean, the SST of the Indian and Pacific Oceans may influence the variability of the Indian monsoon, and in turn, the monsoon winds and rainfall may affect the variability of SST of the oceans. This mutual interaction introduces the possibility that the monsoon and the oceans form a coupled climate system.
- *Snow:* Snow (mainly the Eurasian, Tibetan and the Himalayan snow) is one of the surface boundary conditions that might have some influence on the monsoon pre-

dictability. The snow accumulation during the Himalayan winter and spring is inversely related to the subsequent summer monsoon rainfall over India. The underlying physical mechanism was thought to be a reduction (enhancement) of the typical land-sea thermal contrast and latent heat release that drives the monsoon through the albedo and thermal insulation effects of heavier (lighter) than normal snow cover. Greater (less) than normal snow accumulation in winter and spring would also lead to greater (less) than normal early summer snow melt water that would increase (decrease) the soil moisture and evaporation from the surface keeping the surface cooler (warmer) than normal and like-wise reducing (increasing) the land-sea thermal contrast. Shukla (1987) also pointed out that a heavier than normal snow accumulation in the winter and spring preceding a monsoon season would delay the development of the monsoonal temperature gradient by reflecting more solar energy (albedo effect) and by using more of the insolation energy to melt the anomalous snow. It has been found that snow cover over Tibet and the Himalayas has an influence on both the onset and the interannual variability of monsoon rainfall. Bamzai and Shukla (1999) showed that there is a statistically significant relationship between the snow cover (and probably snow depth) over the northwestern part of Eurasia and the Indian monsoon.

- *Soil moisture:* Matsuyama and Masuda (1998) suggested that there may be a linkage between the soil moisture in the extratropical Eurasia and the Indian monsoon. They found that the enhanced thermal inertia of anomalously high soil moisture in the former Soviet Union could reduce the thermal contrast between the Eurasian land mass and the Indian Ocean and thereby reduce the intensity of the monsoon.

- *Land surface:* The mean annual cycle of the Indian monsoon has long been held to be associated with the surface temperature contrast between the Indian Ocean and the rapidly warming Asian continent in late spring and summer.. It has also been suggested that the interannual variations of the Indian monsoon may be associated with fluctuations of the surface temperature and other surface conditions, notably soil moisture. The effect of soil moisture variability may be either a positive feedback or a negative one. The positive feedback can occur through the increased (decreased) availability of moisture for convection when the soil is wetter (drier) than normal. The negative feedback can arise as follows. An increased (decreased) soil moisture can increase (decrease) evaporation which can cool (warm) the surface temperature and thereby decrease (increase) the temperature contrast that drives the mean monsoon. Generally, surface conditions had a lesser impact on monsoon fluctuations than the internal atmospheric dynamics, but the low frequency behaviour could be affected due to the inertia of soil moisture storage.

- *Orographic features:* There are two major orographic barriers that appear to have significant influence on the atmospheric flow. These are the Himalaya-Tibetan Plateau complex and the Eastern Mountains of Africa. The very large massif of the Himalayas presents a major obstacle to the flow of the atmosphere, both the prevailing westerlies of the extratropics north of the massif and the southerly flow that might be associated with outflow from the convective systems in the tropical latitudes. Because the mountains effectively block the low-level and mid-level flow of the atmosphere, the circulation is significantly altered from what it would be with no mountains present. The high elevation of the Tibetan plateau in the middle of the Himalayas is strongly heated in summer by insolation, creating a mid-tropospheric heat source. This elevated sensible heat source and the radiative cooling in the surrounding environment maintain a strong temperature gradient that drives a vigorous ascent in the region with strong descent in the surrounding regions. This local circulation can interact with the convectively-driven circulation in the monsoon region, influencing the onset of the monsoon as well as its development across the subcontinent and its eventual withdrawal. Thus the Himalayan mountain range acts as a giant geographical barrier to the cold continental winds of central Asia in its north during the northern winter and to the moisture laden southwesterlies during the northern summer. It is the key factor working for the maintenance of the Asian summer monsoon and also allows high temperatures on the Tibetan Plateau to extend low pressure towards the southwest. As a whole, this contributes to the strengthening of the Indian monsoon producing high rainfall over the subcontinent through mechanical/ dynamical and thermodynamic mechanism.

The Western Ghats and the Burma mountain ranges have also been found to influence the monsoon on local scale. The heavy rainfall in the Western Ghats on the other hand was also due to the topographically forced ascent. The downstream side of these ranges (*i.e.*, the leeward side) are devoid of rainfall owing to the high precipitation (and hence loss of moisture content) upstream. This describes the occurrence of drier climate of the peninsula.

- *Atmospheric systems over Bay of Bengal:* The onset of monsoon is characterised by the presence of some synoptic scale disturbances. After onset of monsoon, the monsoonal rain gets highly intensified due to these disturbances. Cyclonic storms or disturbances are a regular and frequent feature of the whole southwest monsoon period. Atmospheric whirls of all degrees of intensity and magnitude pass up from the Bay of Bengal to the coastal districts and interior of India.

Depressions, the principal rain bearing system, generally form over the Bay of Bengal within the monsoonal trough. On an average 6-7 depressions form each year during JJAS. Year to year variation in their number however, is quite large. The energy supplied by the release of latent heat of condensation becomes the major energy source for these depressions. The depressions formed in early June are responsible for the advance of the southwest monsoon. In the months of July and August they usually form north of 18° N in the northwest Bay. By September its origin point shifts to the central Bay. The disturbances originating over the warm ocean water move onto the land, bringing heavy to exceptionally heavy rainfall. Generally an active spell of monsoon is characterised by high frequency genesis of the synoptic scale systems over the Bay, which migrates onto the subcontinent and produces the awaited monsoonal downpour. The zone of maximum rainfall shifts to northwest and then to northeast as the depression moves from northwest to north to northeast. After the break of monsoon, once again, these disturbances pacing westward, reintroduce the rainfall. The convection over the Bay is a vital factor for the formation and variation of the synoptic scale disturbances. On the other hand these disturbances apart from providing rainfall to the subcontinent do play a major role in transport of heat and moisture, thus maintaining the global meteorological balance.

- *El-Nino-Southern Oscillation effect: El-Nino* is a 'warm' ocean current originating along the coast of Peru that replaces the usual 'cold' Peru or Humboldt Current. This warm surface water reaching towards the coast of Peru with *El-Nino* are pushed westwards by the trade winds. Thus, the temperature of the southern Pacific Ocean is raised. A reverse condition is known as *La Nina.*

Southern Oscillation, a phenomenon first observed by Sir Gilbert Thomas Walker, Director General of Observatories in India in 1920s, refers to the see-saw relationship of atmospheric pressures between Tahiti (an island in the central southern Pacific Ocean) and Darwin (situated on the Timor Sea near Australia). Walker noticed that the quantity of rainfall in the Indian subcontinent was often negligible in the years of high pressure at Darwin (and low pressure at Tahiti). Conversely, low pressure at Darwin predicts the precipitation quantity in India. Thus, he established the relationship of Southern Oscillation with quantities of monsoon rains in India. A Southern Oscillation Index (SOI) is formulated based on the pressure difference between Tahiti and Darwin to measure the strength of the Oscillation. Ultimately, it was realized that the Southern Oscillation is just the corresponding atmospheric component of the *El Nino/ La Nina* effect (which happens in the ocean). Therefore, in the context of the monsoon, the two cumulatively came to be known as the ENSO. The ENSO is known to have a pronounced effect on the strength of southwest monsoon over India with the monsoon being weak (causing droughts in India) during the *El Nino* years whereas *La Nina* years had particularly good monsoon strength over India.

- *Indian Ocean dipole effect:* Although ENSO was statistically effective in explaining several past droughts in India, in the recent decades the ENSO-monsoon relationship seemed to weaken in the Indian subcontinent. In 1999, it was discovered that similar to ENSO in the Pacific Ocean, there exist a seesaw ocean-atmosphere system in the Indian Ocean. It was named as the Indian Ocean Dipole (IOD). An index to calculate it was also formulated. IOD develops in the equatorial region of Indian Ocean from April to May peaking in October. With a positive IOD, winds over the Indian Ocean blow from east to west resulting in a much warmer Arabian Sea (western Indian Ocean near African coast) with a colder and drier eastern Indian Ocean around Indonesia. In the negative dipole year, the reverse happens making Indonesia much warmer and rainier. It was demonstrated that a positive IOD index often negated the effect of *El-Nino,* resulting in increased monsoon rains in several years *El-Nino* like the 1983, 1994 and 1997. Further, it was shown that the two poles of the IOD, the eastern pole (around Indonesia) and the western pole (off the African coast) were independently and cumulatively affecting the quantity of rains for the monsoon in the Indian subcontinent.

- *Teleconnections to the NAO:* As noted on the relationship between Eurasian snow and the Indian monsoon, there is a hypothesis that anomalous snow cover and/or depth can alter the albedo and surface wetness characteristics of the Asian land mass in the spring season in such a way as to influence the land-sea thermal contrast that drives the Indian monsoon and thereby introduce variability of the monsoon. It is well known that the climate regimes over western Europe undergo substantial low frequency variability as a result of an oscillation called the North Atlantic Oscillation (NAO) In one phase of the NAO (negative), the north Atlantic winter atmospheric circulation is dominated by a large high pressure anomaly near Iceland that represents a weaker than normal Icelandic low and an associated low pressure anomaly (weaker than normal subtropical high) near the Iberian peninsula. In this phase, with a weaker winter meridional pressure gradient, western Eurasia experiences fewer and weaker storms from the north Atlantic whose trajectory is more zonally oriented than normal. This results in less than normal snow depth across western Eurasia. The opposite (positive) phase of the NAO is associated with more and stronger winter storms that enter Eurasia at higher latitude than normal, producing substantially more snow than normal. Chang *et al.* (2001) noted that the relationship between surface air temperature over western Eurasia and the Indian monsoon rainfall has become stronger in recent years, over about the same period that the relationship between the monsoon and ENSO has diminished. They suggested that, as the ENSO-monsoon relationship has weakened, the possibility for the NAO to influence the monsoon through the above mechanism has increased.
- *Teleconnections to Africa and beyond:* The Indian monsoon is known to be affected by climatic phenomena in other parts of the world and is also known to have a far-reaching influence on remote regions itself. The Indian monsoon has connections to other regions, notably northern Africa and the southern Indian Ocean. In particular, it is clear that the large convective region of the Indian monsoon drives a divergent circulation in the upper troposphere that reaches to north Africa where the large subsidence strengthens the tendency for desert formation in the Sahara. The mechanism connecting the two regions is a lagged circulation change in which pressure changes over India can strongly influence the winds over the eastern sub-Sahara a few days later causing anomalous moist westerlies over the east African highlands. It is also known that fluctuations in the Somali jet and the Findlater jet are associated with variations in Indian monsoon rainfall, both in terms of the onset and the seasonal total. The jet originates over Kenya and crosses the equator, giving it very interesting dynamical importance

insofar as it can transport negative potential vorticity from the Southern Hemisphere into the atmosphere overlying the Arabian Sea, possibly inducing a symmetric instability.

Monsoon Prediction

The study of the Indian summer monsoon and its rainfall pattern has a long history. Long range forecasts of seasonal rainfall are being issued by the India Meteorological Department (IMD) since the late 19th century. A large network of rain gauge stations established after the devastating droughts of 1877 and 1899 has continued to provide a long record of rainfall over India. After the 1899 drought, Sir Gilbert Walker became the Director-General of Observatories in India and conducted systematic studies to provide advance warning of floods and droughts by searching for predictors of seasonal Indian rainfall. While establishing the correlation of the Indian rainfall with variables observed at various global locations, Walker (1924) discovered the Southern Oscillation, the North Atlantic Oscillation and the North Pacific Oscillation. Presently, IMD forecast monsoon every year in April and the revised forecast in June. Recently a private organization Skymet has also been involved in monsoon forecasting.

With advances made in dynamical prediction of weather and seasonal climate using general circulation models (GCMs), the simulation of monsoon by GCMs is an active area of research. Long range forecasts (LRF) of the seasonal mean monsoon have been issued by the IMD for over a hundred years using empirical models. These are statistical models based on the correlation of the monsoon rainfall with local and global climate variables found over a long period of time. However, the statistical forecasts lack the ability to predict the spatial distribution of rainfall and on a time scale shorter than a season. A different approach is the dynamical prediction using GCMs for both daily and seasonal forecasts. There have been several organized international efforts to simulate the Indian monsoon by modeling groups since the mid-1980s.

- *Empirical models:* These empirical models used to predict the monsoon are basically regression models that have undergone modifications, in both technique and predictors used, since the time IMD started issuing LRF. Reflecting the fact that the seasonal mean monsoon is determined by internal dynamics as well as by the influences of slowly varying boundary conditions, the predictors used are both regional and global climate parameters, including SST, surface temperature and SLP at various locations. Forecasts of seasonal monsoon rainfall over large regions of India issued by the IMD during 1924-87 were based on multiple linear regression models. Earlier regression models introduced by Walker (1923) used parameters such as: the snow accumulation over the Himalayas in May and South American pressure during spring. Since 1988, the IMD has been issuing LRF of seasonal mean monsoon rainfall over India as a whole using parametric and power regression models with 16 predictors (Gowariker *et al.* 1989, 1991). The parametric model is purely qualitative, with equal weights given to all the parameters, and it provides forecasts of whether the monsoon rainfall will be normal (within ~10% of long term mean), excess or deficient. The power regression model, however, is quantitative and takes into account the nonlinear nature of the interactions of the local and global forcings with the Indian monsoon. The 16 predictors used by these models include Pacific SST, surface temperature and pressure in India and other global locations, snow cover over the Himalayas and Eurasia, and the 500 hPa ridge positions. The temporal variations in the correlation between monsoon rainfall and some of the predictors, such as: the interdecadal variability in the ENSO-monsoon relation, and the need to modify the list of predictors have been recognized by the modelers. Certain predictors have been discarded over time and new predictors have been added.

- *General circulation models:* Based on the premise that the seasonal mean Indian monsoon has potential predictability because of forcing by slowly varying boundary conditions (Charney and Shukla 1981), the simulation experiments have been conducted with atmospheric GCMs (AGCMs) with observed SST specified as lower boundary conditions. The 1987 El Niño and 1988 La Niña coincided with weak and strong Indian monsoon rainfall seasons, respectively, and provided an opportunity for the modelers to simulate the monsoon with two starkly contrasting Pacific SST boundary forcing. As part of the first AMIP experiment, 32 AGCMs were integrated over the period 1979-98 with the same observed SST specified as boundary conditions (Sperber and Palmer 1996). Some models were also integrated with different initial conditions but with same SST to estimate the potential predictability of the interannual variability.

Recently, dynamical seasonal prediction (DSP), done by integrating GCMs with an ensemble of initial conditions, has been attempted to provide probabilistic seasonal forecasts. The simulation of the Indian monsoon rainfall and circulation is also difficult with coupled ocean-atmosphere models. Dynamical models do not have sufficiently high fidelity to accurately simulate the salient characteristics of the mean monsoon and monsoon variability. More observations and analyses are needed to understand the intraseasonal variability of the monsoon and its relation to the neighboring oceanic regions. Further studies are also required to understand the relationship of the monsoon with global climate features such as: ENSO, NAO and Eurasian snow. The predictability of the monsoon depends on understanding the relative roles of internal dynamics and the influences of boundary conditions. There is much still to learn about what controls the monsoon and its variability. Recently IMD failed to predict the below normal rainfalls in 2004 and 2009, though its prediction for 2014 and 2015 was to the mark.

Recently Stolbova *et al.* (2016) have developed a novel prediction method based on a network analysis of regional weather data. It may be possible now to predict the onset of the Indian monsoon two weeks earlier and the withdrawal of it even six weeks earlier than before.

Effect of Climate Change on ISM

Model improvements are vital for making progress in monsoon prediction. Impacts of climate change remain hugely uncertain for those reasons. In Southeast Asia, between 1955 and 2005 the ratio of rainfall in the wet to the dry seasons increased. Annual total wet-day rainfall has increased by 22 mm per decade, while rainfall from extreme rain days has increased by 10 mm per decade. However, climate variability and trends differ vastly across the region and between seasons. Several studies predict substantial changes in the ISM variability by the end of 21st century indicating its strong sensitivity to global warming. On the seasonal scale, the all-India summer monsoon mean rainfall is likely to increase moderately in future, primarily governed by enhanced thermodynamic conditions due to atmospheric warming, but slightly offset by weakened large scale monsoon circulation. It is projected that the rainfall magnitude will increase over core monsoon zone in future climate, along with lengthening of the season due to late withdrawal. On interannual timescales, it is speculated that severity and frequency of both strong monsoon (SM) and weak monsoon (WM) might increase noticeably in future climate. Active/break spells will be more intense and regionally extended in future climate. SM (WM) could be more wet (dry) in future due to the lengthening of active (break) spells. It is also thought that interannual variability of the monsoon will increase in future.

Substantial changes in the daily variability of ISM are also projected, which are largely associated with the increase in heavy rainfall events and decrease in both low rain-rate and number of wet days during future monsoon. However, future changes in the spatial pattern during active/break phase of SM and WM are geographically inconsistent among different models. The results point out the growing climate-related vulnerability over Indian subcontinent, and further suggest the requisite of profound adaptation measures and better policy-making in future.

Simulations of future climate generally suggest an increase in monsoon rainfall on a seasonal mean, area-average basis. This is due to the twin drivers of an increasing land-sea thermal contrast, but more importantly, warming over the Indian Ocean which allows more moisture to be carried to India. Typically increases in total rainfall over India may be in the region of 5-10 per cent, although some climate models suggest more and some less. Climate simulations also show different patterns of rainfall change, so it is difficult to predict how rainfall might change within India.

Conclusion

The Indian monsoon is remarkably stable as a whole, with a mean total of around 850 mm in the months of June to September, and an interannual (year-to-year) variation of only around 10 per cent in most cases. Even these relatively small variations in the Indian monsoon can influence things like agricultural production and the stocks and commodities market. For many people in India it is the variability of rainfall on shorter time scales that has the biggest impacts. Intense heavy rainfall leads to flooding; breaks in the monsoon of a week or more lead to water shortage and agricultural drought. The intraseasonal and interannual variability of the summer monsoon has a tremendous socio-economic impact on India, especially in the fields of agriculture and health. Since the Indian economy is heavily dependent on summer monsoon rains, understanding its past and present variability is of immense importance in making any attempt in predicting future monsoon variability. Understanding the shift and predicting changing trends of monsoon may be central to managing the floods that impact on millions of people, damage to lives and property, destruction of ecology and farmlands and the long term effect on food security.

The improvement of monsoon prediction depends on the collaboration of both researchers and forecasters to develop a comprehensive understanding of the issues at hand. Knowledge of regional climatology and weather, as well as related generic scientific and application topics, is equally important in achieving a holistic perspective of the complex monsoon systems. Advance in monsoon prediction is possible only if models are improved to adequately represent monsoon physics. Improving the model physics will require better observations with higher spatial and temporal resolutions, as well as a better strategy for validating model physics in specific monsoon regions. Moreover, significant monsoon weather is often associated with variations that are both longer and shorter than the annual cycle, *i.e.,* interannual, interdecadal, and longer climate variations, as well as intraseasonal, synoptic, and mesoscale systems. An example of the former is the relationship between El Nino-Southern and Examples of the latter include the impacts of tropical cyclones on the summer monsoon rainfall. Besides, global warming may increase the variability of the monsoon leading to more challenge in forecasting.

REFERENCES

Basistha A, Arya D.S. and Goel N.K. (2009). Analysis of Historical Changes in Rainfall in the Indian Himalayas. *International Journal of Climatology* 29: 555-572.

Billa Lawal and Singh Ajit (2015). Effect of Climate Change on Seasonal Monsoon in Asia and its Impact on the Variability of Monsoon Rainfall in Southeast Asia. *Geoscience Frontiers* 6: 817-823.

Charney, J.G., and J. Shukla (1981). Predictability of Monsoons. *Monsoon Dynamics,* J. Lighthill, Ed. Cambridge University Press, 99-109.

Gadgil S., Joseph P.V. and Joshi N.V (1984). Ocean–Atmosphere Coupling Over Monsoon Regions *Nature* 312:141-143.

Gowariker, V., V. Thapliyal, R.P. Sarker, G.S. Mandal, and D.R. Sikka (1989) Parametric and Power Regression Models: New Approach to Long range Forecasting of Monsoon Rainfall in India. *Mausam,* 40:115-122.

Gowariker, V., V. Thapliyal, S. M. Kulshrestha, G.S. Mandal, N. Sen Roy, and D.R. Sikka (1991). A Power Regression Model for Long Range Forecast of Southwest Monsoon Rainfall Over India. *Mausam,* 42: 125-130.

Goswami B.N., Venugopal V., Sengupta D., Madhusoodanan M.S. and Xavier P.K. (2006). Increasing trend of Extreme Rain Events over India in a Warming Environment. *Science* 314: 1442-1445. Guhathakurta P and Rajeevan M. (2008). Trends in the Rainfall Pattern Over India. *International Journal of Climatology* 28:1453-1469.

Joshi M.K. and Pandey A.C. (2011). Trend and Spectral Analysis of Precipitation over India during 1901-2000. *Journal of Geophysical Research* 116:

Khare D., Singh R and Shukla R. (2014). Temporal Trend Analysis of Climatic Parameters in Barinallah catchment over Himalayan Region, India. *Environment and We an International Journal of Science and Technology* 9: 29-38.

Kothyari U.C., Singh V.P. and Aravamuthan V. (1997). An Investigation of Changes in Rainfall and Temperature Regimes of the Ganga Basin in India. *Water Resources Management* 11: 17-34.

Kumar V., Jain S.K. and Singh Y. (2010). Analysis of Long-term Rainfall Trends in India. *Journal des Sciences Hydrologiques* 55.

Lal M (2001). Climatic Change – Implications for India's Water Resources. *Journal of Indian Water Resources Society* 21: 101-119.

Mohapatra M. and Mohanty U.C. (2006). Spatio-temporal Variability of Summer Monsoon Rainfall Over Orissa in Relation to Low Pressure Systems. *Journal of Earth System Science* 115: 203-218.

Mohapatra M., Mohanty UC and Behera S (2003). Spatial Variability of Daily Rainfall over Orissa, India, during the Southwest Summer Monsoon Season. *International Journal of Climatology* 23: 1867-1887.

Nair A., Joseph K.A. and Nair KS (2014). Spatio-Temporal Analysis of Rainfall Trends over a Maritime State (Kerala) of India during the last 100 years. *Atmospheric Environment* 88: 123-132.

Parthasarathy B. and Dhar O.N. (1975). Trend Analysis of Annual Indian Rainfall. *Hydrological Sciences* 26: 257-260.

Parthasarathy, B., A. A. Munot, and D.R. Kothawale, (1995). Monthly and Seasonal Rainfall Series for All-India Homogeneous Regions and Meteorological Subdivisions: 1871-1994, Res. Rep. RR-065, 113 pp. Indian Inst.of Trop. Meteorol., Pune.

Patnaik R. Gupta A.K., Naidu P.D., Yadav R.R. Bhattacharyya A. and Kumar M., (2012). Indian Monsoon Variability at Different Time Scales: Marine and Terrestrial Proxy Records. *Proc Indian natn Sci Acad* 78:535-547.

Patra J.P., Mishra A., Singh R. and Raghuwanshi N.S. (2012). Detecting Rainfall Trends in Twentieth Century (1871-2006) over Orissa State, India. *Climate Change* 111: 801-817.

Pattanaik D.R. (2005). Variability of Oceanic and Atmospheric Conditions during Active and Inactive Periods of Storm Over the Indian Region. *International Journal of Climatology* 25: 1523-1530.

Sahai A.K., Pattanaik D.R., Satyan V. and Grimm Alice M. (2003). Teleconnections in Recent time and Prediction of Indian Summer Monsoon Rainfall. *Meteorology and Atmospheric Physics* 84: 217-227.

Sperber, K.R., and T.N. Palmer (1996). Interannual Tropical Rainfall Variability in General Circulation Model Simulations Associated with the Atmospheric Model Intercomparison Project. *Journal of Climatology* 9: 2727-2750.

Somee B.S. and Zadeh R.M. (2011). Testing for Long-term Trends in Climatic Variables in Iran. *Atmospheric Research* 100: 132-140.

Veronika Stolbova, Elena Surovyatkina, Bodo Bookhagen, Jürgen Kurths (2016). Tipping Elements of the Indian Monsoon: Prediction of onset and Withdrawal. *Geophysical Research Letters* DOI: 10.1002/2016GL068392.

Pages 92-108

WATER RESOURCES: MAPPING, MONITORING AND MANAGEMENT
***Edited by*: Dr. Pawan Kumar Tyagi; Dr. Avnish Chauhan & Dr. Pawan Kumar Bharti**
***Edition* : 2017**
ISBN : 978-93-5056-861-3
***Published by* : Discovery Publishing House Pvt. Ltd., New Delhi (India)**

Consequences of Human Activities on Glaciers

A Case Study of Pindari Glacier

Deepak Kholiya[1]
Laxmi Rawat[2]

ABSTRACT

The impacts of the global climate change on the dynamics of snow, glaciers and runoff over the Himalayan Mountain with particular reference to Uttarakhand is of great emphasis. Himalaya, the water tower of Asia, stores a significant quantity of fresh water in the form of seasonal snow covers and glaciers. The seasonal snow and ice melt nourish the Himalayan region and beyond, and flow through the great Indian Plains. Hence, the frozen water in the Himalaya is crucial for the people inhabiting the mountain areas as well as the downstream regions.

The major glacier-fed Himalayan Rivers along with glaciated catchments have regional importance and water from glacier melting sustains stream flow in these rivers during the dry season. Without snow melt, the river flowing down from the Himalaya would remain dry for greater part of the year, thereby seriously affecting the livelihood of people. Therefore, the estimation of snow and glacier melt under changing climatic conditions and their long-term impact is critical, and needs to be addressed using snowmelt runoff models. The scientific and sustainable management is intended to provide science based information on impacts of global change on glaciological and hydrological systems in the Himalayan region.

The Pindari Glacier Trek (District; Bageshwar) form origin source of Pinder river - in the upper reaches of the Kumaon Himalayas, lies between the Nanda Devi and Nandakot peaks and terminates at an altitude of 3627 m. Studies of receding/

1. Department of Environmental Science, Graphic Era Hill University, Dehradun (Uttarakhand), India.
2. HOD and Scientist –'E' Ecol. and Environment Division, Forest Research Institute, Dehradun (Uttarakhand), India.

shifting/melting of Himalayan glaciers point out that trekking and trekkers related activities have led to accelerating rate of deforestation, thereby destroying the habitat for numerous wild animals and the rare high altitude plants. This has resulted the closing down of many Sanctuaries, National Park and Biosphere Reserves for trekkers and shepherds in the past. The past statistics of trekkers to glaciers reveal that Uttarakhand attracted more visitors in comparison to other hill states. This has resulted in faulty road construction, indiscriminate removal of forests, unplanned development of infrastructure and poor resource management, which have accelerated the degradation of natural environment nearby glacier areas.

The present studies was carried out in treks area of Pindari, Sunderdhungha and Kafni glacier areas during 2005 to 2008 to have the idea how many tourists visit these areas, whether their activities are having any impacts on shrinking of glaciers, local vegetation, soil, landscape etc., whether the local people are involved in the tourism and what type of involvement they have and finally recommends strategies for participation of local people in tourism and conservation of environment of the high altitudes glacier areas. The major identified culprits are deforestation, climate warming and overgrazing, as well as the mutual influence of human activities and climate change. Increase in evaporation, reduction in snow cover, and fluctuations in precipitation are key factors contributing to the degradation of glacier ecosystems.

***Keywords*:** Receding, deforestation, overgrazing, climate warming, ecosystem etc.

INTRODUCTION

Glaciers

The exotic geographical location and its nature is the main reason for most tourists to visit the fascinating glaciers of India. Trekking on Indian Glaciers is the most sought after adventure activity, attracting thousand of tourists from all around the globe. Among the large number of glaciers in India, the most popular are: Pindari Sunderdhungha, Kafni, Ralam, Yumnotri and Gangotri Glacier, Nanda Devi Glacier, Milam and Siachen Glacier etc. Glaciers have held an eternal fascination for trekkers the world over, who return, year after year, to recharge themselves in the tranquillity, quietitude and healing surroundings.

Review of Literature

A careful study shows that the construction of 44,000 km., long road in the Himalayan region produced 2,650 million cubic meters of debris and each km., of already constructed roads generate 550 cubic meters of debris by landslides and rock falls. Thus, nearly 24 million cubic meters of debris slides down damaging vegetation and chocking the springs etc. (Valdiya, 1980).

In tourism development, a sustainable environment is of vital importance, more than in any other sector of economic activity. This implies that in tourism projects, contrary to projects in other economic sectors, environmental issues should be taken into account in drawing up the financial cost-benefit analysis. It also implies that government has the responsibility to safeguarding the environment. Safeguarding the environment is synonymous with safeguarding the future earning power of tourism in the national economy (Theuns, 2008).

While mapping the vegetation in Bedni and Ali Bugyals of Roopkund Ram *et al.* (1995) have also mentioned that frequent grazing in these Bugyals by nearby villagers has caused degradation in the existing flora. Maikhuri *et al.* (2000) have also emphasised that the ban on tourism in the core zone of the Reserve has created conflict between local people and Reserve authorities. The local people have severe concern about the significant income it provided.

Study Sites

(i) *Sunderdhunga Glacier* is relatively a lesser-known glacier, can be reached from Khati village. People who are mainly doing Pindari glacier normally visit this site. It is located at a height of 3880 Mts. This massive snow clad mountain provides a picturesque view to the surroundings.

(ii) *Kafni Glacier* near the Pindari glacier is located Kafni glacier, at an altitude of 3853 Mts., Kafni glacier is an exquisite and untouched place. The Kafni Glacier is located in the upper reaches of the Kumaon Himalayas, to the southeast of Nanda Devi. The glacier gives rise to the Kafni River, which is a tributary of the Pindar River. The Pinder River is a tributary to Alaknanda River, which eventually is one of the two headstreams of the Ganges. This is relatively small glacier but a popular trekking destination along with Pindari Glacier.

Fig. 5.1

(iii) *The Pindari Glacier* is a glacier found in the upper reaches of the Kumaon Himalayas, to the southeast of Nanda Devi and Nanda Kot. The Pindari Glacier is located in the Pindar Valley between longitudes 79° 13'-80°02' E and latitudes 30° 15' N. It occupies an area of 339.39 sq km. The glacier flows to the south

for a short distance of about 3 km., (1.9 mi) and gives rise to the Pindari River which meets the Alakananda at Karnaprayag in the Garhwal district. The trail to reach the glacier crosses the villages of Saung, Loharkhet, crosses over the Dhakuri Pass, continues onto Khati village (the last inhabited village on the trail), Dwali, Phurkia and finally Zero Point Pindari, the end of the trail. Though most of the trail is along the banks of the Pindari River, the river is mostly hidden until after Khati. The Pindari Glacier trail provides for a 90 km., (56 miles) round-trip trek that most people find comfortable to complete in six days.

Fig. 5.2

(iv) Pindari Glacier Trek: Pindari Glacier trek is to go up to the Pindari glacier, which is at the edge of Nanda Devi one of the world's great peaks (7816 metres). It sounded like a grand idea, to even get to within 10 km., of Nanda Devi. There is a elevated 'platform' of circumference 110 km., consisting of high mountains, which Nanda Devi is at the centre. Pindari glacier is at the lower edge of this 'platform'. The road part of the trip goes through Bageshwar till 'Song' or till Loharkhet. From there, the trek goes till a place poetically named 'Zero Point', and back. So ordinary hikers go till zero point, and not all the way to Pindari Glacier itself. One has to go by road up to Saung which can be accessed from Almora, Bageshwar and Kathgodam and thereafter one has to trek 45 km., up to zero point (Pindari Glacier). Start walk from Song, Loharkhet, Dhakhuri, Khati, Dwali, Phurkiya, to reach Pindari Zero Point.

The glacier is at an altitude of 3353 m. Covered extensively by trekkers, to get to Pindari one has to get to Bageshwar from there get a local bus to Bharari, from here one goes to Song by bus and then to Lohakhet. Dhakuri is 11 kms., from Lohakhet. The view from Dhakuri provides a spectacular view of the Nanda Devi. From Dhakuri we reach Khati (8 kms.,), following the Pindar we reach Dwali which is the confluence of Pindar and Kaphini rivers. The next halt is Phurkiya, which also has a GMVN rest house. This is the base camp for going upto to the 4000m zero point and the snout of the majestic Pindar glacier. On either side one can see the peaks of Panwali Dhar and Nanda kot.

The valley is drained by the Pindar river that emerges from the Pindari Glacier. The river, in its initial course, flows through sedimentary rocks. Further to the south, it meanders through quarts schist. Granite is found in abundance in this area. The Pindar river has cut a gorge in thick glacial deposits up to nearly 10 km., resulting in the formation of spacious glacial terraces spread on both sides of the gorge. Further down, from Phurkia up to Khati, places enroute to the Pindari Glacier, one comes across numerous waterfalls, hanging valleys and tremendous rolls cliffs as the one of at Dwali. The colour of Pindari Glacier is very white and at some places, spots of light blue and brown may also be seen.

Trek

- Base Camp Saung
- Saung to Loharkhet 3 km., trek
- Lohaekhet to Dhakuri 11 km.
- Dhakuri to Khati 8 km.
- Khati to Dwali 11 km.
- Dwali to Phurkia 7 km.
- Phurkia to Pindari Glacier 5 km.

By Road

- Saung to Bageshwar 36 km.
- Saung to Almora 109 km.
- Saung to Kathgodam 199 km.

Altitude Graph

Seasonal trekkers take about 8-10 days to complete the two way journey. There are adequate arrangements for night halts at Loharket, Dhakuri, Khati, Dwali and Phukia. Khati, a village lies at the confluence of the Pindari and Sunderdunga rivers. The simplicity and warmth of the village folk touches you. The trek to Phukia is breathtaking as the tree line gives way to bugyals, the Kumaonic equivalent of Alpine meadows.

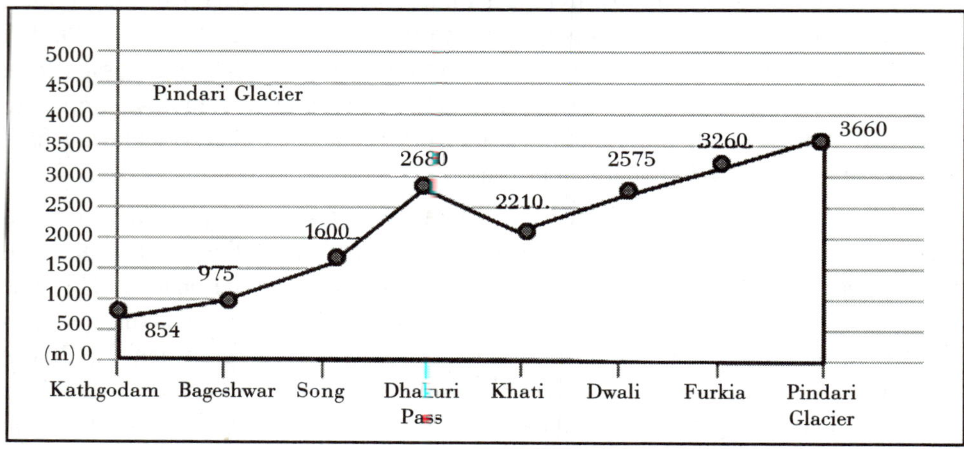

Fig. 5.3

One should start early from Phurkia so that the glacier can be reached by sunrise. The trek to zero point takes a couple of hours. The last 3.5 km., are extremely steep and trekkers are advised to carry glucose sachets to combat any fall in energy levels. Coming face to face with the glacier, one follows the little trickle of ice and soon gazes up at the expanse of the frozen river. Trekkers should start their descent by 11 a.m at the latest, as inclement weather tends to make the journey hazardous later on. The downhill trek is fairly easy and one can enjoy the journey dotted with rhododendrons, bhojpatras and exotic wild flowers.

On the way from Phurkiya towards Zero Point

A km., before Zero Point, have the 'best seats in the house', and a Babaji has built himself a lovely place. It is like an amphitheatre, where we are ringed by snow-capped peaks. They are piercingly clear; a sight to behold. It's an amazing place, and it's possible to pitch tent here. One can see the Pindari glacier from here. It is 0.5 km., wide and 4 km., long. Babaji serves food to anyone who makes it up there. Babaji has built himself a sweet little den, complete with a solar panel which he uses to recharge NiCd batteries that drive a CFL. His rooftop makes for a striking image, mixing solar photovoltaics with a trishul.

A Few Suggestions

If you think of doing this trip, the following ideas will help:

- Get the Survey of India *Trekking Map Series* map of Kumaon.
- Dress in layers that are convenient to add and delete. The temperature can swing around by 10 degrees in a few minutes. It rains almost every day, so it's useful to have a raincoat or a windcheater. Gore-tex would be ideal.
- There is electricity at only one place: A generator at Khati. Carry spare charged batteries.
- You don't need the KMVN package trek. At Bageshwar, you can line up the unbundled components. The components are: Porter (can carry 30 kg, and costs Rs. 200/day), beds at KMVN huts (Rs. 150/night), a guide (who is voluble, unlike porters, and acts like a majordomo at the camps), transportation to and from Song, etc. This gives you more flexibility in designing your own trip, and making changes on the fly. The package treks are too restrictive; they are useful if you have never ever done a trip in the region before and have no clue about how things work.
- The maps identify all KMVN huts. You can landup at a KMVN hut without any advance warning. If they have a bed, you'll get it. If they don't, they'll spring a sleeping bag and/or a mattress and accomodate you anyway. They will make dinner for you. It's cool.
- The water is not clean when it is near human habitation.
- If you must contract with KMVN in Delhi (or anyplace other than Bageshwar), be sure to have a written definition of what you have contracted.

- It is nice to have a tent, that gives choices other than the KMVN huts.
- KMVN food planning is low on trail chow and protein.
- There are leeches and flies-that-bite. Full sleeves and long pants make sense.

Management Strategies

- Proper entries of tourists/visitors, guide potters, ponies/mules, sheep, goats etc., within the carrying capacity of the areas must be made at Song in the Forest Chowki register to have correct number of tourists visiting the area.
- Two Chawkidars be posted at Forest Chowki, Song to have regular entries made and entry fees collected to regenerate maintenance revenue.
- More participation of local people should be as porters, guide, restaurants/hotel owners etc.
- Encourage local youth to involve more in ecotourism to avoid their migration to urban areas/metropolitan cities for earning.
- Financial assistance to local to participate in tourism related business like: Hotels, Dhabas, paying guest house etc.
- Display of local crops like: Rajma, Phaphad etc., and Ringal (hill bamboo) items with proper name tag, price tag etc., should be done along the trek route, which can increase the earning of local people and can popularize these items among tourists.
- Local people need to know the importance of water and to conserve it by arresting them in tanks (Rain Water Harvesting) at higher elevation, then to distribute at lower lying villages for their needs.
- Renovation of Rest house of CPWD, TRC should be done periodically to provide better amenities to the tourists and to increase the number of the tourists.
- Renovation of bridges along the route, almost all the wooden bridges were damaged during our recent visit in June 2008.
- Local people should be made aware of solid waste collection/disposal how dangerous these could be if not managed properly.
- Local people should be motivated for conservation of natural resources. The area has rich flora and fauna of rare/endangered species.
- Awareness programmes/meetings should be organised for local residents about eco-tourism. Tourists should be made aware of the area by distributing the brochures with information about local customs, foods, traditions along with do's and don'ts for in the Pindari area.
- Local people must be involved in the decision-making process related to tourism in their areas.

- Provide alternative fuel (*e.g.*, Solar panel, Biogas plant, LPG) to minimize cutting of trees for cooking purposes.
- Grazing by sheep and goats disrupting the alpine meadows, grazing must be allowed rotation wise at different meadows (*viz*; Bedni and Ali Bugyals).
- Integrated tourism development with other sectors of local economy and encourage local entrepreneurs to the greatest possible extent.
- Pindari, Kafni and Sunderdhungha Glaciers can be promoted for adventure tourism, for which registered societies of various adventure sports *viz*; Skiing. Rock climbing, Mountaineering etc., can be formed by issuing license.
- For trekking master plan of trek routes can be prepared with basic facilities like: drinking water, toilets, shelters etc., at fixed points only.
- Availability of tents, equipments, trained guides and porters be ensured.
- Guidelines be prepared for tourists which should be strictly implemented.
- Construction of permanent building near 'O' Point may enhance receding/melting of glaciers. In Pindari, base camp at Phurkia should be strictly practiced by tourists. No camping should be allowed near within 5 km., area of Glaciers.
- Proper solid waste disposal through educating tourists and local people.
- Recycling of wastes must be practiced for which recycling machines can be provided to the locals.
- Hence, management strategies can be in the following major ways on the basis of Anon (2006).

Preventive Measures

- Conduct periodic cleaning operations along the trek route.
- Establish refuse collection areas at base camps, which should be cleaned regularly.
- Construct micro hydroelectric power units for power supply to remote areas, this along with adoption of firewood technology/providing alternative fuel will restrict cutting of trees from these fragile areas.

Improvement Measures

- Organise afforestation programmes with best adapted local species to help the local economy.
- Plant native mixed vegetation on barren sites to control further deterioration of the site.
- Construct latrines suiting local environment, adoption of proper sewage system.

Information Measures

- Train porters/guides/local people in local administration and in elected bodies through lectures, slide shows/film shows pamphlets etc.

Incentive Measures

- Publicize the positive work of locals/tourists, who have helped in preserving the mountain/local ecology and environment.

Management Policies

- Periodically close Peaks and Bugyals to control damage due to over use or overgrazing.
- Campaign to promote winter tourism in order to reduce congestion during the summer peak season.

Conclusions

The construction of roads, treks and other infrastructure are indispensable for efficient transport and communication system for tourism development, but these activities accelerates increase in GHG resulting to global warming, hill slope instability, deforestation, soil erosion, pollution of air and water etc., especially along the road sides and around most of the Himalayan tourist resorts. The construction of accommodation facilities like: rest houses, tourist bungalows, buildings, seasonal accommodation units, recreation centres etc., have posed the most serious menace to the region; not only does it accelerate soil erosion but also causes damage to crops, animals, plants, housing and public properties. Heavy siltation in adjacent areas particularly in the valley of mountainous regions is also caused due to these activities.

Ecotourism planning and development need to be conceived in the context of overall development of the area. The current need is to promote community based ecotourism and biodiversity conservation; implement impact assessment and monitoring studies on environment, take care of social and cultural aspects of ecotourism, give more emphasis on local employment, popularize local tradition/products etc., Revenue generated through entry fee collection should be invested on conservation and community development programmes. Stakeholders need to be actively involved in the planning of ecotourism development at local, regional and national levels. Monitoring and evaluation have to be an integral part of the planning system with participation, supervision and overall control by stakeholders. Little efforts have been made to view ecotourism and its impact from the perspective of the local communities (Anon, 2006).

It is a need of the hour to maintain a balance of intricate linkages between socio-cultural, ecological, economic and physical systems that could lead to sustainability in the Indian Himalayan region. Prior attention needs to be given to the preservation of fragile mountain ecosystem, indigenous knowledge system and sustainable use of natural resources. The further studies is needed to seek the impact on the local economy, identification of model eco-trekking/expedition routes and potential sites, and designing appropriate strategies/action plans for sustainable ecotourism. This will not only help to resolve the local people-policy conflicts and improve the local economy but will help to achieve the biodiversity conservation goal.

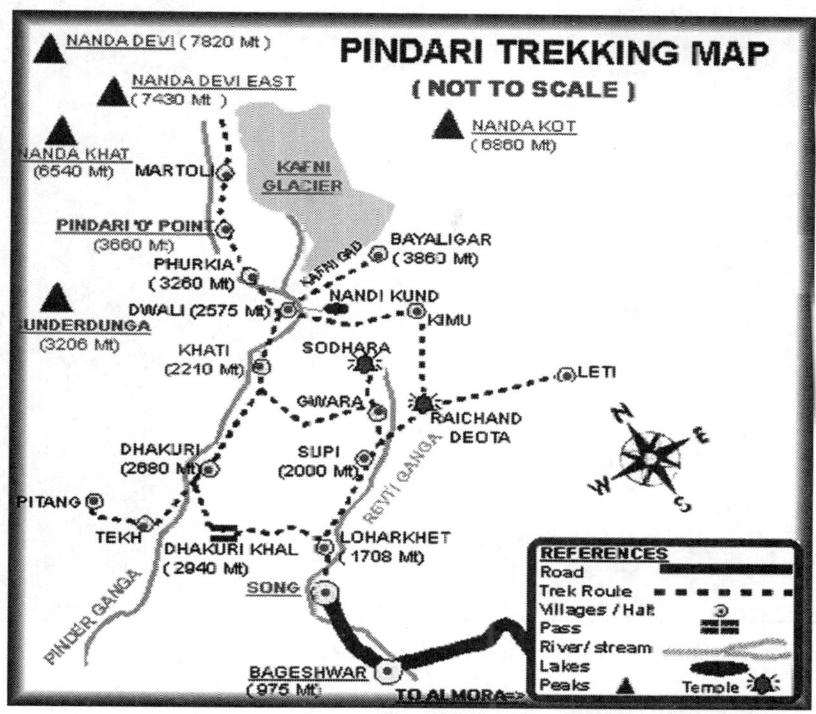

Trekking Route from Loharket Village towards Pindari

Temporary Wooden Bridge to Cross Pinder River

Camping near Bugyal

Steep Slope (timberline) Starts on the way near Bugyal

Construction near Pindari 'O' Point

Pindari Glacier view from PWD Pinadri 'O' Point sign board

At foothill of Pindari Glacier

Problem of Overgrazing in the Nearby Pindari - Bugyal areas

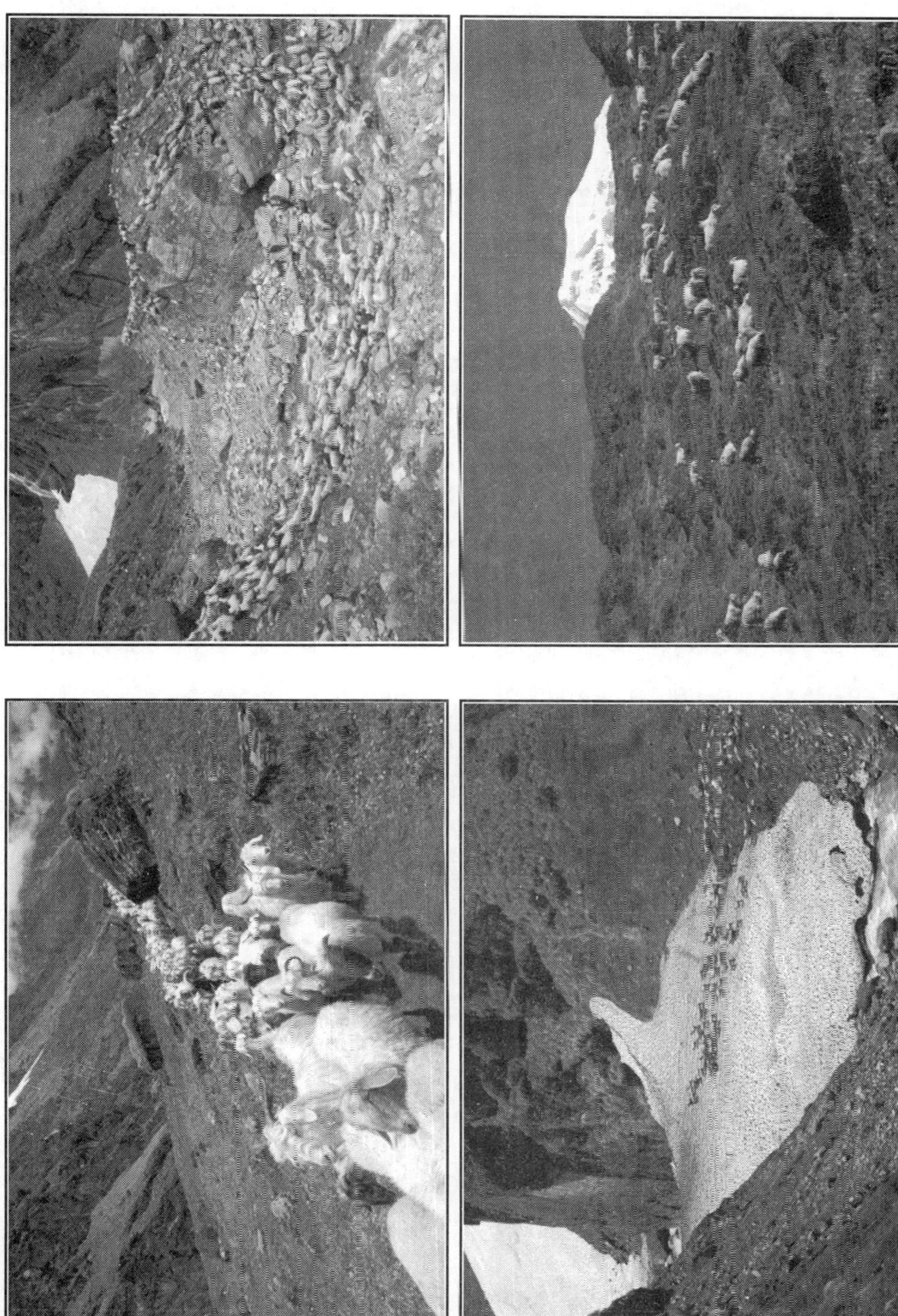

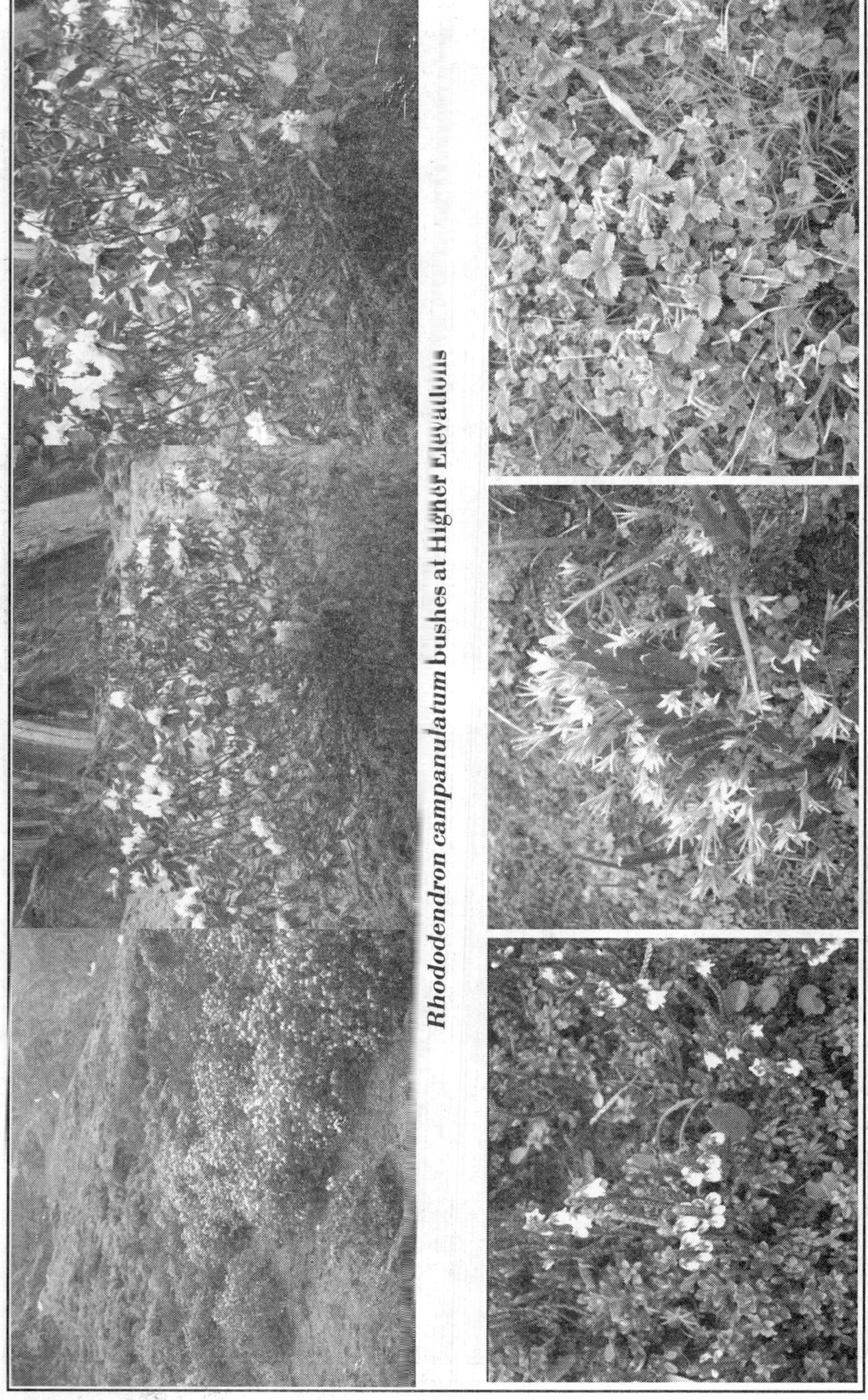

Rhododendron campanulatum bushes at Higher Elevations

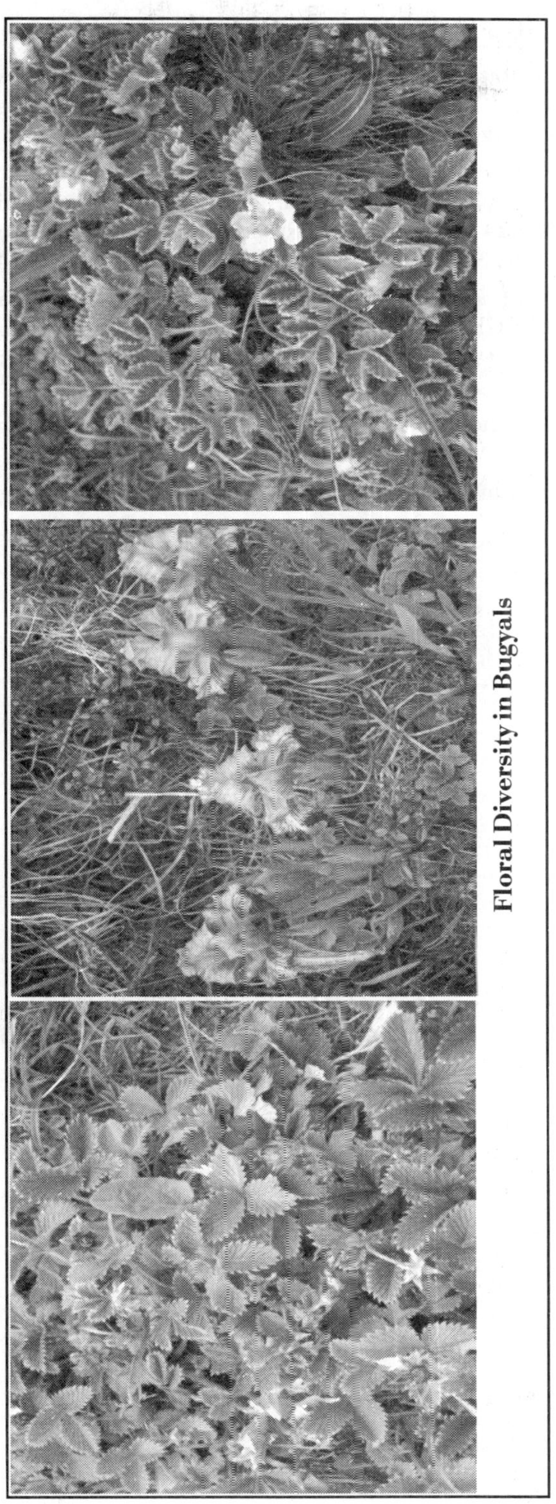

Floral Diversity in Bugyals

REFERENCES

Anon, (2006). Developing eco-tourism for Nanda Devi Biosphere Reserve (A world heritage site): Strategies and Action Plan. G.B. Pant Instt. of Himalayan Environment and Development, Garhwal University, Post Box 92, Srinagar, Garhwal, Uttaranchal - 246174 with Financial support from UNESCO, New Delhi. March 2006. pp. 14.

Maikhuri, R.K., U. Rana, K.S. Rao, S. Nautiyal and K.G. Saxena. (2000). Promoting Ecotourism in the Buffer Zone areas of Nanda Devi Biosphere Reserve: An Option to Resolve People-policy Conflict. *Int. Jour. of Sustainable Dev. and World Ecology*, 7(4): 333-342.

Ram, Jeet, G.L. Shah and S.P. Singh. (1995). Vegetation Mapping in Higher Himalaya: Beidni – Alee Bugyal – A case. In: Glimpses of Central Himalaya – A Socio-Economic and Ecological Perspective. Part I (eds. B.R. Pant and M.C. Pant) Radha Publication New Delhi, pp. 379-397.

Theuns, H. Leo. (2008). Globalization and Tourism: Pros and Cons. *Tourism Recreational Research*, 33 (1): 99-105.

Valdiya, K.S., (1980). Geology of Kumaun Lesser Himalaya. Wadia Institute of Himalayan Geology, Dehradun, 291.

Pages 109-151

WATER RESOURCES: MAPPING, MONITORING AND MANAGEMENT
***Edited by* : Dr. Pawan Kumar Tyagi; Dr. Avnish Chauhan & Dr. Pawan Kumar Bharti**
***Edition* : 2017**
ISBN : 978-93-5056-861-3
***Published by* : Discovery Publishing House Pvt. Ltd., New Delhi (India)**

Filtering Contaminants and Efficient Management Strategies of Water Resources

A Perspective Outlook

Bina Rani[1], Murtaza Abid[2]
Upma Singh[3], M.M. Abid Ali Khan[4*]
Shailendra Patni[5], V.K. Swami[6]
Ashok K. Kakodia[7], Sukhraj Punar[8]
Raaz K Maheshwari[8]

ABSTRACT

With rising population and dwindling groundwater resources, the groundwater quality of deteriorating day-by-day. From an acute public health perspective, the quality of drinking water in India is a major concern. It is estimated that the annual impact of water borne disease in this country affects 37.7 million persons annually including the loss of 73 million working days and the death of 1.5 million children from diarrhea alone. Based on the deteriorating condition of the country's water supply, proper usage of water resources has become the utmost priority in India and many efforts to conserve and protect the water supply are being made at national and state levels. India has witnessed unprecedented economic growth but at what environmental price? Contamination threatens natural water sources and without regulatory enforcement,

1. Department of Chemistry and Environmental Engineering, Poornima College of Engineering, Jaipur, Rajasthan.
2. Department of Biochemistry, KGMU, Lucknow, U.P., India.
3. Department of Applied Chemistry, School of Vocational Studies, Gautam Buddha University, Greater Noida, UP.
4. Department of Botany, Shia PG., College, Lucknow, U.P., India.
5. Department of Zoology, SRKP Girls' College, Kishangarh, Ajmer, Rajasthan.
6. Department of Chemistry, Lohia Government PG College, Churu, Rajasthan.
7. Department of Chemistry, SGG Government PG College, Banswara, Rajasthan.
8. Department of Chemistry, SBRM Government PG College, Nagaur, Rajasthan.

consumers have to treat water using point-of-use devices. There are numerous technologies that help one to move the water quality from 'As is' to 'As required'. Some methods have been tried and tested for ages which altogether change the scale and method in some variation, while there are a few newly discovered methods originating from the variety of inventions carried out in different streams of science. Ozone (O_3) and Ultraviolet (UV) are both matter particulates carrying energy which can be used technically and economically for the treatment of water and wastewater. An overview of drinking water issues in the country including UV, UF and RO treatment technology is delineated in this manuscript precisely.

INTRODUCTION

India holds 17.5 per cent of the world's population yet it only contains 4 per cent of the world's fresh water resources, which are declining in terms of both supply and quality. Although drinking water was once considered safe in India, today providing the nearly 1.2 billion inhabitants with access to safe drinking water is an increasingly difficult challenge. Groundwater sources are being rapidly depleted, surface water sources are largely contaminated and the infrastructure needed to deliver drinking water both in urban and rural areas is either non-existent or needs substantial upgrades to meet demand. Over the last quarter century, the excessive extraction of groundwater needed to meet the demands of the country's growing agriculture and industrial sectors has decreased the per capita availability of fresh drinking water. Not only has the salinity of groundwater in coastal areas increased due to seawater intrusion from the continuous withdrawal of groundwater, but both ground and surface water sources now face greater contamination from industrial effluents, sewage, agricultural waste. Depletion of groundwater and its increasing pollution could be leading to a silent, nationwide public health crisis as aquifers in many stretches across India are becoming unfit for drinking, according to the government's own figures. Groundwater in pockets of 158 out of the 639 districts has gone saline. It says in pockets across 267 districts, groundwater contains excess fluoride; in 385 districts, it has nitrates[24] beyond permissible levels; in 53 there's arsenic[16] and there's high level of iron in 270 districts. Besides this, aquifers in 63 districts contain heavy metals like: Pb, Cr and Cd, the presence of which in any concentration poses a danger[1].

The stealthily growing health crisis could be worse in rural India where facilities to even detect chronic health problems arising out of water contamination do not exist. Nearly 80 per cent of India's rural drinking water comes from underground sources. Today we are more quality and health conscious than our ancestors. We have been forced to be so because of the increased levels of pollution in the environment and higher contaminants in water as well as food items. Right from the beginning of the day, the air we breathe, the water we drink and the food we eat, is becoming increasingly infectious because of higher pollution and utilization of several harmful chemicals at different stages. Drinking fluoride-laden water beyond safe levels can lead to fluorosis which hits teeth and bones[15]. Arsenic causes problems in the nervous system, reduces IQ level in children and in extreme cases can also cause cancer. Cr is a known carcinogen. Presence of nitrates[6] in drinking water leads to what is commonly called as *methaemoglobinaemia* BBS (blue baby syndrome) which hits infants and can lead to respiratory and digestive system problems. These chemicals have appeared in the water sources either due to too much water being drawn from deeper and deeper in the ground, or due to industrial and human waste contamination[2].

Arsenic and fluoride[3] are typically found in groundwater where chemicals have leeched from the bedrock due to over-exploitation of the source. Heavy metals are likely to flow in from industrial waste dumped untreated into water-systems. Nitrates are likely to appear in groundwater because of excess or repetitive use of fertilizers over time. Government reports have shown that water withdrawal from underground aquifers is higher than the annual recharge levels in almost 15 per cent of the country's geographical area. The number of wells are increasing rapidly and so are the depths to which people are plumbing to bring water out as the sources dry up[3].

Sources, Supply and Distribution of Water in India

Both ground and surface water are sources of drinking water for the rural and urban Indian populations. However, the quality, supply and distribution of both sources present problems for human consumption.

In India, approximately 85 per cent of the rural population, comprised of more than 700 million people, is dependent on groundwater. However, groundwater is currently being depleted at a fast rate and many sources contain excessive concentrations of fluoride[13], arsenic and nitrate.

It is estimated that ~ 66 million Indians use water sources containing excess fluoride and another 10 million have excess arsenic in their groundwater[25]. Additionally, septic effluent percolation to the water table is another source of groundwater contamination that presents an added public health risk. On the other hand, an estimated 60 per cent of the urban population is dependent on surface water. Similar to groundwater, the availability and quality of source water presents major concerns. While the majority of municipalities treat drinking water using conventional treatment technologies prior to distribution, there are often significant issues within the distribution system itself including cross-connections, leakage and loss of pressure that may cause a vacuum in the system leading to untreated surface water intrusion[4].

Untreated surface water intrusion of the distribution system may introduce contaminants such as: Pb, As[18], Cd, Hg, Fe, F^- (fluoride), NO_3^- (nitrate), high hardness, insecticides and surfactants into the potable drinking water supply. Even worse, issues within the distribution systems can lead to wastewater being mixed with treated drinking water, which introduces a host of microorganisms including: bacteria, virus and protozoans. The introduction of pathogenic organisms such as: bacteria (*E. Coli, Shigella, V. Cholerae*), viruses (*Hepatitis A, Polio, Rotavirus*) and parasites (*E. Histolytica, Giardia*) can lead to many diseases including: but not limited to, diarrhea, typhoid fever, dysentery, cholera, para-typhoid, viral hepatitis, polio, amoebiasis, and giardiasis[5].

To address these issues, public water suppliers routinely use chlorine to treat for microbiological contaminants. However, depending on the organic content of the water, treatment with chlorine and other halogenated disinfectants can lead to the formation of chlorination by-products, many of which are reportedly known carcinogens. The Indian government is working to address problems inherent in the sources, supply and distribution of drinking water. However, unlike other countries, there is not currently a set of enforceable drinking water regulations.

Drinking Water Regulations in India

A provision of clean drinking water was given priority in the constitution of India, conferring the duty of providing clean drinking water and improving public health standards to the state governments. More recently, water quality monitoring has been accorded a high priority and institutional mechanisms have been developed at both a national and state level.

The Ministry of Drinking Water and Sanitation (MDWS) and the Government of India are proposing to implement a uniform drinking water quality monitoring protocol to ensure the systematic examination of all drinking water sources. If enforced, this protocol will lead to the regular monitoring of all water sources to assess the quality of the water and identify chemical and microbiological contaminants.

The MWR (Ministries of Water Resources), UDPP (Urban Development and Poverty Prevention), RDEF (Rural Development, Environment and Forests), and HFW (Health and Family Welfare) also play a major role in providing drinking water of adequate quantity and potable quality to meet the health needs of the community. Rural water supply agencies are currently working to identify suitable technologies to address chemical contamination with a particular focus on the most common pollutants in India: arsenic, fluoride, iron, nitrate, and salinity. And, although microbiological contamination is still a serious health concern in India, source protection and improving microbiological quality through various treatment methods are already well established through regulations on waste disposal.

However, given the number of concerns with the contamination of ground, fresh and treated water, a first critical step to protect public health is to continuously monitor for chemical and microbial contaminants. The quality of drinking water supplied in India by public agencies is presently governed by the BIS (Bureau of Indian Standards) which has developed IS 10500:1991 to standardise monitoring of chemical and microbiological constituents in drinking water. This guideline specifies the acceptable levels of chemical and microbiological constituents in drinking water and also provides information on the implications of drinking water in which these contaminants exceed their guideline value. A similar standard, IS 14543, specifies monitoring guidelines for packaged water. However, without enforceable regulations for both the monitoring and treatment of drinking water, it is increasingly necessary for Indian consumers to treat their water using POP (Point-of-Use) devices.

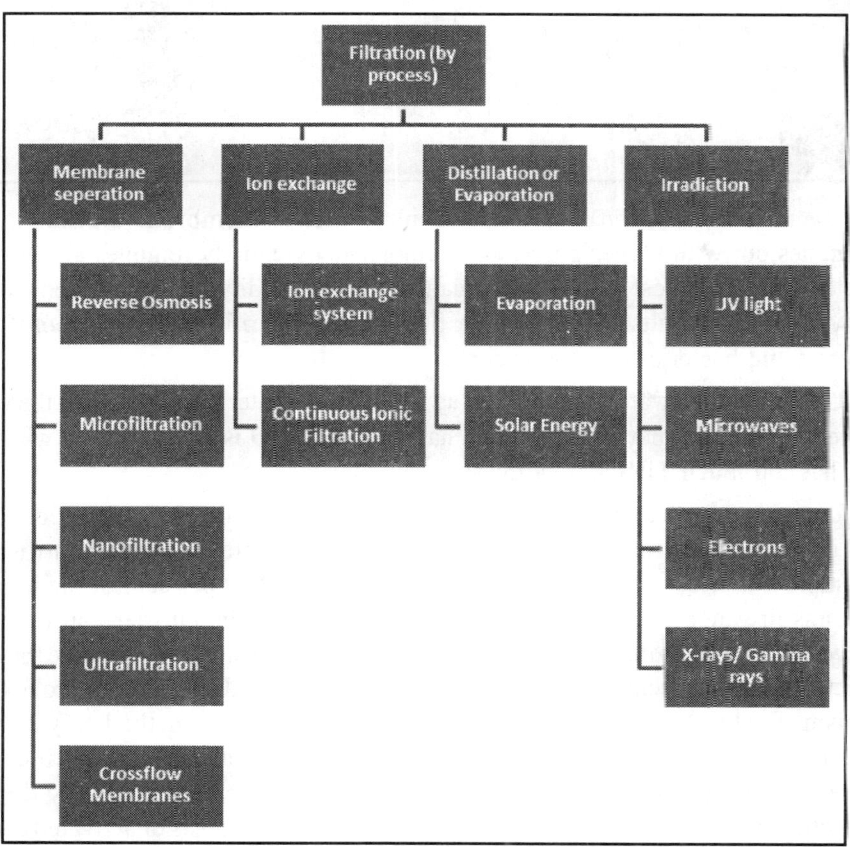

Drinking Water Treatment Technologies

With the vast array of pollutants that can potentially contaminate drinking water, a single technology may not be sufficient for potability. Multi-technology devices are widely used in India. In general, POU units will contain both sediment and activated carbon filters combined with a disinfection technology such as: UV, UF, or RO. Furthermore, in some cases a combination of disinfection technologies are used such as: RO and UV. Reverse osmosis is the most widely used water purification method. RO uses membrane technology to remove dissolved salts, impurities and germs from water[7].

The semi-permeable membrane separates germs and dissolved chemicals from water. The membrane has very fine pores that allows only water to pass through it leaving behind all the harmful chemical, dissolved salts and microbes suspended in water (*size of RO membrane pore is ~ 0.0005 μ which is slightly > the size of water molecule and < bacteria*). The drawback of RO is that it alters the taste of water and may remove some essential mineral from water.

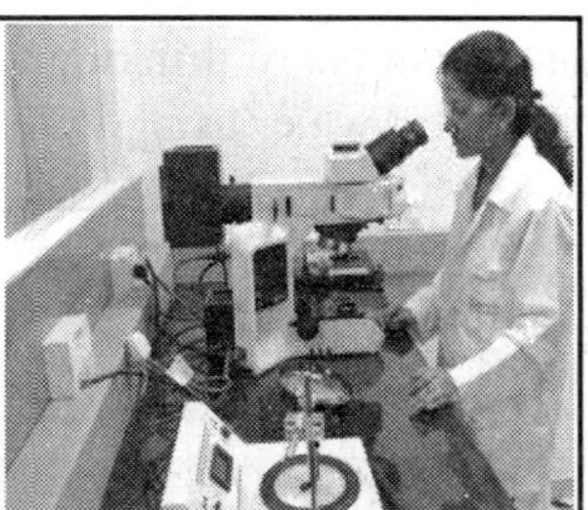

UF (*Ultra filtration*) purification method uses membrane similar to RO membranes but with bigger pores. UF membranes essentially removes all colloidal particles including most pathogenic organisms and turbidity but fails to remove the dissolved solids and salts. Unlike UV purifier, UF water purifier physically removes all the germs and bacteria from the water.

Ultra-filtration water purifiers are as good as RO water purifiers when the water supplied to homes is not very hard and has less TDS. RO is only required when the water has too much TDS and hardness.

UV water purification is a method of water filtration which uses ultra-violet light to kill all germs, bacteria, microbes, cysts, etc., in water. Ultraviolet water purification is a simple but effective process that destroys around 99.99 per cent of the harmful organisms in water. There is a tiny mercury lamp inside the purifier that produces short wave UV radiations[7]. These radiations irradiate the water and penetrate the cells of bacteria and viruses, destroying their ability to reproduce. The microbes and organisms fail to multiply and eventually die. This purification method only kills the germs but the bodies of the dead germs remain in the water. Separate filters are required to remove the germs physically. UV water purification is usually done in conjunction with other forms of filtration such as: reverse osmosis or activated carbon filters. Water purifiers with candle type filter have a very basic operating mechanism.

The candle has very minute pores. Any particle which has the size larger than the pores gets blocked out and cannot pass on to the clean side. It does not require any electricity for operation. But the downside is that it fails to block microbes and so water still needs to be boiled before consumption. Also the candle needs to be cleaned up frequently for effective operations. This water purifier use activated carbon filters for purification process. The carbon filters can remove chemicals like chlorine, pesticides and impurities to a great extent. The filtration changes the taste and odor of water. It does not require electricity for operation. But it is also not very effective in removing microbes from water.

Ozone has been utilized for decades to purify water, mainly due to its germicidal effect on microorganisms present in water – effects that exceed those of any other disinfectant, primarily chlorine. Although ozone was discovered in the mid 19th century, it was only during the last several decades that its numerous applications and benefits have become evident. Growing international concern for water quality has called for 'cleaner' chemicals to be used in treatment technologies, and ozone has swiftly become a major ingredient and a preffered choice among water bottlers worldwide. Ozone (O_3) is the triatomic oxygen, an extremely effective oxidant. The property which makes it the most efficient broad-spectrum microbiological control substance in addition to being environmentally friendly, safe and a very reliable disinfectant. It is highly reactive, very unstable and converts back into oxygen after the process of disinfection. Ozone is generated by excitation of molecular oxygen, causing some of it to dissociate into oxygen atoms, which recombines with oxygen to produce ozone. The energy for the process of ozone production is supplied by electrical energy. A commercial ozone generator has two electrodes separated by an air gap. A high voltage potential is applied between the two electrodes containing a dielectric between them, and a corona discharge is developed. The feed gas containing oxygen is allowed to pass between the narrow gap, where ozone is produced by recombination of oxygen atoms.

Ozone will oxidize both organic and inorganic substances. Ozone disinfection doesn't leave a trail behind. Like the formation of tri-halomethanes (THMs) as is the case, when chlorine is used for water disinfection. Once a THM is formed, it's difficult to oxidize, even with ozone. Compared to other disinfectants, ozone has emerged as the distinctive victor.

Bacteria are microscopically small, single-cell creatures with a primitive structure. The bacteria body has a solid-cell membrane. Ozone attacks the cell wall, causing molecular rupture of the outer membrane in a few seconds. Thus the cytoplasm of the bacteria is thrown out – an irreversible problem. Viruses are small independent species, built of structure and macromolecules. Unlike bacteria, they multiply only within the host cell. They transform protein of the host cell into proteins of their own. Ozone destroys viruses by dispersing through the protein coat into the nucleic acid core, damaging the viral RNA. At higher concentration, ozone destroys the capsid, or exterior protein shell by oxidation of DNA (Deoxyribonucleic acid), or RNA (Ribonucleic acid) structures of the microorganism are affected.

Today in all the advanced countries, drinking water is disinfected by ozone. The utilization of ozone is increasing day-by-day – because of the availability of economical and more reliable ozonation systems in addition to the development of techniques for ozone dissolution in water.

ECAR Technology for the Removal of Arsenic

It is serious concern to express over the extent of arsenic contamination in groundwater that has affected nearly 70 million people in 86 districts across 10 States. As many as 38 countries, including: Bangladesh[29], Nepal and Pakistan, are affected by arsenic contamination in ground water. In India, the problem has assumed alarming proportions in many States – the worst being West Bengal where it is 'grave.' Of the 19 districts in the State, 79 blocks in eight districts – Malda, Murshidabad, Nadia, North 24 Parganas, South 24 Parganas, Bardhaman, Howrah, Hooghly and Kolkata – have reported high arsenic concentrations in tube-wells, exceeding the permissible limit. Other States affected by high arsenic content in ground water are: Assam, Bihar, Jharkhand, Chhattisgarh, Haryana, Karnataka, Manipur, Punjab and UP.

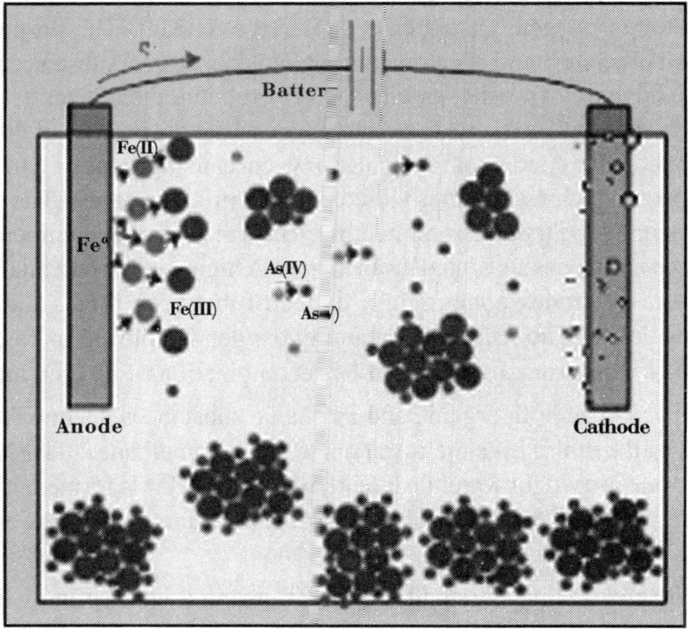

About 100 million people worldwide are exposed to toxic concentrations of naturally occurring arsenic in groundwater supplies, the vast majority living in rural Bangladesh and India (West Bengal, Bihar). Other arsenic-affected areas are found in Vietnam, Thailand, Argentina, Chile, Mexico, China and the United States. The slow accumulation of arsenic in the body causes skin lesions, gangrene, multiple types of cancer, cardiovascular diseases, reduced IQ in children, neuropathy and premature death. Over 60 million people in Bangladesh and West Bengal (India) drink groundwater contaminated with naturally occurring arsenic. Although the WHO's recommended maximum limit for arsenic in drinking water is 10ppb (parts per billion), the arsenic levels can exceed 1000 ppb. Forty thousand people in Bangladesh are already showing signs of arsenic poisoning, in what is rightly called the largest case of mass poisoning in history. A recent 10-year long cohort study published in *The Lancet* showed that 1 in 5 of all adult deaths in Bangladesh are now due to arsenic.

Although there are numerous proposed solutions to this devastating problem, many of them are expensive and/or ineffective at decreasing arsenic in drinking water to acceptable levels. Scientists at Lawrence Berkeley National Labs have developed two methods to affordably and effectively remove arsenic from drinking water. The first method is called (ARUBA (Arsenic Removal Using Bottom Ash). Bottom ash, a widely available waste material from coal-fired power plants, is coated with iron rust, which binds to arsenic. The arsenic can then be removed from the water through settling and/or filtration. The second method is called EASR (Electro Chemical Arsenic Remediation). Engineers from (JU) (Jadavpur University) with technical help from the UC (University of California) have developed an inexpensive water filter which removes AS (arsenic) besides other impurities.

A team of civil engineers from JU and the UC has successfully installed the water filter plant which produces 10,000 litres of water per day at a school near Baruipur in South 24 Parganas district, an affected area. They employed As-contaminated ground water and filtered it using ECAR (electro-chemical arsenic remediation) technology to produce potable water which is not only free of As, but all other contaminants. Used successfully in countries like Bangladesh and Cambodia already, ECAR was developed by NRI scientist Ashok Gadgil in his Berkeley lab on EWR (Energy and Water Research). The technology uses electricity to quickly dissolve Fe (iron) in water which leads to the formation of a type of rust that readily binds to As in the water. As the rust aggregates forming larger particles, it is separated from the water through filtration. This is a very simple and cheap technology. Once commercialised the cost of drinking water can be as low as one rupee a litre. "We have taken only the know-how from outside. Rest everything is indigenous. Even the materials we procured for making the plant are locally-sourced. Our students in School of Environment Engineering know how to do everything," coordinator of the team, Prof Joyashree Roy stated. The cost, researchers said, is very low as none of the components need to be imported. The cost of licensing the technology is also little because the project is a joint collaboration between the DST (Department of Science and Technology of the GoI (Governement of India) and the US government for transfer of technology for public health benefit.

Mercury-free UV Lamps for Water Purifiers

The CSIR (Council of Industrial Research) - CEERI (Central Electronics Engineering Research Institute) Pilani has developed MFP (mercury-free plasma) UV-lamp for water disinfection systems which will enable its users to have water free of environmentally and health hazardous Hg (mercury). This new technology has been transferred to 2 companies for its mass production.

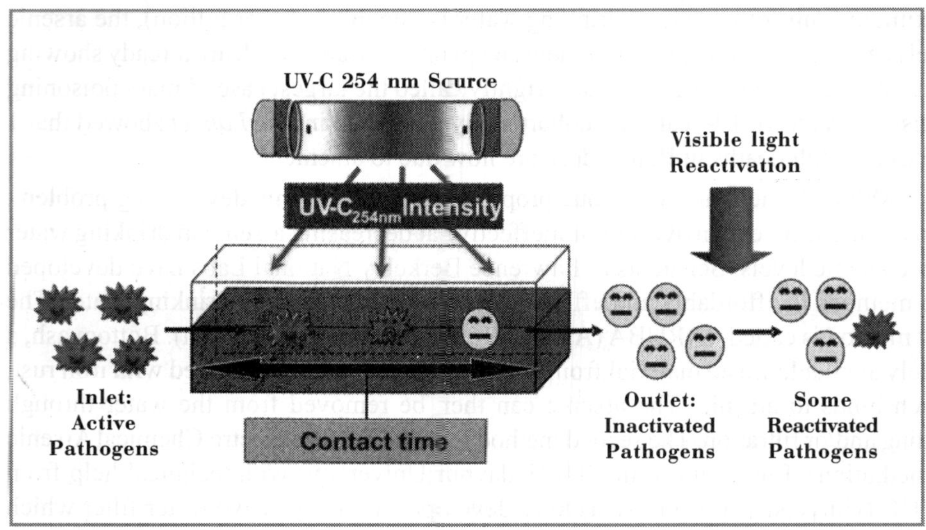

The developed MFP-UV-lamp is a better alternative for Hg-based UV lamps. "It is Hg free, operates at room temperature. It has a zero start-up time and is also easily repairable," said Ram Prakash, a scientist and one of the team members at CSIR-CEERI who developed this technology "This is an indigenous technology developed for the first time in the country by our scientists. This technology has been well-tested in the household water purifier systems. They are planning to scale it up for municipality and sewage wastewater treatment plants with the help of Indian industries. This would certainly bring a new revolution worldwide in the water industry specially by eliminating Hg from the existing UV-lamps. It can be used for sterilization of food, medical equipment, surfaces, ill-skin conditions, air-conditioners and air fresheners for hospitals, etc., titanium coated toilet sterilization in trains, water supply in trains and buses, portable water purifiers for soldiers, outdoorsmen, farmers, etc. The developed technology is now available for commercialization after licencing of know-how agreements and will soon be available in the market.

Defluoridation

Defluoridation is the removal of excess fluoride from water. Fluoride cannot be removed by typical water treatment means like boiling, UV treatment etc. Synthetic ion exchange and precipitation processes, activated alumina filters, and reverse osmosis are typically used to remove fluoride from water in the developed world , there is no universally accepted or routinely used defluoridation techniques in the developing world. Thus, defluoridation is a prime example of field in the need for further development of appropriate technologies.

Nalgonda Technique

The National Environment Engineering Research Institute in Nagpur, India in 1975 has evolved an economical and simple method of defluoridation, which is referred

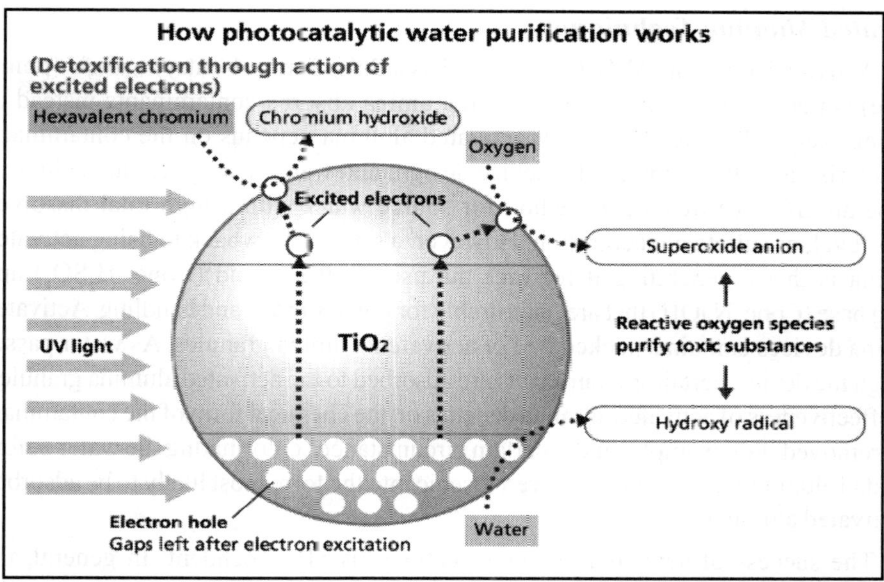

to as the Nalgonda technique. [1, 2, 3, 4] The Nalgonda technique has been repeatedly proven to be an economical and effective household defluoridation technique. In this commonly used technique, fluoride is precipitated using 500 mg/L of alum and 30 mg/L of lime. The Nalgonda technique is a means of fluoride removal that depends on the flocculation, sedimentation, and filtration of fluoride with the addition of Potash alum or aluminum sulfate and lime.

Aluminum sulfate ($Al_2(SO_4)_3 18H_2O$) is added to the water to acts as a flocculent. Though aluminum sulfate is commonly used in general water treatment as a flocculent, the amounts used in defluoridatoin are much higher (150 mg/mgF or 1000mg/L or 20 × norml). As is typical with flocculation processes, the water must be thoroughly stirred to ensure dispersal of the flocculating agent . Because the reaction results in an excess of H^+ ions, Lime ($Ca(OH)_2$) is added to the water during the process to help maintain a neutral pH and hasten the settling of the sediment. The amount of lime added is typically 5 per cent (by mass) of the aluminum sulfate added though some sources say significantly more (20-50% of alum by mass) should be added. The chemical processes, though admittedly are not fully understood , can be seen below:

$$Al_2(SO_4)_3 18H_2O \Rightarrow 2Al + 3\,SO_4 + 18H_2O$$
$$2AL + 6H_2O \Rightarrow 2Al(OH)_3 + 6H^+$$
$$F^- + Al(OH)_3 \Rightarrow \text{Al-F Complex + undefined product}$$
$$6Ca(OH)_2 + 12H^+ \Rightarrow 6Ca^{2+} + 12H_2O$$

Additionally, some of the fluoride is able to form precipitate with calcium. [$Ca(OH)_2 + 2F^- \Rightarrow CaF_2 + 2OH^-$

Activated Alumina Technique

Activated alumina [Al_2O_3] can be used as a PoE (point-of-entry) or PoU (point-of-use) water treatment device. Activated alumina absorbs contaminants instead of filtering them. The effectiveness of activated alumina depends on the contaminant, characteristics of the alumina, the device design, and water quality. ctivated alumina can be an effective treatment method for source water with a high total dissolved solids level, or sulfate concentration. However, a serious drawback to using activated alumina is that regenerating it requires the use of strong acid (Conc. H_2SO_4) and strong base (Conc. NaOH) that are undesirable for home storage and handling. Activated alumina devices contain a packed bed of activated alumina granules. As water passes through the device, certain contaminants are adsorbed to the activated alumina granules. The effectiveness of activated alumina depends on the chemical form of the contaminant to be removed. For example, under certain circumstances chlorinating the water before activated alumina treatment will convert arsenic into the form most likely to be adsorbed by activated alumina.

The success of activated alumina treatment is pH dependent. In general, the water pH should < than 8.5. For fluoride, a pH between 5 and 6 is optimum. For arsenic, a pH of 7 is recommended. Pretreatment to reduce pH may be necessary for activated alumina to be effective.

When the untreated water contains suspended solids, pre-treatment with a 5-μ cartridge sediment filter is required to prevent clogging of the activated alumina bed. In addition, if iron and manganese are present, their concentrations should be below the EPA Secondary Drinking Water Standards of 0.3 mg/L for iron and 0.05 mg/L for manganese. Flow rate and contaminant removal capacity are the two factors in determining the total capacity of an activated alumina device. Flow rate is dependent on the surface area of flow, the pore size of the activated alumina granules, and the available water pressure. As flow area increases, the flow rate increases, assuming other factors are equal. Flow rate decreases as pore size decreases. Household water pressure is usually sufficient for producing adequate amounts of treated water. Point-of-use activated alumina units with a separate faucet can generate ~ 1 gpm (gallon per minute) of treated water at household pressures. PoE devices may produce as much as 7 to 10 gallons per minute. If additional flow capacity is needed and a larger device is not available, two devices can be used in parallel. The contaminant removal capacity depends mostly on the amount of alumina in the device.

CDI Technology

Potable water as well as water for agriculture and industry is critical to human habitation on this planet. We have been squandering and polluting this precious resource and are now inneed of finding cost competitive newer technologies for reclaiming this valuable life-sustaining liquid. Capacitive deionization (CDI) is an electrochemical water treatment process that holds the promise of not only being a commercially viable alternative for treating water but for saving energy as well. CDI works by sequestering ions, or other charged species, in the electrical double layer of ultra capacitors. While removing these ions, one actually stores capacitive energy. If one recovers this energy efficiently ,this process likely consumes less power than any competing technology. This paper reviews current methods for treating water in comparison to the state of art –of - the CDI process.

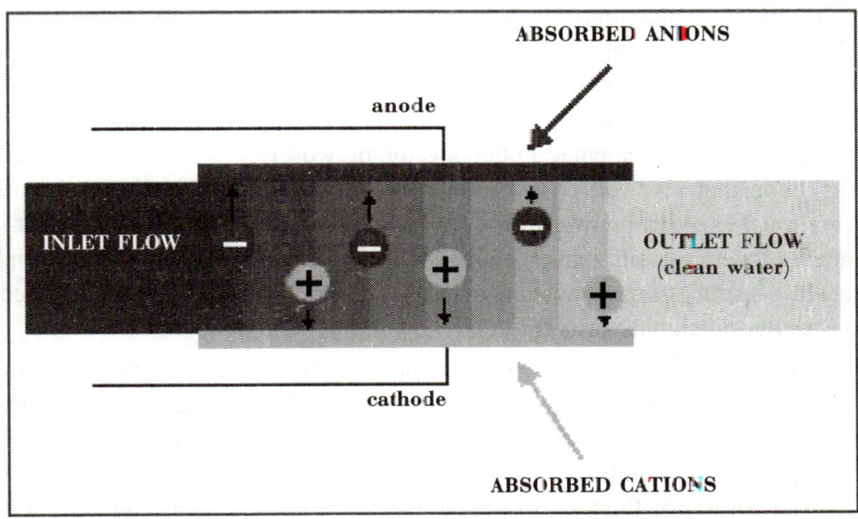

(...) cations (metals are absorbed on the cathode and conversely for the anode (...) the process is electrostatic, not electrochemical

RO Technology: An Emerging State-of-the-art Contrivance for Producing Safe Drinking Water

This technique has attracted the interest of the community investigating water treatment technologies since the mid-1960s. The technology is based on the recognition that high-surface-area electrodes, when electrically charged, can quantitatively adsorb ionic components from water, thereby resulting in desalination. The article reviews the theoretical and technological background of CDI, the history of its development, and past and present attempts towards scaling up and commercialization.

As the name suggests, RO (reverse osmosis) is the opposite phenomenon of osmosis. Osmosis describes the spontaneous flow of water from a dilute solution to a more concentrated solution, when separated from each other by a suitable membrane. As may be evident by now, the reverse osmosis process is best known for its use in desalination (removing the salts from seawater to get safe water), but also get to purified naturally occurring water for medical, industrial and other rinsing applications. In the production of bottled packaged drinking water, the water passes through a reverse osmosis water processor to remove contaminants and pathogens. Rain water collected from the sever drains is purified with reverse osmosis processor and used as tap water in some countries of the world, in case of water scarcities. In industry, reverse osmosis is used to remove minerals from boiler water. It also finds application in cleaning effluent and brackish groundwater Reverse osmosis is a technology that has been used more successfully in the developed world than the developing world. This process is achieved by applying high pressure to water against a semi permeable membrane that is capable of rejecting undesired ions from passing through. [51] A variation of this process is known as electro dialysis that relies on DC potential to remove specific ions. In fact, reverse osmosis can be used to remove a variety of undesired quantities from the water depending on the nature of the membrane used. Being a purely physical process, it eliminates many of the problems seen with other de fluoridation techniques, like pH balancing and the need for regeneration. Reverse Osmosis has been shown to successfully treat water with fluoride concentrations up to 12 mg/L.[3,13] Unfortunately, reverse osmosis has not been successfully implemented in the developing world for a number of reasons. The primary being that it is a very costly de fluoridation option. Additionally, reverse osmosis requires much electrical power to operate. Also, 20-40 per cent of water is lost in this treatment process, possibly much more. Technological improvements in materials and larger scale operations may someday make this technology affordable to more people in need of defluoridation technology.

How did Reverse Osmosis (RO) technology get started? Let's begin with a close look into osmosis. One of the most interesting and fascinating natural phenomena, osmosis is the basis for the fastest growing desalination technology called RO. Natural osmosis governs how waters transfer between solutions with different concentrations. It's also the basis for the way in which human skin and organs function, and how flora and fauna maintain a water balance.

Figure of Reverse Osmosis Process

Due to the nature of the RO process it can't be characterised as a filtration or as treatment.

As in natural process, water tends to flow from a solution with a lower concentration to a solution with a higher concentration (Henniker, 1949). As shown on Figure 6.1, where there is a semi-permeable barrier such as: a membrane, when pressure id applied to a concentrated solution that exceeds osmotic pressure, clean water will be displaced out of the concentrated solution while salts will remain in the concentrated solution. Theoretically, salts shouldn't salts should not pass through the membrane, but in practice we observe salt leakages as a result of diffusion, despite the fact that membrane 'openings' are much larger than the molecules of water (H_2O) and many other ions in the water that may pass the membrane (Polack, 2012).

Reverse osmosis Thnology

This method was invented in 1959 by Professor Reid of the University of Florida and was into practical use by Sidney Loeb and Srinivasa Sourirajan. Reverse osmosis (Report on Industry Consortium........2004) is a mineralization process that relies on a semi-permeable membrane to affect the separation of dissolved solids from a liquid. The semi-permeable membrane allows liquid and some ions to pass, but retains the bulk of the dissolved solids. Semi-permeable membrane (Suratt, 1995) made up of thin films of cellulose acetate, polymethyl methacrylate and polyamide polymers.

Although many liquids (solvents) may be used, the primary application of RO is water-based systems. Hence, all subsequent discussion and examples will be based on the use of water as the liquid solvent. To understand hoe RO works, it is first necessary to understand the natural process of osmosis. (Scott, 2012). Osmosis is a natural process where water flows through a semi permeable membrane from a solution of low concentration of dissolved solid to a solution with high concentration of dissolved solids. Picture a cell divided into 2 compartments by a semi permeable membrane, as shown in Figure 6.1. This membrane allows water and some ions to pass through it, but is impermeable to most dissolved solids (salts). One compartment in the cell has a solution with a high concentration of dissolved solids. Water will continue to flow through the membrane until the concentration is equalized on both sides of the membrane. In equilibrium, the concentration of dissolved solids is the same in both compartments. Now, there will not be more flow from one compartment to the other. However, the compartment that once contained the higher concentration solution now has a higher level than other compartment. The difference in height between the two compartments corresponds to osmotic pressure of the solution that is now at equilibrium, RO is the process by which an applied pressure, greater than the osmotic pressure, is exerted on the compartment that once contained the high-concentration solution, forcing water to move through the semi permeable membrane in the reverse direction of osmosis. Once contained the high-concentration solution. This pressure forces water to pass through the membrane in the direction reverse to that of osmosis. Water now moves from the compartment with the high concentration solution to that with the low concentration solution (Figure 6.1).

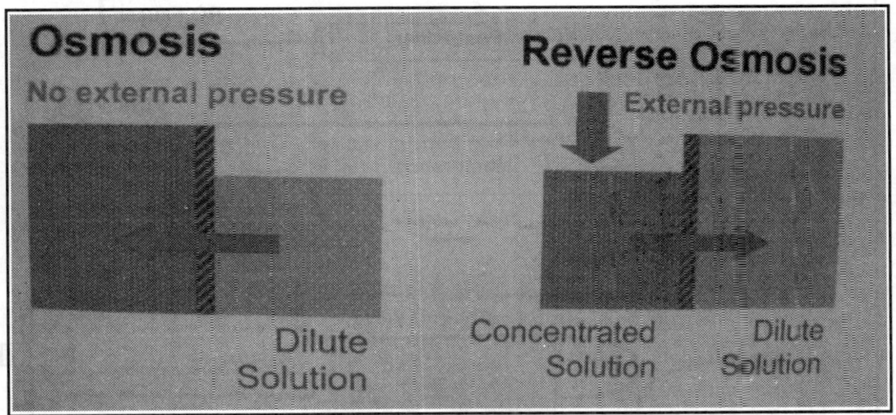

Fig. 6.1: **Schematic of Osmosis and Reverse Osmosis**

In this manner, relatively pure water passes through membrane into the one compartment while dissolved solids retained in the other compartment. Hence, the water in the one compartment is purified or 'demineralized', and the solids in the other compartment are concentrated or dewatered (Scott, 2012). Due to added pressure of the membrane, the applied pressures required to achieve RO are significantly higher than the osmotic pressure. For example, for 1,500 ppm TDS (Total Dissolved Solids) brackish water, RO operating pressure as high as 1,500 psi may be required. The factors that affect the performance of RO system are:

- Water temperature.
- Incoming water pressure.
- Type and number of TDSs in the tap water.
- The quality of filters and membranes used in the RO system.

This process which removes both dissolved organics and salts. Feed water is pressurized and flows across a membrane, with a portion of the feed permeating the membrane. The balance of the feed sweeps parallel to the surface of the membrane to exit the system without being filtered. The filtered stream is permeating because it has permeated the membrane. The second stream is the concentrate because it carries off the concentration contaminants, rejected by the membrane. Because the feed and concentrate flow parallel to the membrane and not perpendicular to it, the process is called 'cross flow filtration'. Depending on the size of the pores engineered into the membrane, cross flow filters are effective in the classes of separation known as RO.nan filtration, ultrafiltration and microfiltration Basic components of a RO system are shown in Figure 6.2.

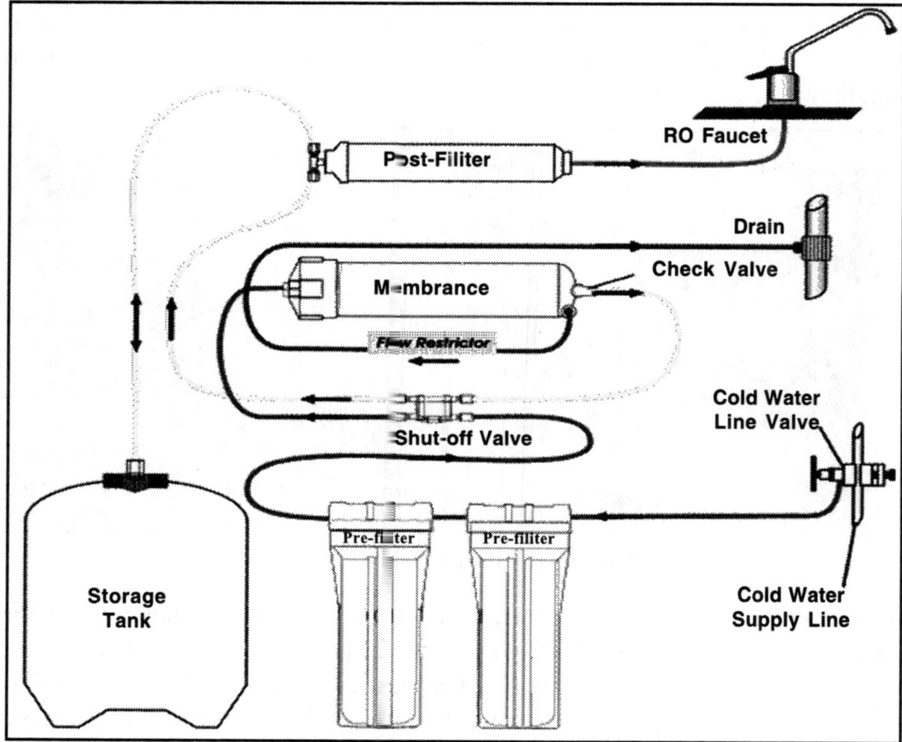

Fig. 6.2: **Major components of RO technology**

- *Cold Water Line Valve:* Valve that fits onto the cold water supply line. The valve has a tube that attaches to the inlet side of RO pre-filter. This is the water source for the RO system.

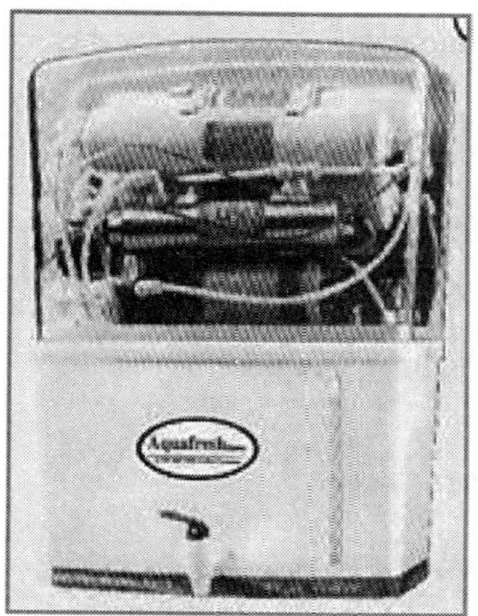

Model of RO System - 1

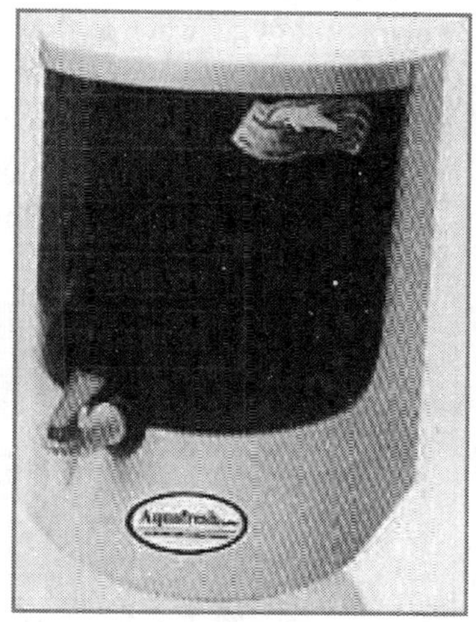

Model of RO System - 2

- *Pre-filter(s):* Water from the cold water supply line enters the RO pre-filter first. There may be more than one pre-filter used. The most commonly used pre-filters are sediment filters. These are used to remove sand, silt, dirt and other sediments. Additionally, carbon filter may be used to remove chlorine, which can have a negative effect on TFC (Thin Film Composite) and TFM (Thin Film Material) membranes. Carbon pre-filters are not used in the RO system contains CTA (Cellulose Tri-Acetate) membranes.
- *Reverse Osmosis Membrane:* The reverse osmosis membrane is the central part (external kidney) of the system (Figure 6.3). The most commonly used is a spiral wound of which there are two options: the CTA, which is chlorine tolerant, and the TFC/TFM, which is not chlorine content. A selection of RO membranes can be used to treat different feed water scenarios. It can meet almost all water standards with a single pass system and all water standards with a double pass system. The process achieves rejections of 99.9 per cent of viruses, bacteria and pyrogens. A reverse osmosis will remove impurities and particles larger than 0.001 μ (microns).
- *Post filter(s):* After the water leaves the RO storage tank, but before going to the RO faucet, the product water goes through the post filter(s). The post filter(s) is generally carbon (either in granular or carbon blocks form). Any remaining tastes and odours are removed from the product water by post filtration.
- *Automotive Shut-off Valve:* To conserve water, the RO system has an automatic shut-off valve. When the storage tank is full (this may vary based upon the

incoming water pressure) this valve stops any further water from entering the membrane, thereby stopping water production. By shutting off the flow this valve also stops water from flowing to the drain. Once water is drawn from the RO drinking water faucet, the pressure in the tank drops and the shut-off valve opens, allowing water to flow to the membrane and waste-water (water containing contaminants) to flow down the drain.

- *Check Valve:* A check valve is located in the outlet end of the RO membrane housing. The check valve prevents the back flow or product water from the RO storage tank. A backward flow could rupture the RO membrane.

Model of industrial RO system - 3

- *Flow Restrictor:* Water flows through the RO membrane is regulated by a flow control. There are many different style of flow controls. The device maintains the flow rate required to obtain the highest quality drinking water (based on the gallon capacity of the membrane). It also helps maintain pressure on the inlet side of the membrane. Without the flow control very little potable water would be produced because all the incoming tap water would take the path of at least resistance and simply flow down the drain line. The flow control is located in the RO drain line tubing.
- *Storage Tank:* The standard RO storage tank holds up to 2.5 gallons of water. A bladder inside the tank keeps water pressured in the tank when it is full.
- *Faucet:* The RO unit uses its own faucet, which is usually installed on the kitchen sink. In areas where required by plumbing codes an air-gap faucet is generally used.

- *Drain Line:* The line runs from the outlet end of the RO membrane housing to the drain. This line is used to dispose of impurities and contaminants found in the incoming water source (tap water). The flow control is also installed in this line..

Membrane Characteristics and Continuance

The material of the membrane has to be inert to the liquids it is exposed to, at the same time having mechanical strength to withstand the high pressure of operation. It should not support scale formation or organic growth, which will block the pores and reduce the performance of the unit. It should be resistant to acid and alkaline cleaning chemicals which are used to recover the membrane over a period of time. In the manufacture of RO membranes, Thin Film Composites (TFC) are used. These are semi-permeable membranes manufactured principally for use in water purification. They also have use in chemical applications such as: batteries and fuel cells. In essence a TFC material is a molecular sieve constructed in the form of a film from two or more layered materials. Membranes used in RO are, in general, made out of Polyamide, chosen primarily for its permeability to water and relative impermeability to various dissolved impurities including salt ions and other small molecules that cannot be filtered. It can withstand twice the temperature as compared to cellulose acetate membranes. Figure 6.5 shows a cutaway section of the modern RO membrane. Earlier versions of membranes were very different from the present cylindrical spirally wound membranes. They were flat sheets assembled with inter layers of collectors. But they were not as easy to install and maintain as the modern ones. Membranes formed from spiral wound layers of membranes/spacer/collector come in different sizes; the most popular sizes are the membranes of diameter 4 inches and 8 inches, with length of 40 inches. The effective area is 7 to 8m^2 for each module. Domestic models of RO plants use smaller membranes while larger diameter and length are made for special applications. Membranes are housed in pressure vessels with end connections for joining the inlet feed water, and outlets for the pure permeate and the concentrate. Housings come in different lengths to suit up to 8 membranes in a single housing. These are chosen depending on applications (Wilson *et al.* 2012; Kaushik, 2012).

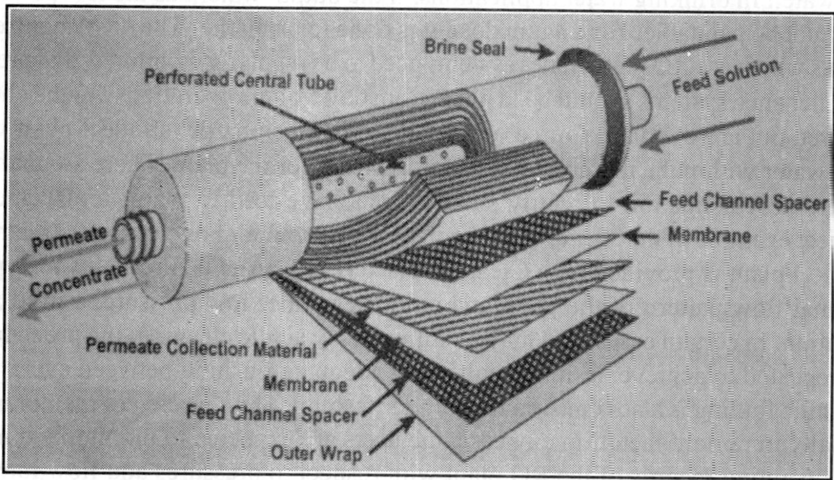

Fig. 6.3: **Cutaway section of the modern RO membrane**

It has become a practice to select RO plants as a commodity. Whereas, the membranes required for a specific application has to be selected-based on several parameters, the most important being the quality of raw water, the flow rate, and its end use. Manufacturers of membranes have a fact sheet to be submitted to be submitted to them for specific applications, from which, data is used to run a software programme which will specify among others, the number of membranes, its configuration, and the operating pressure, another factor to be considered is the utilisation of the reject stream. The ideal situation would be one where the reject could be put to alternate use. But given the rate of depletion of groundwater, the available water already has a high concentration of salts, resulting in the reject being hardly useable. High recovery plants will produce reject water which cannot be discharged as per pollution norms. They have to be evaporated by approved means. However, higher recoveries also mean the plant will operate at greater pressures, incur higher operating cost, become service and power intensive. Hence a holistic approach is needed to get an optimum water balance over the different conditions. In order to maximize the performance of the RO membranes, pre-treatment of the feed water is done. Physical impurities are removed by sand filters. If the feed water has been chlorinated at the source, the chlorine has to be 'leached', since the membranes are sensitive to chlorine. High amount of dissolved iron has to be removed by oxidation. Likewise, colloidal silica causes fouling of the membrane which is difficult to remove by simple means. Nevertheless, it has to be tackled. Dosing pumps are used to dose various chemical formulations which aid in the pre-treatment of feed water (Kozisel, 2003).

If the feed water is from an open source like well or lake, higher level of organics will be present which will grow on the membrane surface, like-wise, in high salinity waters and sea water, the presence of organics is extreme since the salinity sustains it. To overcome this, special formulations called antiscalents are dosed before the water enters the membranes. Sometimes post-treatment is done depending on the end use of the water. In drinking water applications, if the output water has the low pH, the taste may not be palatable. Here again dosing is done to bring the pH to 7. Water treatment plants which use RO membranes systems need to be regularly monitored, and preventive maintenance systems should be in place from day 1 of the operations. As the chemicals filtered out are the main source of damage to the membrane, an ideal plant with the raw water within the membrane is a major hazard for the plant. There are many cases where procrastination to rectify small effects have lead to major replacements – a perfect example of the adage, 'A stitch in time saves nine'. For cleaning of membranes, the RO plant is provided with Clean-in-place (CIP) systems; this helps to bypass the normal flow pattern of the plant and circulates under low pressure, a mild alkaline solution. In certain cases, this may be followed by acidic cleaning; the procedure may be repeated to achieve desired results with adequate flushing between every change. Organic fouling is also removed in a similar fashion. The sourcing of membranes is as equally important factor. In any case, the users are expected to monitor and maintain the operating records of the RO plant with respect to pressures and flow rates of the equipment, along with the details of cleaning cycles. Reject streams of large plants discharge water at almost the operating pressure. Hence is a source of energy. Today large plants are built with patented energy recovery systems. So, that part of the wasted energy is used to run the plant and reduces the overall power consumption. Very large plants are complex in design and operation but in the long run are more economical as the unit cost of treated water could be attractive. If the plant is not going to be used the membranes have to be de-watered and preserved with chemicals. Otherwise the permeability of the membrane is lost irreversibly. Despite the fact that RO system is composed from a number of RO membrane elements properties, there are a number of design and operation techniques that can make RO system design and operation extremely flexible.

The RO process attracted the attention of many researchers in middle of the twentieth century; however efforts to develop a commercial RO membrane were unsuccessful until the late 1950s. In 1959, a group of researchers at the University of California Los Angeles (UCLA) led by Sidney Loeb and Srinivasa Sourirajal demonstrated an RO membrane that worked. The asymmetric or anisotropic cellulose acetate membrane demonstrated by the researchers provided adequate salt rejection at that time. This was the beginning of desalination by RO and membrane desalination. Besides membrane desalination, this was also the beginning of the commercial development of membrane technologies for solid-liquid separation. The RO separation process can be shown in the simple diagram in Figure 6.4.

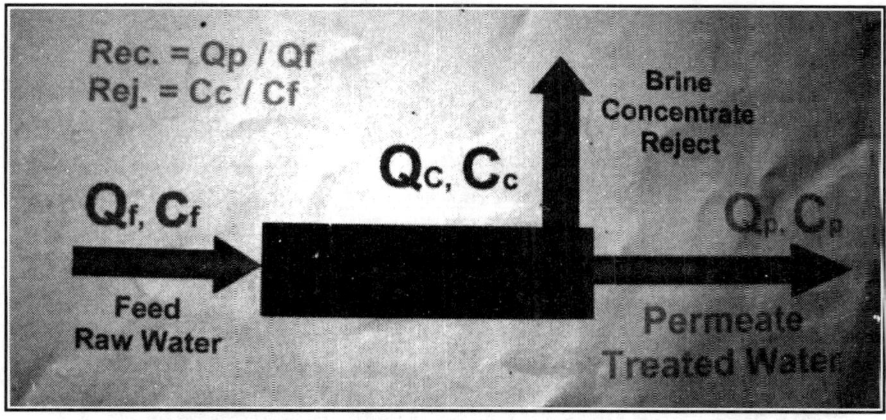

Fig. 6.4: **Schematic of major reverse osmosis stream**

The RO process has three major streams: *(a)* Feed; *(b)* Permeate (product water); *(c)* Concentrate (reject or brine).

The mass balance for the entire system can be represented as follows:

$$Q_f \times C_f = Q_c \times C_c + Q_p \times C_p$$

Where: Q_f - feed flow (m³/hr); C_f - salt concentration in feed water (ppm); Q_c - concentrate flow (m³/hr); C_c - salt concentration in concentrate (ppm); Q_p - product flow (m³/hr); C_p - salt concentration in product water (ppm).

The smallest module of the RO system of the RO system is the RO membrane element. As RO technology developed, the industry came to a consensus on manufacturing standard size RO membrane elements. The major diameters of the spiral – wound elements are 2.5', 4' and 8' with the standard length of single elements at 40' and 60'. More recently, the RO industry has developed larger RO elements with diameters o 16', 17', 18', and 18.5'. While there is currently no consensus on a standard for large diameter RO, each supplies produces a different size, this situation may change as time passes. Each model of the RO element has certain 'fixed' properties that are described and can be found in the element's specification sheet. Little variation is allowed from the membrane element specification when each element is subjected to factory wet seta *e.g.*, the produced elements must meet the specification. In a full scale system the RO elements are encapsulated in pressure vessels that can hold from one single element up to 8 elements in single vessel as shown on Figure 6.5.

Fig. 6.5: RO **membrane inside the pressure vessel**

Fig. 6.6: **Reverse Osmosis rack**

A number of vessels are mounted on the RO rack and can be operated in parallel or in series as shown on Figure 6.6.

Potable Water and its Essential Characteristics (*Bis Stand Ards*)

Essential Characteristics	Is Requirement Limit	Is Permissible Limit	Who Guidelines	Us EPA Limit
Colour (in Hazen units)	5	25	15	15
Odour	Unobjectionable	-	-	-
Taste	Agreeable	-	-	-
Turbity (in NTU)	5	10	5	-
pH	6.5 – 8.5	6.5 – 8.5	-	6.5 -8.5
Total Hardness (as $CaCO_3$)	300	600	-	-
Iron	0.2	1.0	0.3	0.3
chloride	250	1000	250	250
Residual free chlorine	0.2	-	-	-

Potable Water and its Essential Characteristics (*BIS StandARDS*)

Essential Characteristics	Is Requirement Limit	Is Permissible Limit	Who Guidelines	Us EPA Limit
Ddisssolved soilds	500	2000	1000	500
Calcium	75	200	-	-
Copper	0.05	1.5	2	1.3
Managenese	0.1	0.3	0.5.	0.05
Sulphate	200	400	200	200
Nitrate	45	100	50	10
Fluoride	1.0	1.5	1.5	4
Phenolic Compounds	0.001	0.002	-	-
Mercury	0.001	0.002	0.001	0.001
Cadmium	0.01	0.001	0.001	0.002
Seleniu	0.01	0.001	0.001	0.002
Arsemic	0.05	0.05	0.01	-
Cyanide	0.05	0.05	0/07	0.2
Lead	0.05	0.05	0.01	0 0
Zinc	5	15	3	5
Anionic detergents	0.2	1.0	-	-
Chromium	0.05	0.05	0.05	0.1
Poly nuclear hydrocarbons	-	-	-	-
Mineral oil	0.01	0.03	-	-
Alkalinity	0200	600	-	-
Aluminium	0 03	0.2	0,2	0,05 – 0.2
Pesticides	0.0	0.001	-	-

All units in mg/litres unless mentioned otherwise.

US EPA standards are Maximum Contaminants Level Goals (MCLG) and are non-enforceable.

Advantages of RO System

- It is simple and reliable process.
- Capital and operating expenses are low.
- Compact design requires less space for installation.
- Fully automatic operation with auto-start abd auti-off.
- Suitable for raw water from all types of sources like: bore well, overhead storage tanks, water tankers and even municipal taps.
- Colloidal SiO_2 (Silica) can be removed by RO, which cannot be removed by other methods.
- The life of semi permeable membrane is about 2 years and it can be easily replaced within few minutes, thereby nearly uninterrupted water supply can be provided.

Typical Rejection Characteristics of RO Membranes

Contaminant	% Normal Rejection
Sodium	85-94
Sulphate	96-98
Calcium	94-98
Potassium	85-95
Nitrate	90-95
Iron	94-98
Zinc	95-98
Mercury	95-98
Selenium	94-96
Phosphate	96-98
Lead	95-98
Arsenic	92-96
Magnesium	94-98
Nickel	96-98
Fluoride	92-95
Manganese	94-98
Cadmium	95-98
Barium	95-98
Cyanide	84-92
Chloride	85-92

% may vary based on membrane type, water pressure, temperature and TDS.

Major Improvements in Reverse Osmosis Technology

Three major improvements in the technology can be identified.

1. *Improvements of the RO Technologies and RO Process*: Membrane materials, energy optimization, large scale plants, design optimization, construction and procurement optimization.
2. *Nanomaterials and Nanoparticles*: Modification of the RO materials utilizing nanomaterials and nanoparticles to achieve lower energy demand for the process and higher permeability of the membranes while keeping membrane fouling low or comparable to the existing commercial RO membrane materials.
3. Forward Osmosis (FO) utilizing draw solution with high osmotic pressure when utilizing Ammonia and Carbon dioxide or other ingredients for the draw solution. Water purification is the removal contaminants from untreated water to produce potable water that is pure enough for the most critical of its intended uses, usually for human consumption. Substances that are removed during the process of potable water treatment include: suspended particles, pathogens, fertilizers, pesticides, algae, fungi, minerals and other chemical pollutants.. The goal of all water purification process is to remove existing contaminants in the water, or reduce the concentration of such contaminants so the water becomes fit for domestic and industrial use, medical and many other uses. One use is returning water that has been used back into the natural environment without adverse ecological impact. A combination selected from the following processes is used for municipal drinking water treatment worldwide:

Screening - removing floating matter like: wood pieces, leaves, etc., from water; Sedimentation - for flocculation, that is, removal of suspended solids; Coagulation - for flocculation *i.e.,* to convert small particles to larger particles which are easily removed by sedimentation. Coagulation aids, also known.

Low-cost, Low-maintenance, and Effective Disinfection System-based Solar Purification Irradiation Technology

Conventional technologies used for disinfection of unpotable water include: ozonation, chlorination, and artificial UV radiation. These technologies are capital intensive, require sophisticated equipment, and demand skilled operators. At the household level, boiling water for about 10 min or the use of certain chlorine compounds available in tablets (halazone or calcium hypochlorite) or solutions (sodium hypochlorite at 1 to 2 drops per liter) is commonly used to disinfect drinking water. A lack of resources and/ or distribution infrastructure makes the application of these procedures extremely limited in developing countries where waterborne diseases are prevalent. Even if these methods are available and affordable, their implementation could be environmentally unsound or hygienically unsafe when performed by a layperson. Boiling, for example, requires about 1 kg of wood/liter of water, and misuse of sodium hypochlorite solution poses a safety hazard. The use of solar irradiation for treatment of chemically and biologically contaminated water is not a new phenomenon. Solar radiation removes a wide range of organic chemicals and pathogenic organisms by direct exposure, is relatively inexpensive, and avoids generation of harmful by-products of chemically driven technologies. More importantly, the economics of the process are almost volume independent. The bacterial inactivation rate in a contaminated water sample is proportional to the intensity of sunlight and atmospheric temperature and inversely proportional to the water depth. While sunlight can penetrate into water, its intensity decreases with the depth of penetration due to scattering caused by suspended particles present in the water. The reduction in intensity varies with wavelength; for wavelengths ranging from 200 to 400 nm the reduction in intensity does not exceed 5 per cent/m of water depth; however, it rises as high as 40 per cent/m for longer wavelengths.

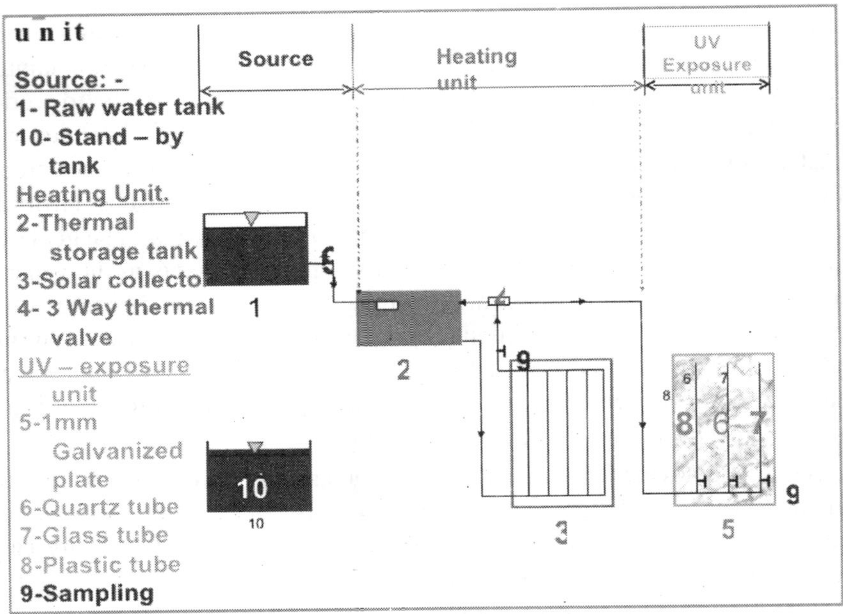

The synergistic effects of two irradiation wavelengths and of light and heat and the action of light on bacteria and living cells have been well documented. The most effective wavelengths for microbial destruction are the near-UV-A band (320 to 400 nm) and to a lesser extent the visible band of violet and blue light, 400 to 490 nm. While there was no appreciable difference in the rate of bacterial inactivation for sample temperatures ranging from 12 to 40°C, when the water temperature was increased to 50°C, the same fraction of the initial population of *Escherichia coli* was inactivated by a much lower fluence (a threefold reduction. This reduction was presumably due to the synergetic effects of solar radiation and thermal water treatment While pasteurization of water occurs at 72°C (161°F) in a minimum of bacterium-free water can be obtained by solar irradiation at lower temperatures with much longer residence times. Many researchers have reported results from limited laboratory studies under narrowly defined radiation bands. The polychromatic nature of solar light and its varying intensity with geographic location of incidence complicate extrapolation of these results and their implementation in actual designs. Additionally, different microorganisms behave differently when subjected to multiple irradiation wavelengths.

Not only can you build a solar water-purification system, you can also design it. The system shown here uses distillation, a process that can remove salts, microorganisms, and even chemicals such as: arsenic, leaving you with pure H_2O. Here's how it works: If you leave salty or contaminated water in an open container, the water evaporates and leaves the contaminants behind. If you heat the water, the process speeds up considerably. After the water evaporates, the water vapor condenses on the glass window and drips down into the catch trough. Tilt the catch trough just slightly and put a bottle or other container underneath the low end, and voila! Purified water.

As 13 states struggle with drought, scientists in a corner of India have devised a way to make potable water - 6.3 million litre of it every day - from sea water. They have also developed certain filtration methods that ensure groundwater containing As and U are safe to drink. The pilot plant at Tamil Nadu's Kalpakkam, built by scientists of BARC (Bhabha Atomic Research Centre) use waste steam from a nuclear reactor to purify the seawater. Its capacity is 6.3 million litre every day. Currently, the fresh water is being used at the Kudankulam nuclear reactor. But this reporter tasted the purified water - it tasted like fresh water, not saline at all. Several membranes have also been developed by BARC that can produce purified drinking water out of contaminated groundwater at a meager cost. Plants employing such membranes have been installed in Punjab, as well as West Bengal, Rajasthan, said KN Vyas, Director, BARC, Mumbai, MS. A bicycle that had a water purifier installed on it has also been created having use of peddles.. It turns dirty contaminated water into potable water. Turning the pedals produces the energy the purifier needs.

The nuclear scientists have also made several household water purifiers that are being marketed all over drought-hit Marathwada. Some these use thin membranes and special filters to separate the contaminants.

MIT: Graphene could tap the Seven Seas for Drinking Water

A team of researchers at MIT (Massachusetts Institute of Technology) has developed a way to use atom-thin sheets of graphene for water filtration, which could lead to an inexpensive and energy-efficient way to desalinate seawater. Currently, the desalination method of choice is a process called reverse osmosis. The drawback is that it requires a significant level of water pressure, which in turn requires a copious amount of energy. One solution has been to improve the efficiency of conventional reverse osmosis. The MIT research represents a significant break from reverse osmosis technology. The team has fabricated a sheet of graphene containing a precise series of holes, just one nanometer across. With the addition of other materials, the edges of the holes interact on a molecular level with water to either repel or attract. Since the graphene process is based on a chemical interaction, it requires very little water pressure compared to reverse osmosis. In terms of energy use, a graphene-based system could generate desalinated water at a far greater rate using the same amount of energy, or it could simply be run at lower pressure. That flexibility could provide graphene desalination systems with a greater range of applications, using small-scale solar power and other forms of renewable energy rather than having to rely on a relatively large supply of fossil fuels. Graphene is an ultra-thin, ultra-strong sheet of carbon atoms that has superior properties as a semi-conductor.

SMD to Coordinate Research on Membrane Disposal

A coalition to coordinate applied research programmes to alleviate the disposal of used desalination and water treatment membranes has been launched recently in Singapore. The Coalition for SMD (Sustainable Membrane Development) was founded by a group of not-for-profit and NGOs, equipment manufacturers and water utilities to develop innovative solutions to manage the growing volumes of used membrane elements that a discarded each year from desalination, water-reuse and drinking-water plants around the world. The group seeks to proactively develop market/social mechanisms to turn waste into a resource that can benefit developing communities and reduce the environmental footprint of the world's membrane industry. Their focus is to coordinate applied research programmes to alleviate the disposal of used membranes. The accumulation of used or spent membranes of all types, typically more than 10,000 tonnes globally per annum, are sent to landfill, and it is now a waste issue in all countries. The sooner the international industry identifies the disposal issue as an opportunity, the better. The potential availability of recovered and recycled membranes from water plants in developed countries can be readily applied to simple gravity potable-water installations in Africa with incredible impact. Each recovered ultrafiltration membrane that is typically sent to landfill can be utilized in a small community water kiosk to provide safe water for 500-1,000 people per day.

JST: Water-Saving Technology for Greenhouse Agriculture

The Government of Japan, through the JST (Japan Science and Technology) Agency's CREST programme, has initiated a targeted funding grant in 2009, with a total envelope of USD 75 million, as a means to support the nation's water scientists in accelerating research into innovative water technologies. The researchers have developed a precise control technique for water supply to meet the demand of plant growth. A key point is to detect and adjust a small reduction in water potential around the rooting zone when the plant absorbs water. They call it a precision subsurface irrigation approach, *i.e.,* apply the correct amount of water at the correct time and correct location through the correct method. The proposed technology is for microscopic super-saving uses. If the water needs evaluations show a lower level of water supply use, researchers can provide solutions while keeping up the productivity. On the other hand, the conventional concept on irrigation tends to just strengthen the capacity of water supply with big facilities without correcting water demand or needs. The overall significance of water-saving greenhouse systems is to reduce constraints on water resources for cultivation not only in arid areas but also in urban zones in which conflicts for resources between agriculture and industry or citizens seem to occur.

UWA: Eyeing Geothermal Energy for Desalination

The UWA (University of Western Australia) has announced that researchers at the university will investigate the use of geothermal energy to desalinate groundwater in Western Australia. It was the first phase of a feasibility programme to investigate and encourage use of geothermal and waste-heat resources for heat-driven pretreatment and desalination of brackish and saline water. The NCCDA (National Centre of Excellence in Desalination Australia) provided USD 124,000 funding for the project, which was driven by a desire to boost water supplies for the Integrated Water Supply Scheme. The scheme services Perth and Mandurah by treating brackish water that is currently available but unused. This use of geothermal power to desalinate water through multi-effect distillation, preheating and reverse osmosis can also work in regional and remote areas where the cost of water and energy is far higher. The project would provide WA government and industry with an economic, technical, and market analysis of geothermal energy coupled with water production. It will also identify areas in the state where the technology may be best applied.

Cheaper Method Employing Glucose and Enzymes to Filter Water

Removal of organic toxins from groundwater requires chemical additives, which are expensive and environmentally hazardous. Now researchers at the University Kentucky in UK have developed a novel technique to breakdown such contaminants. The new purification system uses two highly porous membranes to generate purifying hydroxyl radicals. Till now organic compounds were degraded using Fenton reactions – a method based on the concept that some metals like iron have a strong catalytic power to generated highly reactive hydroxyl radicals. The radicals react with, and ultimately degrade, the organic impurities. Other than the use of chemicals the process also requires acidic conditions. This approach immobilizes the iron in a membrane pore and thus reaction can be carried out at near neutral pH conditions. The new device has two porous, microfiltration membranes. To purify water, glucose is added to it and then passed through the first membrane. Here an enzyme – glucose oxidase – converts the glucose to hydrogen peroxide. In the second membrane hydrogen peroxide reacts with the iron, and thus purifies the water.

The details of this remediation system were published in the April issue of *Proceedings of the National Academy of Sciences*. 'The concept has been developed for organic detoxification, but can be extended for disinfection and virus inactivation', says Dibakar Bhattacharya, one of the authors of the study. The researchers say as the level of hydrogen peroxide in the filter can be controlled, and because iron is trapped in the membranes, no additional chemicals need to be supplied. The operating cost of purification is estimated to be about seven cents per 1,000 litres. The energy cost is also low since highly porous microfiltration membranes; the materials are commercially available. In contrast to commercial membranes that reject impurities, in this purification system pollutants are allowed the reactants to convert contaminants to non-toxic end products. Reviewing the purification system, Pawan Labhasetwar, researcher at the NEERI (National Environment and Engineering Research Institute), says the technology can be used in India. But several factors such as: membrane fouling (accumulation of unwanted materials), filtration efficacy, inlet water characteristics and their impacts on the system must be studied in detail.

Purification of Potable Water Employing Various Adsorbents

Clean drinking water is one of the utmost requirements for a healthy human population. However with growing industrialization and extensive use of chemicals the quantity of unwanted pollutants in the drinking water has taken a heavy toll in developing countries like: India. The entry of potentially hazardous substances into the nearby water bodies has been increasing day-by-day. In the absence of an effective alternative, the only way to maintain safer water bodies is to develop efficient purifying technologies. One such important and beneficial procedure that has been in use is that of purification of water by using 'adsorbents'. Various minerals and natural plants products have been proved as an effective marker for removing many pollutants *viz*; fluoride, arsenic, nitrate, heavy metals and pesticides. Adsorbents which are derived from carbon, alumina, zeolite, clay minerals, iron ores, and natural products *viz*; parts of the plants and herbs offer promising results of removal. In the past few years efforts have been made to develop process involving screening or activation using alkalies, acids, alum, lime and other chemicals that are effective in increasing adsorption efficiency. The characteristics and chemical nature of these adsorbents briefly describes the mechanism of the process. It is important to observe that capacities of the adsorbents may vary depending on their characteristics, chemical modifications and concentration of the individual adsorbent. Experimental conditions *viz*; pH, concentration of the adsorbate, quantity of the adsorbent and temperature are found to be the basis of removal kinetics. As suggested, adsorption capacities in batch and column modes of various adsorbents were reviewed with isotherm models.

Drinking water quality deteriorates due to the presence of excess fluoride, arsenic, natural organic matters, heavy metals and variety of pathogens that plays a vital role in causing various water-borne diseases. The tremendous increase in the use of heavy metals over the past few decades has inevitably resulted in an increased flux of metallic substances in the aquatic environment (Gaikwad, 2004; Tseng, 2007; Yoon *et al.* 2008). These pollutants enter the water bodies through wastewater from metal plating industries, batteries, phosphate fertilizer, mining, pigments and stabilizers alloys (Low and Lee, 1991). However, many preventive measures have been adopted to remove pollutants but these methods are not found suitable for removing heavy metals. In the recent years, use of adsorbents have gained much attention because they have metal binding capacities and are able to remove unwanted pollutants from contaminated water at low cost. Various materials have been studied for the adsorption of pollutants, for example, bark and other tannin - rich materials, lignin, chitosan, dead biomass, xanthate, zeolite, clay and peat moss (Orhan and Buyukgungor, 1993; Bryant *et al.* 1992; Rorrer *et al.* 1993; Hsien and Rorrer, 1995; Roy *et al.* 1993; Sharma and Foster, 1993). Among these adsorbents, chitosan, zeolite, lignin and seaweed (Kertman *et al.* 1993) showed high adsorption capacities. Presence of various functional groups in coffee residues makes them a potential pollutant adsorbent. Tea leaves are also used as adsorbent (Bailey *et al.* 1992).

Of many adsorbents, natural zeolite came into significant interest, due to its valuable properties such as: ion exchange capability. Clay minerals are found to be an important inorganic component in the soil and their sorption capabilities are due to high surface area and exchange capacities. Industrial byproducts such as: waste slurry, lignin, ferric hydroxide and red mud have been explored for their technical feasibility to remove pollutants from contaminated water (Kumar *et al.* 2000). In recent years, various adsorption processes have been developed using a wide variety of adsorbents. Activated carbons, activated mineral surfaces (silica, bauxite, alumina), fly ash, industrial waste, agricultural wastes and coral limestone have also been used as adsorbents.

- *Advantages of Adsorption:* The search for new technologies involving the removal of toxic pollutants from wastewater has given attention to adsorption, based on binding capacities of various biological materials (Babel and Kurniawan, 2003). The major advantages of sorption over conventional treatment methods include: low cost, high efficiency, minimization of chemical and biological sludge, regeneration of sorbents, and possibility of metal recovery (Ahalya *et al.* 2003).
- *Adsorption - Equilibrium and its types:* Adsorption capacity of the adsorbent can be determined by making a feasible contact between the adsorbate and adsorbent. Adsorption Equilibrium is the phenomenon in which the residual concentration is reached which will remain unchanged with time. Adsorption process has been characterized into two types: *(a)* Physical adsorption is a reversible phenomenon and it results from the action of van der Waals forces. It is usually dominant at low temperatures and is multilayered. *(b)* Chemisorption is generally irreversible due to involvement of chemical interactions between the adsorbate and adsorbent. pH, temperature, adsorbent quantity, and particle size including other chemical properties of the adsorbate and adsorbent are the major factors affecting the adsorption process.
- *Isotherm Models - An Interpretative Tool:* It is the relationship between the amount of adsorbate adsorbed on the surface of adsorbent and equilibrium concentration of the adsorbate at a certain temperature and other conditions. Brunauer (Brunauer *et al.* 1972) classified adsorption isotherm into six types. These types may be monolayer, multilayer or condensation in pores/capillaries. An isotherm model is a suitable tool to assess the adsorption capacities in batch and column study. In Batch study an adsorbate is made to contact with a definite quantity of adsorbent in a batch stirred system. Then the mixture is agitated to facilitate the adsorption process. In column study, adsorbent is packed into a column reactor and almost no flow or movement of adsorbent takes place inside the column. Different theoretical and empirical models have been proposed to describe the different types of isotherms in batch study. Most commonly used models are discussed here which are generally used for the interpretation of adsorption isotherms.
- *Langmuir Isotherm:* In this type of isotherm, surface of the adsorbent is homogeneous in nature *i.e.,* all the adsorption sites have equal affinity for the adsorbate molecules and adsorption at one site does not affect adsorption at an adjacent site (Langmuir, 1918; Weber 1972). The Langmuir equation may be written as:

$$q_e = \frac{Q^o bC_e}{1+bC_e} \quad \text{(non-linear form)} \quad (1)$$

$$\frac{C_e}{q_e} = \frac{1}{Q^0 b} + \frac{1}{C_e Q^0} \quad \text{(linear form)} \quad (2)$$

where q_e is the amount of solute adsorbed per unit weight of adsorbent (mg g^{-1}), Ce = Equilibrium concentration of solute in bulk solution (mg l^{-1}), Q^c = Monolayer adsorption capacity (mg g^{-1}) and b = constant related to the free energy of adsorption/ desorption ($bae^{-AG/RT}$). Sorbents with highest possible Q^o and high b value are desirable for a process.

- *Freundlich Isotherm:* Herbert Max Finley Freundlich, a German physical chemist, presented an empirical adsorption isotherm. It states that the equilibrium is reached only on heterogeneous surfaces of the adsorbent. The Freundlich isotherm is the earliest known relationship describing the adsorption equation and is often expressed as:

$$qe = K_F C_e^{1/n} \qquad \text{(non-linear form)} \qquad (3)$$

where q_e is the adsorption density (mg of adsorbate per g of adsorbent), C_e is the concentration of adsorbate in solution (mg l^{-1}), K_f and n are the empirical constants dependent on several environmental factors and n is greater than one. The linear form of the above equation is conveniently used by taking the logarithmic of both sides as:

$$\ln q_e = \ln K_F + 1/n \ln C_e \qquad (4)$$

A plot of $\ln C_e$ against $\ln q_e$ yielding a straight line indicates the confirmation of the Freundlich isotherm for adsorption. The constants can be determined from the slope and the intercept. 1/n is the intensity of the adsorption process, K_F is the relative adsorption capacity of the adsorbent (mg g^{-1}) (Freundlich, 1906).

- *BET Isotherm:* This isotherm uses the assumption that the multilayer adsorption of adsorbate molecules are felt on adsorbent surfaces (Brunauer *et al.* 1972; Weber 1972).

$$q_e = BCQ^0 / (Cs - C)[1 + (B - 1)(C/Cs)] \qquad \text{(non-linear form)} \qquad (5)$$

$$qe = C / (Cs\text{-}C) q_e = 1 / Bq^0 + \{(b-1) / Bq^0\} \qquad C/Cs \text{ (linear form)} \qquad (6)$$

where q_e is the amount of solute adsorbed per unit weight of adsorbent (mg g^{-1}), B = A constant related to the energy of interaction with the surface, C = The equilibrium concentration of adsorbate in solution (mg l^{-1}), Q^o = The number of moles of adsorbate per unit weight of adsorbent to form a complete monolayer, and Cs = The saturation concentration of the adsorbate.

- *Adsorbents as Alternatives and their Efficiency*: In recent years, various natural products have gained importance for serving the role as adsorbents for the removal of heavy metals, nitrates, arsenic, fluorides, natural organic materials, because of their good performance and low cost. The adsorbent developed offers a viable alternative to traditional metal removal technologies. There are several adsorbents commonly used for the removal of arsenic (Katsoyiannis and Zouboulis, 2002; Elson *et al.* 1980), fluorides (Srimurali *et al.* 1998; Ramos *et al.* 1999; Fan *et al.* 2003; Chaturvedi *et al.* 1990), heavy metals, natural organic matter (Korshin *et al.* 1997; Mall and Upadhyay, 1998; Chiang *et al.* 2002; Daifullah and Girgis 1998; Bernard *et al.* 1997) and trihalomethanes from drinking water, which give better results after blended with certain chemicals. The most common adsorbent widely used is activated carbon. Bituminous coal is used in the manufacturing of activated carbon which is used for pollution control. It can also be made from agricultural wastes, wood and petroleum. Oxygenates and mercaptans from hydrocarbons and fluorides from water are commonly removed with the help of activated alumina. The adsorption properties of materials of biological origin have been investigated: chitosan (Elson *et al.* 1980) amine modified coconut coir (Baes *et al.* 1997). Natural organic matter can be adsorbed on iron oxide.

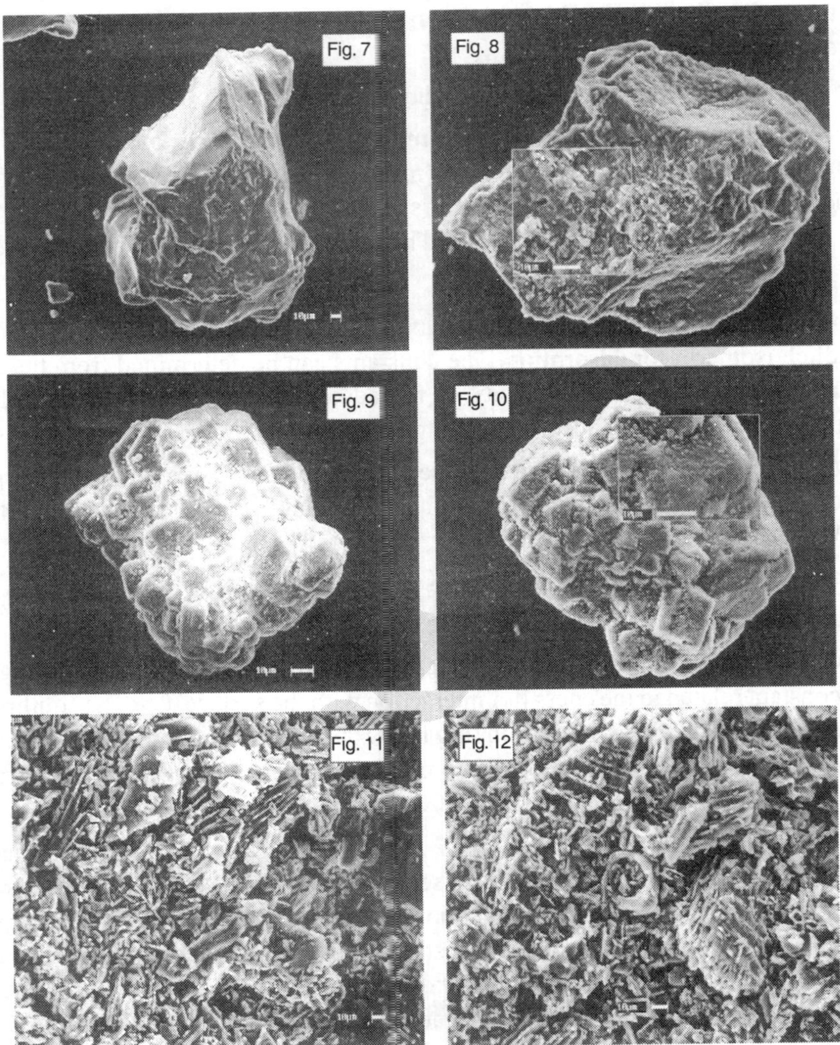

Scanning electron microscopy (SEM): Fig. 6.7: **Uncoated sand,** Fig. 6.8: **$FeCl_3$ coated sand,** Fig. 6.9: **Activated alumina,** Fig. 6.10: **Iron oxide coated activated alumina,** Fig. 6.11: **Activated carbon powder,** Fig. 6.12: **Carbonized ground nut husk**

Surface area, pore size, and polarity are the major factors that affect the capacity of an adsorbate. Enhancement of porous structure is done by the activation process which is essential for effective adsorption. Activation process is basically are of two types that are widely used *i.e.*, chemical and physical activation. Chemical activation is a process in which material having the vegetable origin is carbonized wit the addition of the activating agents. Physical activation or gas activation is a process in which inactive carbonized product is allowed to react with suitable substance, usually gaseous (carbon dioxide or steam). The sorption capacities for the sorbents are usually very low before activation and the maximum sorption capacity rarely exceeds 0.1-0.2 mmol g^{-1}. In the case of chitosan, arsenic sorption capacity is significantly lower than the levels reached with other metal ions (Guibal *et al.* 1995; Guibal *et al.* 2000; Jansson Charrier *et al.* 1996). For increasing the efficiency of sorbents for metal ion uptake several processes have been developed especially ligand grafting. The chemical modification of silica surface by using chemical ligating groups provides scope for trapping metal ions specially and selectively even at ultra trace level (Jal *et al.* 2004). NOx adsorption on KOH impregnated activated carbon also give positive support to this concept that chemical impregnation increase the removal efficiency of the adsorbent (Lee *et al.* 2002). Activated carbon was produced from almond shells through chemical activation, by several activating agents (H_3PO_4, $ZnCl_2$, K_2CO_3 and Na_2CO_3). $ZnCl_2$ activated material was noticed to be the best product with high adsorption capacity (Bevla *et al.* 1984a; Bevla *et al.* 1984b).

Activated carbons were prepared from untreated and phosphoric acid treated coconut shells, and increased adsorption capacity was found (Laine *et al.* 1989). Ammonium chloride, untreated almond shell and hazelnut shell samples were tested for their surface area at different temperatures. Chemical activation carried out at 350°C gave products with surface area values above 500 m^2 g^{-1}. However, the surface area values observed for the products obtained from untreated raw materials were reported about half of this value. It was also observed that, the surface area of products obtained from NH_4Cl impregnated samples reached values of over 700 m^2 g^{-1} when the carbonization temperature was increased to 700°C (Balci *et al.* 1994). The granular activated carbon samples activated, either chemically, with H_3PO_4, or physically, with CO_2, under a variety of conditions. The product obtained by chemical activation had higher BET surface areas and greater product yields than the CO_2-activated carbons. The products were also compared with the commercial activated carbon, which have higher adsorption ability (Toles *et al.* 1997). Phosphoric acid impregnated apricot stones were carbonized at 300, 400 and 500°C respectively, were found to increase the BET surface area increased from 700 m^2 g^{-1} up to 1400 m^2 g^{-1} with rise in temperature. The highest BET surface area was obtained from the sample that was mixed with 30 per cent (vol) phosphoric acid and carbonized at 500°C (Girgis and Daifullah, 1998). Activated carbons were produced from canes from Arundo donax, a rapid-growing plant, by phosphoric acid activation under four different activation atmosphere, to develop carbons with substantial capability to adsorb Cd(II) and Ni(II) ions from dilute aqueous solutions. Surface areas and total pore volumes of the activated carbons used were of around 1100 m^2 g^{-1} It is established that, the content of carbons' polar or acidic surface oxygen functional groups, with their development depending on the atmosphere used, influenced predominantly metal adsorption. Carbons derived under flowing air, possessing the largest total content of these groups, showed the best adsorption effectiveness (>90%) for both ions, even superior to that determined for a commercial sample used as a reference (Basso *et al.* 2002). Denizli *et al.* (1997) incorporated dye ligand onto synthetic polymers to enhance their metal ion sorption properties. Similar modifications have been performed on activated carbon; the impregnation with metal ions significantly enhances arsenic sorption on activated carbon (Huang and Vane, 1989; Rajakovic, 1998).

- *Adsorbents – Nature and Characteristics:* The characteristics of the products and spent adsorbent may be identified to understand the process mechanics. Various techniques have been discovered for determining the nature of the adsorbent like; amorphous and crystalline nature of the adsorbent can be determined by the use of X-ray Diffraction XRD. Like-wise, adsorbents composition can be determined with the help of IR spectra. The specific surface area of the adsorbent can be calculated from the N_2 - BET equation (Mohan *et al.* 2005). Other Instruments like: surface area analyzer and mercury porositimeter are used for the determination of porosity. Scanning electron Microscopy (SEM), Extended X-ray adsorption fine structure, nuclear magnetic resonance (NMR) and high performance liquid chromatography (HPLC) may give the details regarding the texture (Huggins *et al.* 2002; Singh *et al.* 2003) and depicts the mechanism of process of the water purification. The trace element contents of the coals have been determined by a combination of instrumental neutron activation analysis (INAA), inductively coupled plasma mass spectrometry (ICP-MS) and ICP atomic adsorption spectroscopy (ICP-AES) (Shtepenko *et al.* 2005). Study of sorbent and the metal speciation on the sorbent were analysed using X-ray photoelectron spectroscopy (XPS). Desorption studies were also carried out to elucidate the interactions between the metal and the sorbents. A sorbent for metal removal has been produced from anhydrous calcium silicate/ aluminate by means of an accelerated carbonation process. Production from iron treatment increases the adsorption capacity by 10 - fold. Shifts in XPS spectra suggest that dichromate binding occur with the iron at active adsorption sites (Fathima *et al.* 2005). Surface-reaction phenomenon of adsorbent caused by the KOH impregnation and NOx adsorption were investigated by using SEM, time of flight secondary ion mass spectrometry (ToF - SIMS) and SIMS depth profile.

- *Safety Evaluation – A Prior Concern:* It is our prior duty to assure that the water quality is same as of recommended by regulatory and health agencies, which are desired in the daily intake of the drinking water (Gopal *et al.* 2004). The physio-chemical and bacteriological characteristics of the produced water may be compared with the test water as per the standard methods (APHA, 2005). It is apparent that synthesis of large amount of the product is required in the process of adsorption of the minerals/plant products, in which large amount of sludge is also generated. Once this sludge is added to the soil, the leachates ultimately find its way to the surface water. Living organisms present in soil and water, assists in the process of biotransformation and biodegradation of the material and also the translocation of the energy into food chain. Therefore the standard protocols are to be developed for the safety evaluation of the products and spent wash/solid waste. Multispecies testing *e.g.,* fish bioassay chironomus, daphnia, earthworm and algal bioassays are recommended protocols that may be carried out for ecotoxicological assessment (OECD, 2002). In case of community water supply identification of suitable disposal sites should be of prior concern.

Conclusion

Groundwater pollution is caused due to natural, agricultural, industrial and other man-made sources. There are certain ways to minimize groundwater contamination, like proper drainage pipes, safe storage of chemicals, safe disposal of waste. Groundwater pollution cannot be prevented completely. As there are varied sources, it is not always practical to prevent the contamination of groundwater. However, there is no doubt that individuals can contribute in many ways to reduce pollution of groundwater. Some of the basic tips are proper disposal of waste, waterproof storage of household chemicals (paints, medicines, detergents) and agricultural chemicals to avoid leaching, etc. Proper installation of septic systems along with regular cleaning will reduce groundwater contamination. It is very difficult and costly to treat contaminated groundwater. Hence, it is better to minimize the risk of groundwater pollution. Public awareness programmes about the importance of groundwater and ways to minimize its contamination should be implemented. Typical concentration of dissolved salts in seawater and brack-ish water are 35,000 and 1000mg/L, respectively. The most widely used processes for desalination include membrane separation systems: reverse osmosis (RO), and electrodialysis (ED); and thermal separations including: multistage flash distillation (MSF), multi-effect distillation (MED) and mechanical vapor compression (MVC). Among these processes, RO and MSF methods are employed in the bulk of the plants (90%) to desalinate seawater worldwide. Electrodialysis has the particularity that, while being a membrane process, the driving force is apotential applied between two electrodes; the same driving force as the CDI process.

REFERENCES

1. Raaz U., Rani B., Maheshwari RK. (2016). Water Issues Including Pollution and Management Strategies in India. *Proceedings of National Seminar on Innovative Technologies for Sustainable Sanitation, Health and Environment* Poornima College of Engineering, April 22, 2016, pp. 17-22. Jaipur, Rajasthan.
2. Rani B., Singh U., Maheshwari R.K. (2011). New Perspectives of Safe Water Generation. *The Ecoshhere: An International Journal of Life Sciences* 3(1):85-89.
3. Maheshwari, R.K., Sharma, S., Chauhan , A.K. and Sharma, M. (2013). To Confiscate Fluoride from Groundwater. *International Journal of Pharmaceutical and Bio-Science,* 2 (3), pp. 06-313.
4. Maheshwari, R.K. (2013). Zero Valent Iron (ZVI) for Mitigation of Chromium (VI) in Contaminated Water. *ISST Journal of Applied Chemistry* 4 (1):15-19.
5. Rani B., Maheshwari R.K., Garg A., Prasad M. (2012). Bottled Water – A Global Market Overview. *Bulletin of Environment, Pharmacology and Life Sciences* 1(6):01-04.
6. Rani B., Yadav R.K., Singh U., Trivedi A., Pathak R.K., Bagdodiya P., and Maheshwari R.K. (2014). Scourge of Nitrate Toxicity: Its Clinical Manifestations and Remediation Employing RO Technology. *Journal of Industrial Pollution Control* 30(1):97-108.
7. Rani B., Yadav R.K., Guta V.K., Maheshwari R.K. (2013). Disinfection of Contaminated Water Employing Ozone and UV Processes. *International Journal of Physical Sciences* IV(1&2):19-33.
8. Maheshwari R.K., Rani B., Sharma M (2012). Effect of Solar Disinfection on Water Quality. *International Journal of Chemical Sciences* III (II): 99-104.
9. Rani B., Singh U., Maheshwari R.K. (2011). How does Water Affect our Health. *The Ecosphere – An International Journal of Environment and Biological Sciences,* 2 (1 & 2): 55-59.
10. Parihar, S., Rani, B., Chauhan, A.K., and Maheshwari, R.K. (2013). Defluoridation of Contaminated Water Employing Opentiadilleni. *International Journal of Chemistry and Pharmaceutical Sciences,* 1 (6), pp. 187-182.

11. Bhati, I., Dhawan, N.G. and Maheshwari, R.K. (2013). Greener Route to Prevent Pharmaceutical Pollution. *International Journal of Pharmaceutical and Chemical Sciences,* 2 (4), pp. 1781-1787.

12. Maheshwari, R.K. and Parihar, S. (2013). To Defluoridate Groundwater Employing *Moringaolefera* Seeds and Potash alum. *International Journal of Chemistry and Pharmaceutical Sciences,* 1 (1) 76-79.

13. Maheshwari R.K., Garg A., Katyal P., Kumar M., Rani B., Sharma M., Prasad M., Gaur M. (2012). Mitigating Fluoride Toxicity Occurring in Groundwater of Nagaur City (Rajasthan), Employing Various Bioadsorbents. *Bulletin of Environment and Life Sciences* 1(7):50-53.

14. Maheshwari R.K., Rani B., Chauhan AK. (2009). Groundwater Contamination (Environmental Management for Sustainable Future) *Proceedings of National Seminar on Changing Geohydrological Scenario and its Environmental Impact* (Geological Society of India) July 6-8, 2009, pp. 28-32, Bhikampura, Alwar, Rajasthan.

15. Maheshwari R.K., Bansal N. (2006). Excess Fluoride in Groundwater: Its Clinical Manifestations, Preventive Measures and Mitigation Processes. *Proceedings of National Conference on Environmental Conservation,* BITS, September 1-3, 2006, pp. 495-502, Pilani, Rajasthan.

16. Maheshwari R.K., Singh U., Singh P., Rani B. (2009). Arsenic Toxicity in Groundwater: Clinical Manifestations and Mitigation Strategies for the Sustainability of Future Perspectives. *Proceedings of National Conference on Technological Innovations for Sustainable Development,* Govt Engineering College, August 29, 2009, pp. 14-26, Bikaner, Rajasthan.

17. Oren Y. (2008). Capacitive Deionization (CDI) for Desalination and Water Treatment – Past, Present and Future (A Review). *Desalination* 228(1-3):10-29.

18. Anderson M.A., Cudero A.L., Palma J. (2010). Capacitive Deionization as an Electrochemical Means of Saving Energy and Delivering Clean Water. Comparison to Present Desalination Practices: Will it Compete? *ElectrochimicaActa55* (2010) 3845–3856. doi:10.1016/j.electacta.2010.02.012

19. Caslake L.F., Connolly D.J., Menon V., Duncanson C.M., Rojas R., Tavakoli J J. (2004). Disinfection of Contaminated Water by using Solar Irradiation *Appl Environ Microbiol* 2004 Feb; 70(2): 1145-1150 doi: 10.1128/AEM.70.2.1145-1150.2004 PMCID: PMC348911.

20. Singh U., Maheshwari R.K., Rani B. (2013). Conscientious of Environmental Biotechnology for Decontaminating Polluted Water. *Souvenir and Conference book on National Conference on Energy, Environment and Biotechnology Research,* Mewar Institute of Management, October 5-6 , 2013 pp. 77-85, Ghaziabad, UP.

21. Maheshwari R.K., Rani B., Singh P. (2007). Scourge of Arsenic Hydrotoxicity: Its Mitigation Technologies and Management for Sustainable Future. *Proceedings of Indian Water Works Association* 39th Annual Convention , Nehru Place, February 1-3, 2007, pp. 27-37, Mumbai, MS.

22. Rani B., Maheshwari R.K., Garg A., Prasad M. (2012). Addressing Water Scarity: A Worldwide Crisis. *Research in Biological Pharmaceutical Sciences* 1(1):67-69.

23. Rani B., Singh U., Maheshwari R.K. (2015). Problems of Groundwater Pollution and their Management Strategies Published in Impact of *Global Warming and Climate Change on Human and Plant Growth,* Chapter 28: 291-304; Edited by Arya A and Patel VS Daya Publishing House, New Delhi.

24. Rani B., Kumar D., Yadav R.K., Maheshwari R.K. (2008). Cleaning up of Pollutants by Phytoremediation Published in A Novel Approach for Sustainable *Development, Advances in Applied Biotechnology and Microbiology*, Chapter 19:117-123; Edited by Jatkar, Parihar and Parihar, Agrobios Publications, Jodhpur, Rajasthan.

25. Rani B. (2013). Collective Conscientiousness for Water Conservation and Safe Water. *Proceedings of National Conference on Hydrology with Special Emphasis on Rain Water Harvesting*, Poornima University, September 13-16, 2013, Jaipur, Rajasthan.

26. Paptel B. (2007). Water Conservation: A Shared Responsibility. *Water Digest* pp. 6-7.

27. Maheshwari R.K., Rani B., Nathawat N.S. (2007). Nitrate: A Hydrotoxicant in Groundwater of Zone (Rajasthan – Sikar, Jhunjhunu Districts). *Water digest* pp. 84-87.

28. Maheshwari R.K., Rani B., Singh P. (2007). Field-based Experimental Approaches for Arsenic Remediation of Contaminated Water: Recent Developments for Sustainable Perspectives. *Water Digest* pp. 26-38.

29. Rani B., Singh U., Maheshwari. (2011). Nitrate Toxicity in Groundwater - Clinical Manifestations, Prevention and Remediation Strategies. *Everything About Water*, pp. 10-118.

30. Maheshwari R.K., Rani B., Gupta N. (2007). Fluoride Toxicity. *Everything About Water* pp. 31-37.

31. Rani B., Maheshwari R.K., Yadav R.K., Pareek D., Sharma A. (2013). Resolution to Provide Safe Drinking Water for Sustainability of Future Perspectives. *Research Journal of Chemical and Environmental Science* 1(1): 50-54.

32. Rani B., Maheshwari R.K., Prasad M., Chauhan V. (2011). Arsenic Contamination in Groundwater of Bangladesh: Its Hazards and Mitigation Strategies. *Bulletin of Geological Science* 7(1):7-15.

33. Maheshwari R.K., Rani B. (2006). Safe Water: Best Gift to the Future's Mankind (Towards Conserving the Elixir of Life). *Proceeding of National Conference on Environmental Conservation* BITS, September 13, 2006, pp. 495-502. Pilani, Rajasthan.

34. Henniker, J.C. (1949). The Depth of Surface Zone of a Liquid.*(Reviews of Modern Physics* 21:322.

35. http://www.who.int/water_sanitation_health/publications/combating_diseasepart1lowres.pdf.

36. http://www.who.int/water_sanitation_health/waterforlife.pdf.

37. Kaushik, M.R. (2012). Reverse Osmosis – A Unique Technique of Water Purification. *Journal of Biological and Chemical Research*, 29(2): 73-81.

38. Kozisek, F. (2003). Health Significance of Drinking Water, Calcium and Magnesium, http://www.who.iny/water_sanitation_health_dwg/chemicals/en/hardness.pdf.

39. Maheshwari, R. (2012). Dawn of Reverse Osmosis Technology. *Advances in Bioresearch*, 3 (2):10-11.

40. Polack, G. (2012). Water Science. University of Washington, Pollack Laboratory. http://faculty,washington.edu/ghp/rresearcthemes/water-science. Water has three Phases – Gas, Liquid, and Soli; but Recent Findings from our Laboratory Imply the Presence of a Surprisingly Extensive Fourth Phase that Occurs at Interfaces, Retrieved 0.5-25.

41. Scott, B. (2012). Chemical Nomenclature. Widener University, Department of Chemistry, http://science.widener.edu/svb/pset/nomen_b.html, Retrieved 05-25.

42. WHO (World Health Organization). 2003. Hardness in Drinking-water, http://www.who.int/water_sanitation_health/dwg/chemicals/en/hardness.pdf

43. Ahalya, N., T.V. Ramachandra and R.D. Kanamadi: Biosorption of Heavymetals. *Res. J. Chem. Environ.*, 7, 71-79 (2003). APHA: Standard Methods for the Examination of Water and Wastewater. 21st.

44. Edn., Washington D.C. (2005). Babel, S. and T.A. Kurniawan: A Review: Low Cost Adsorbents for Heavy Metals Uptake from Contaminated Water. *J. Haz. Mat.*, B97, 219-243 (2003).

45. Baes, A.U., T. Okuda, W. Nishijima, E. Soto and M. Okada: Adsorption and Ion Exchange of some Ground Water Anion Contaminants in an Amine Modified Coconut Coir. *Wat. Sci. Technol.*, 35, 89-95 (1997). Bailey, R.P., T. Bennett and M.M. Benjamin: Sorption onto and Recovery of Chromium using Iron-Oxide Coated Sand. *Water Sci Tech.*, 26, 1239-1244 (1992).

46. Balci, S., T. Dogu, and H. Yucel: Characterization of Activated Carbon Produced from Almond Shell and Hazelnut Shell. *J. Chem. Tech. Biotechnol.*, 60, 419-426 (1994).

47. Basso, M.C., E.G. Cerrella and A.L. Cukierman: Activated Carbons from a Rapidly Renewable Biosource for Removal of Cadmium (II) and Nickel (II) Ions from Dilute Aqueous Solutions. *Ind. Eng. Chem. Res.*, 41, 180-189 (2002).

48. Bernard, S., Ph. Chazal and M. Mazet: Removal of Organic Compounds by Adsorption on pyrolusite (P - MnO_2). *Water Res.*, 31, 1216-1222 (1997).

49. Bevla, F.R., D.P. Rico and A.F.M. Gomis: Activated Carbon from Almond Shells. Chemical Activation. 1. Activating Reagent Selection and 88 Variables Influence. *Ind. Eng. Chem. Prod. Res. Dev.*, 23, 266-269 (1984a).

50. Bevla, F.R., D.P. Rico and A.F.M. Gomis: Activated Carbon from Almond Shells. Chemical Activation. 2. $ZnCl_2$ Activation Temperature Influence. *Ind. Eng. Chem. Prod. Res. Dev.*, 23, 269-271 (1984b).

51. Brunauer, S, S.P.H. Emmett and E. Teller: Adsorption of Gases in Multi Molecular Layers. *J. Am. Chem. Soc.*, 60, 309-319 (1972).

52. Bryant, P.S., J.N. Petersen, J M. Lee and T.M. Brouns: Sorption of Heavy Metals by Untreated Red Fir Sawdust. *Appl. Biochem. Biotech.*, 34/ 35, 777-788 (1992).

53. Chaturvedi, A.K., K.P. Yadava, K.C. Pathak and V.N. Singh: Defluoridation of Water by Adsorption on Fly Ash. *Water Air Soil Pollut.*, 49, 51-61 (1990).

54. Chiang, H.L., C.P. Huang and P.C. Chiang: The Adsorption of Benzene and methylethylketone onto Activated Carbon: Thermodynamic aspects. *Chemosphere*, 46, 143-152 (2002).

55. Daifullah, A.A.M. and B.S. Girgis: Removal of some Substituted phenols by Activated Carbons Obtained from Agricultural Waste. *Water Res.*, 32, 1169-1177 (1998).

56. Denizli, A., B. Salih, M.Y. Arica, K. Kesenci, V. Hasirici and E. Piskin: Cibacron blue F3GA-Incorporated Macroporous poly (2-hydroxyethyl methacrylate) Affinity Membranes for Heavy Metal Removal. *J. Chromatogr. A.*, 758, 217-226 (1997).

57. Elson, C.M., D.H. Davies and E.R. Hayes: Removal of As from Contaminated Drinking Water by a Chitosan/chitin Mixture. *Water Res.*, 14, 1307-1311 (1980).

58. Fathima, N.N., R. Aravindhan, J.R. Rao and B.U. Nair: Solid Waste Removal Toxic Liquid Waste: Adsorption of Chromium (VI) by Iron Complexed Protein Waste. *Environ. Sci. Technol.*, 39, 2804-2810 (2005).

59. Freundlich, H.: Uber die Adsorption n losungen Z. *Phys. Chem.*, 57, 385-470 (1906).

60. Fan, X., D.J. Parker and M.D. Smith: Adsorption kinetics of Fluoride on Low Cost Materials. *Water Res.*, 37, 4929-4937 (2003).

61. Girgis, B.S. and A.A. Daifullah: Removal of some Substituted Phenols by Activated Carbon Obtained from Agricultural Waste. *Wat. Res.*, 32, 1169-1177 (1998).

62. Gopal, K., S.B. Srivastava, S. Shukla and J.L. Bersillon: Contamination in Drinking Water and its Mitigation using Adsorbent. *J. Environ. Biol.*, 25, 469-475 (2004).

63. Guibal, E., I. Jansson Charrier Saucedo, P. Le Cloirec: Enhancement of metal ion sorption Performances of Chitosan: Effect of the Structure on the diffusion Properties. *Langmuir*, 11, 591-598 (1995).

64. Guibal, E., C. Milot and J. Roussy: Influence of Hydrolysis Mechanism on Molybdate Sorption using chitosan. *Sep. Sci. Technol.*, 35, 1021-1038 (2000).

65. Hsien, T.Y. and G.L. Rorrer: Effects of Acylation and Cross linking on the Material Properties and Cadmium ion Adsorption Capacity of Porous chitosan Beads. *Sep. Sci. Technol.*, 30, 2455-2475 (1995).

66. Huang, C.P. and L.M. Vane: Enhancing As^5+ removal by Fe^2+ - treated Activated Carbon. *J. WPCF*, 61, 1596-1603 (1989).

67. Huggins, F.E., G.P. Huffman, A. Kolker, S.J. Mroczkowski, C.A. Palmer and R.B. Finkelman: Combined application of XAFS Spectroscopy and Sequential Leaching for Determination of As Speciation in Coal. *Energy and Fuels*, 16, 1167-1172 (2002).

68. Jal, P.K., S. Patel and B.K. Mishra: Chemical modification of silica surface by immobilization of Functional Groups for Extractive Concentration of Metal Ions. *Talanta*, 62, 1005-1028 (2004).

69. Jansson Charrier, M., E. Guibal, B. Delanghe and P. Le Cloirec: Vanadium (IV) sorption by chitosan: Kinetics and equilibrium. *Water Res.*, 30, 465-475 (1996).

70. Katsoyiannis, I.A. and A.I. Zouboulis: Removal of As from Contaminated Water Sources by Sorption onto Iron Oxide Coated Polymeric Materials. *Water Res.*, 36, 5141-5155 (2002).

71. Kertman, S.V., G.M. Kertman and Z.S. Chibrikova: Peat as a Heavy Metal Sorbent. *J. Appl. Chem. USSR*, 66, 465-466 (1993).

72. Korshin, G.V., M.M. Benjamin and R.S. Sletten: Adsorption of Natural Organic Matter (NOM) on Iron Oxide: Effects on NOM Composition and Formation of Organo-halide Compounds during Chlorination. *Water Res.*, 31, 1643-1650 (1997).

73. Kumar, S., K. Gopal and P.K. Seth: A Process for the Preparation of alum Impregnated tea Leaves Carbon for defluoridation of Drinking Water. Patent Apl. No. NF-34 (2000).

74. Laine, J., A. Calafat and M. Labady: Preparation and Characterization of Activated Carbons from Coconut Shells Impregnated with phosphoric Acid. *Carbon*, 27, 191-195 (1989).

75. Langmuir, I.: The Adsorption of Gases on Plane Surfaces of Glass, mica and Platinum. *J. Am. Chem. Soc.*, 40, 1361-1367 (1918).

76. Lee, Y.W., D.K. Choia and J.W. Parkb: Performance of fixed-bed KOH Impregnated Activated Carbon Adsorber for NO and NO Removal in the Presence of Oxygen. *Carbon*, 40, 1409-1417 (2002).

77. Low, K.S. and C.K. Lee: Cadmium uptake by Moss Calempess Delcsertiis Beasch. *Bioresor. Technol.*, 38, 1-6 (1991).

78. Mall, I.D. and S.N. Upadhyay: Studies on Treatment of Basic Dyes Bearings Wastewater by Adsorptive Treatment using Fly Ash. *Ind. J. Environ. Hlth.*, 40, 177-188 (1998).

79. Mohan, D., K.P. Singh and V.K. Singh: Removal of Hexa Valent Chromium from Aqueous Solution using Low-cost Activated Carbons Derived from Agricultural Waste Materials and Activated Carbon Fabric Cloth. *Ind. Eng. Chem. Res.*, 44, 1027-1042 (2005).

80. OECD: Test Guideline 404. OECD Guideline for Testing of Chemicals. Washington D.C. (2002).

81. Orhan, Y. and H. Buyukgungor: Removal of Heavy Metals by using Agricultural Wastes. *Wat. Sci. Technol.*, 28, 247-255 (1993).

82. Rajakovic, J.V.: The Sorption of As onto Activated Carbon Impregnated with Metallic Silver and Copper. *Sep. Sci. Technol.*, 27, 1423-1433 (1998).

83. Ramos, R.L., J.O. Turrubiartes and M.A. Sanchez-Castillo: Adsorption of fluoride from Aqueous Solution on Aluminium-impregnated Carbons. Carbons, 37, 609-617 (1999).

84. Rorrer, G.L., T.Y. Hsien and J.D. Way: Synthesis of Porous-magnetic Chitosan Beads for Removal of Cadmium Ions from Waste Water. *Ind. Eng. Chem. Res.*, 32, 2170-2178 (1993).

85. Roy, D., P.N. Greenlaw and B.S. Shane: Adsorption of Heavy Metals by Green Algae and Ground Rice Hulls. *Environ. Sci. Hlth.*, 28, 37-50 (1993).

86. Sharma, D.C. and C.F. Foster: Removal of Hexa Valent chromium using sphagnum moss Peat. *Water Res.*, 27, 1201-1208 (1993).

87. Shtepenko, O.L., C.D. Hills, N.J. Coleman and A. Brough: Characterization and Pre-liminary Assessment of a Sorbent Produced by Accelerated Mineral Carbonation. *Environ. Sci. Technol.*, 39, 74-79 (2005).

88. Srimurali, M., A. Pragathi and J. Karthikeyan: A Study on Removal of Fluorides from Drinking Water by Adsorption onto Low-cost Materials. *Environ. Pollut.*, 99, 285-289 (1998).

89. Toles, C.A., W.E. Marshall and M.M. Johns: Granular Activated Carbons from Nutshells for the uptake of Metals and Organic Compounds. *Carbon*, 35, 1407-1414 (1997).

90. Tseng, Chin-Hsiao: Metabolism of Inorganic Arsenic and Non-cancerous Health Hazards Associated with Chronic Exposure in Humans. *J. Environ. Biol.*, 28, 349-357 (2007).

91. Weber, Jr.W.J.: Physiochemical Processes for Water Quality Control. New York: Wiley Interscience (1972).

92. Yoon, Seokjoo, Sang-Seop Han and S.V.S. Rana: Molecular Markers of Heavy Metal Toxicity - A New Paradigm for Health Risk Assessment. *J. Environ. Biol.*, 29, 1-14 (2008).

Pages 152-166

Water Resources: Mapping, Monitoring and Management
***Edited by*: Dr. Pawan Kumar Tyagi; Dr. Avnish Chauhan & Dr. Pawan Kumar Bharti**
***Edition* : 2017**
ISBN : 978-93-5056-861-3
***Published by*: Discovery Publishing House Pvt. Ltd., New Delhi (India)**

Climate Change and Indian Agriculture

Alok Kumar Patra[1]
Pulak Kumar Patra[2]
Ranjan Kumar Patra[3]

ABSTRACT

Agriculture is the backbone of India's economy. Although there has been overall growth in agricultural production in the country over the years, there is also substantial variability about the trend. Weather variability is regarded as the primary cause of year-to-year fluctuations in yields. Despite technological advances, such as: improved crop varieties, genetically modified organisms, and irrigation systems, weather is still a key factor in agricultural productivity, as well as soil properties and natural communities. Altering cropping seasons, increasing incidence of pests and diseases, rationing water supply, loss of agricultural biodiversity and limiting food supply are all evidences of climate change. These factors force farmers to adapt using meagre resources. A significant effect of global climate change is the altering of rainfall patterns, which affects agriculture in a big way. The adverse effects of climate change on agriculture have become a major course of concern in recent years. The length of the growing season and the type of crop grown are both affected by changes in temperature. Climate change will also modify the availability of water, which will have a profound effect on agricultural productivity.

1. Associate Professor (Agronomy), All India Co-ordinated Research Project on Integrated Farming Systems, Orissa University of Agriculture and Technology, Bhubaneswar - 751 003, Odisha, India.
2. Associate Professor, Department of Environmental Studies, Institute of Science, Visva-Bharati, Santiniketan - 731 235, West Bengal, India.
3. Professor (Soil Science and Agricultural Chemistry), College of Agriculture, Orissa University of Agriculture and Technology, Bhubaneswar - 751 003, Odisha, India.

To deal with effects of climate change, both adaptive measures and mitigation measures are to be taken. The impact of climate change on agriculture can be minimized through better preparedness, mitigation measures and improved response mechanisms. By issuing accurate forecasts and warnings in a form that is readily understood by the farming community can save the crops and farm animals from the risk of weather variability.

INTRODUCTION

Many aspects of the global climate are changing rapidly. Evidence for changes in the climate system abounds, from the top of the atmosphere to the depths of the oceans. The climate system is the highly complex system consisting of five major components; the atmosphere, the hydrosphere, the cryosphere, the land surface and the biosphere, and the interactions among them. The climate system evolves in time under the influence of its own internal dynamics and because of external forcings such as: volcanic eruptions, solar variations and human-induced forcings such as: the changing composition of the atmosphere and land-use.

The term 'climate variability' is often used to denote deviations of climatic statistics over a given period of time (*e.g.*, a month, season or year) from the long-term statistics relating to the corresponding calendar period. In this sense, climate variability is measured by those deviations, which are usually termed anomalies.

'Climate change' refers to a statistically significant variation in either the mean state of the climate or in its variability, persisting for an extended period (typically decades or longer). Climate change may be due to natural internal processes or external forcings, or due to persistent anthropogenic changes in the composition of the atmosphere or in land use. The United Nation's Framework Convention on Climate Change (UNFCCC) defines 'climate change' as 'a change of climate behaviour which is attributed directly or indirectly to human activity that alters the composition of the global atmosphere and which is in addition to natural climate variability observed over comparable time periods' The UNFCCC thus makes a distinction between 'climate change' attributable to human activities altering the atmospheric composition, and 'climate variability' attributable to natural causes. Climate change is a long-term shift in weather conditions measured by changes in temperature, precipitation, wind, snow cover, and other indicators. It can involve both changes in average conditions and changes in variability, including, for example, changes in extreme conditions.

A key difference between climate variability and change is in persistence of 'anomalous' conditions. In other words, events that are used to be rare occur more frequently, or *vice versa*. Occasionally, an event or sequence of events occurs that has never been recorded before, such as: the exceptional tsunami in the Indian Ocean in 2004 or hurricane season in the Atlantic in 2005. Yet even that could be a part of natural climate variability. If such a season does not recur within the next 30 years, by looking back it could be called as an exceptional year, but not a 'climate change'. Only a persistent series of unusual events taken in the context of regional climate parameters can suggest that a potential change in climate has occurred.

Causes of Climate Variability and Change

Climate change is a movement in the climate system because of internal changes within the climate system or in the interaction of its components, or because of changes in external forcing either by natural factors or anthropogenic activities (IPCC, 1996). Natural variability is a characteristic of the global climate and occurs on both long and short time scales.

Some external influences, such as: changes in solar radiation and volcanism, occur naturally and contribute to the total natural variability of the climate system. Other external changes, such as: the change in composition of the atmosphere that began with the industrial revolution, are the result of human activity. The influence of solar irradiance changes and volcanic eruptions has been very small relative to the influence of human emissions of greenhouse gases since the beginning of the industrial revolution. The build-up of greenhouse gases in the atmosphere is the primary cause for concern about climate change now and into the immediate future.

The causes of climate change can broadly be divided into two categories, natural and human causes (Patra, 2012). The natural variability and the climate fluctuations of the climate system have always been part of the earth's history; however, there have been changes in concentrations of greenhouse gases in the atmosphere growing at an unprecedented rate and magnitude.

Natural Causes

The earth's climate can be affected by natural factors, such as: volcanic eruptions, ocean current, the earth's orbital changes and solar variations.

1. *Volcanic eruptions:* When a volcano erupts it throws out large volumes of sulphur dioxide, water vapour, dust and ash into the atmosphere. Large volumes of gases and ash can influence climatic patterns for years by increasing planetary reflectivity causing atmospheric cooling. Tiny particles called aerosols are produced by volcanoes. Because they reflect solar energy back into space they have a cooling effect on the world. Volcanic eruptions are episodic and have relatively short-term effects on climate.
2. *Ocean current:* The oceans are a major component of the climate system. Ocean currents move vast amounts of heat across the planet. Winds push horizontally against the sea surface and drive ocean current patterns. Interactions between the ocean and atmosphere can also produce phenomena such as: *El Nino* which occurs every 2 to 6 years. The oceans play an important role in determining the atmospheric concentration of CO_2. Changes in ocean circulation may affect the climate through the movement of CO_2 into or out of the atmosphere.
3. *Earth's orbital changes:* The earth makes one full orbit around the sun each year. It is tilted at an angle of 23.5° to the perpendicular plane of its orbital path. Changes in the tilt of the earth can lead to small but climatically important changes in the strength of the seasons; more tilt means warmer summers and colder winters; less tilt means cooler summers and milder winters. Slow changes in the

earth's orbit lead to small but climatically important changes in the strength of the seasons over tens of thousands of years.

4. *Solar variations:* The sun is the source of energy for the earth's climate system. Although the sun's energy output appears constant from an everyday point of view, small changes over an extended period of time can lead to climate changes. As the sun is the fundamental source of energy that is instrumental in our climate system it would be reasonable to assume that changes in the sun's energy output would cause the climate to change. Current global warming however cannot be explained solely by solar variations.

Human Causes

Climate change can also be caused by human activities, such as: the burning of fossil fuels and the conversion of land for forestry and agriculture. Since the beginning of the industrial revolution in the 19th century, these human influences on the climate system have increased substantially. Carbon dioxide is the most important greenhouse gas in the atmosphere. Changes in land use pattern, deforestation, land clearing, agriculture, and other activities have all led to a rise in the emission of carbon dioxide. Methane is another important greenhouse gas in the atmosphere. It is released from animals such as: dairy cows, goats, pigs, buffaloes, etc. Methane is also emitted during the process of oil drilling, coal mining, leaking gas pipelines, landfills and waste dumps. It is this human-induced enhancement of the greenhouse effect that is of concern because ongoing emissions of greenhouse gases have the potential to warm the planet to levels that have never been experienced in the history of human civilization. This change in the climate parameter, also known as global warming, has occurred faster than any other climatic change recorded by humans. Such climate change could have far-reaching and/or unpredictable environmental, social, and economic consequences.

- *Greenhouse gases:* The earth has a natural greenhouse effect where certain gases, known as greenhouse gases, in the atmosphere allow the sunlight to enter and absorb the heat radiation. Because these gases absorb the heat, they keep the average surface temperature on earth around 14°C. Without the natural greenhouse effect, the earth's average surface temperature would be around – 19°C. Since the industrial revolution, human activity has increased the amount of greenhouse gases in the atmosphere. The increased amount of gases which absorb heat, has directly lead to retention of more heat in the atmosphere and thus an increase in global average surface temperatures. This change in temperature is known as global warming. The increase in temperature is also leading to other effects on the climate system. Together these effects are known as anthropogenic climate change. The three main causes of the increase in greenhouse gases observed over the past 250 years have been fossil fuels, land use and agriculture (IPCC, 2006).

The principal greenhouse gases (GHGs) include carbon dioxide, methane, nitrous oxide and chlorofluorocarbons (CFCs). Carbon dioxide constitutes only a small part of the atmosphere, but it is one of the most important GHGs. CO_2 is released naturally into the atmosphere through volcanic eruptions and animal respiration but it is also released through human activities such as: deforestation and the burning of fossil fuels for energy. CO_2 also spends a long time in the atmosphere increasing its impact. Methane, the second most important GHG, is produced both naturally and through human activities. The most significant sources of methane come from the decomposition of organic matter under anaerobic conditions. Another large source is from the digestion of ruminants. Methane is a stronger GHG than CO_2 because it can absorb more heat; however it is much less abundant in the atmosphere. Nitrous oxide, a very powerful greenhouse gas is released during the production and use of organic fertilisers. It is also produced when burning fossil fuels. Chlorofluorocarbons are the manmade compounds which are mainly used in refrigerants and air conditioners.

Since the beginning of the 20th century industrial activity grew 40-fold, and the emissions of greenhouse gases grew 10-fold. The amount of CO_2 in the air increased from some 280 parts per million by volume (ppmv) at the beginning of the century to 389 ppmv at the end of 2010. It is predicted that the level will be 450 ppmv in 2050 resulting in increase in temperature by 1.8 to 3°C. The amount of CO_2 varies throughout the year as the result of the annual cycles of photosynthesis and oxidation. Similarly, methane rose from a pre-industrial atmospheric concentration of around 700 parts per billion by volume (ppbv) to about 1789 ppbv by 2007. The change in major green house gases since the industrial revolution is presented in the Table 7.1.

Table 7.1: Change on major greenhouse gases since the industrial revolution

Gas	Pre-1750 Tropospheric Concentration	Recent Tropospheric Concentration (2012)	Increased Radiative Forcing (W/m^2)
Carbon dioxide (ppm)	280	395.4	1.88
Methane (ppb)	722	1893	0.49
Nitrous oxide (ppb)	270	326	0.17
Tropospheric ozone (ppb)	237	337	0.40

Source: IPCC, 2013.

- *Aerosols in the atmosphere:* Atmospheric aerosols are able to alter climate in two important ways; they scatter and absorb solar and infrared radiation and may change the microphysical and chemical properties of clouds and possibly their lifetime and extent. The scattering of solar radiation acts to cool the planet, while absorption of solar radiation by aerosols warms the air directly instead of allowing sunlight to be absorbed by the surface of the earth. Human activity contributes to the amount of aerosols in the atmosphere in several ways. Dust is often a bi-product of agricultural processes. Biomass burning and industrial processes produce a wide variety of aerosols depending on the type of raw materials and products. Exhaust emission from transports generates pollutants that are either aerosols from the outset, or are converted by chemical reactions in the atmosphere to form aerosols.

- *Land use change:* Land-use changes (*e.g.*, cutting down forests to create farmland) have led to changes in the amount of sunlight reflected from the ground back into space (the surface albedo). The scale of these changes is estimated to be about one-fifth of the forcing on the global climate due to changes in emissions of greenhouse gases. The largest effect of deforestation is estimated to be at high latitudes where the albedo of snow-covered land, previously forested, has increased. This is because snow on trees reflects only about half of the sunlight falling on it, whereas snow-covered open ground reflects about two-thirds. Another contributing cause of climate change is when agriculture alters the earth's land cover, which can change its ability to absorb or reflect heat and light. Land use change such as: deforestation and desertification, together with use of fossil fuels, are the major anthropogenic sources of carbon dioxide release into the atmosphere.
- *Deforestation:* The rainforests form part of a delicate ecosystem that has taken millions of years to evolve. Rainforests every year help to absorb almost 20 per cent of manmade CO_2 emissions; therefore, deforestation can be classed as a major contributor to the causes of climate change. Cutting down rainforests faster than they can be replaced has a devastating effect on the carbon emission cycle producing an extra 17 per cent of greenhouse gases. Deforestation by means of cutting down and burning these tropical rainforests usually pave the way for agriculture and industry which often produce even more CO_2. Fossil fuels release carbon dioxide into the atmosphere contributing to global warming and climate change. Forest alleviates this change by converting carbon dioxide to carbohydrate during photosynthesis. The world's forests contain about 125 per cent of the carbon found in the atmosphere. This carbon is stored in the form of wood and vegetation through 'carbon sequestration'. Trees possess about 20 per cent carbon by weight and biomass of forest acts as a 'carbon sink'. The soil organic matter produced by the decomposition of dead plant material also acts as a carbon store.

Climate Change Scenario in India

Climate change in India may pose additional stresses on ecological and socio-economic systems that already face tremendous pressures from rapid urbanisation, industrialisation and economic development. India Meteorological Department (IMD) maintains a well distributed network of more than 500 stations in the country for more than a century. Meteorological data collected from these stations from 1901 to 2009 was analysed and the trend in change of climate parameters in India was published (Attri and Tyagi, 2010).

Temperature

The annual mean temperature for the country as a whole has risen by 0.56°C over a period of 1901-2009. It may be mentioned that annual mean temperature has been generally above normal (normal based on period, 1961-90) since 1990. This warming is primarily due to rise in maximum temperature across the country, over larger parts of the data set. However, since 1990, minimum temperature is steadily rising and rate of its rise is slightly more than that of maximum temperature. Spatial pattern of trends in the mean annual temperature shows significant increasing trend over most parts of the country except over parts of Rajasthan, Gujarat and Bihar, where significant decreasing trends were observed. Season wise, maximum rise in mean temperature was observed during the post-monsoon season (0.77°C) followed by winter season (0.70°C), pre-monsoon season (0.64°C) and monsoon season (0.33°C).

Precipitation

The country as a whole does not show any significant trend with respect to the all India annual and monsoon rainfall for the period 1901-2009. Similarly rainfall for the country as whole for the same period for individual monsoon months also does not show any significant trend. However, during the winter season, rainfall is decreasing in almost all the subdivisions except in Himachal Pradesh, Jharkhand, Nagaland, Manipur, Mizoram and Tripura. Rainfall is decreasing over most parts of the central India during the pre-monsoon season. However during the post-monsoon season, rainfall is increasing for most of the sub-divisions.

Extreme Rainfall Events

A large amount of the variability in rainfall is related to the occurrence of extreme rainfall events. Number of heavy rainfall events is increasing almost over the entire landmass. Also the frequency and intensity of extreme events defined as one-day maximum precipitation shows increasing trend everywhere except some northern parts of the country. Country's highest observed one day point rainfall (156.3 cm) and also world's highest 2-day point rainfall (249.3 cm) occurred in Cherrapunji in the year 1995 (IMD, 2006). The exceptionally heavy rainfall of 944 mm over Mumbai on 26th July, 2005 was very unprecedented in nature, which led to many more studies on frequency and variability of heavy rainfall events.

General Effects of Climate Change

Climate is changing naturally at its own pace since the beginning of evolution of the earth. But presently it has gained momentum due to inadvertent anthropogenic disturbances. Today, climate change is a global concern. The earth is facing one of the greatest environmental, economic and social threats through climate change. Stronger and more frequent typhoons, warmer nights, and longer and hotter days are some of the most common evidences of climate change. The general consequences of climate change are discussed below.

1. *Ecological imbalance:* Climate change can make summer months warmer or cold months cooler than usual. These changes in temperature can cause animals to migrate to more suitable places or force them to adapt with adverse effects on their physical conditions. Some may even die and become extinct because of their inability to adapt to extreme environmental conditions. Biodiversity is thus at more risk now than ever because of climate change.

2. *Extreme climate variability:* Climate variability refers to short-term changes in climate such as: longer dry or rainy season, intense heat during summer, more or scanty rains during rainy months.
3. *Increasing temperature:* Global warming is the biggest threat being faced by mankind today. It refers to the observed and projected increase in the earth's average temperature due to natural or anthropogenic causes. The measured average atmospheric temperature near the earth's surface rose by 0.74ºC during the last 100 years, 1906-2005 (IPCC, 2007). Cold days, cold nights and frost have become less frequent and hot days, hot nights and heat waves more frequent. Diurnal temperature range has also decreased. It is estimated that average annual temperature will rise by 1.8 to 4ºC within the next 100 years. Gases created through industrial and agricultural practices increase the heat-reflecting potential of the atmosphere, thereby raising the planet's average temperature.
4. *Limited food supply:* Climate change can alter the schedule and duration of cropping seasons. Farmers can become confused as to when they should plant crops, thereby affecting length of cropping season, time of harvest and food supply. Water shortage during dry months can also affect crop growth and overall food production.
5. *Increased occurrence of pests and diseases:* Climate change can affect the life cycle of pests by increasing their population at a different time. Farmers may be unaware of or caught unprepared for these changes. Diseases can also become prevalent based on the environmental conditions resulting from climate change.
6. *More powerful typhoons.* Global warming increases ocean temperature and rate of evaporation. As water vapour in the atmosphere increases, the typhoons carry more rains. Climate change, through global warming has increased the frequency and intensity of typhoons over the years.
7. *Rise in sea levels:* Increasing global temperature causes glaciers and polar icecaps to melt, thereby making sea levels rise. If sea levels continue to increase, more land could be submerged under water permanently. The IPCC estimates that sea levels rose 17 cm in 20th century and it may further increase by 18-59 cm by the year 2100.
8. *Glacier retreat and disappearance:* The continued retreat of glaciers will have a number of different quantitative impacts. In the areas that are heavily dependent on water runoff from glaciers that melt during the summer months, a continuation of the current retreat will eventually deplete the glacial ice and substantially reduce or eliminate runoff. A reduction in runoff will affect the ability to irrigate crops and will reduce summer stream flows necessary to keep dams and reservoirs replenished. Approximately 2.4 billion people live in the drainage basin of the Himalayan rivers. India, China, Pakistan, Afghanistan, Bangladesh, Nepal and Myanmar could experience floods followed by severe droughts in coming decades. In India alone, the Ganges provides water for drinking and farming for more than 500 million people.

Effect of Climate Change on Agriculture

Agriculture is the largest human activity in the world which depends on climatic parameters. Climate change and agriculture are interrelated processes, both of which take place on a global scale. Despite technological advances, such as: improved crop varieties, genetically modified organisms, and irrigation systems, weather is still a key factor in agricultural productivity, as well as soil properties and natural communities. The effect of climate change on agriculture is related to variabilities in local climates rather than in global climate patterns. The growth, development and reproductive processes in both plants and animals are also temperature dependent. All these physiological processes show their maximum activity, hence good productivity, only at their optimum temperature. A genotype gives good yield only under suitable climatic conditions and other management practices. For each plant variety, there is an optimal temperature for vegetative growth, with growth dropping off as temperature increases or decreases. Similarly, there is a range of temperatures at which a plant will produce seed. Outside of this range, the plant will not reproduce. More than 50 per cent differences in yield are due to climatic variations. Thus climate change has a profound effect on agricultural practices.

Most significant feature of the Indian-subcontinent climate is its monsoon circulation. The south-west monsoon contributes about 80 per cent of the total annual rainfall in a major part of the region. Although the summer monsoon rainfall exhibits a remarkable stability over time - as evidenced by past data of more than a century, displays a variety of temporal and spatial variations. While a large part of the seasonal anomalies in the monsoon is accounted by the inter-annual variability, decadal and longer term changes manifest themselves as changing frequencies of extreme anomalies (Gupta *et al*. 2009).

Altering cropping seasons, increasing incidence of pests and diseases, rationing water supply, loss of agricultural biodiversity and limiting food supply are all evidences of climate change. These factors force farmers to adapt using meagre resources. A significant effect of global climate change is the altering of rainfall patterns, which certainly affects agriculture. Extended drought can cause the failure of small and marginal farms with resultant economic, political and social disruption.

Impact of Climate Change on Crop

Climate change projections made up to 2100 for India, indicate an overall increase in temperature by 2-4°C coupled with increase in precipitation, especially during the monsoon period. The available evidence shows significant drop in yields of important cereal crops like rice and wheat under climate change conditions (Mall *et al*. 2006).

Changes in temperature, amount of carbon dioxide (CO_2), and the frequency and intensity of extreme weather could have significant impacts on crop yields. Many weeds, pests and fungi thrive under warmer temperatures, wetter climates, and increased CO_2 levels.

Warmer temperatures may make many crops grow more quickly, but warmer temperatures could also reduce yields. Crops tend to grow faster in warmer conditions. However, for some crops, faster growth reduces the length of time available for seeds to grow and mature. In the case of an annual crop, the duration between sowing and harvesting will shorten. The shortening of such a cycle could have an adverse effect on productivity because senescence would occur sooner. Thus, yield potential of the crops may not be fully exploited. In some areas, warming may benefit the types of crops that are typically planted there. However, if warming exceeds a crop's optimum temperature, yields can decline. Increase in temperature also increases crop respiration rate and alters partitioning of photosynthates to economic products.

Higher CO_2 levels can increase yields. The yields for some crops, like: wheat and soybeans, could increase by 30 per cent or more under a doubling of CO_2 concentrations. However, some factors may counteract these potential increases in yield. For example, if temperature exceeds a crop's optimal level or if sufficient water and nutrients are not available, yield increases may be reduced or reversed.

More extreme temperature and precipitation can prevent crops from growing. Extreme events, especially floods and droughts, can harm crops and reduce yields. Dealing with drought could become a challenge in areas where summer temperatures are projected to increase and precipitation is projected to decrease. As water supplies are reduced, it may be more difficult to meet water demands. Extreme climate conditions may affect quality of fruits, vegetables, tea, coffee, aromatic and medicinal plants.

Decrease in stratospheric ozone may increase biologically dangerous ultraviolet radiation on earth's surface. Ultra violet radiation may damage nucleic acids creating long term effects. Excess ultraviolet radiation can affect plant physiology either directly or indirectly through changed pollinator behaviour and cause massive amounts of mutations. Tropospheric ozone causes foliar injury. This may reduce productivity of many crops.

More detailed analysis of rice yields by the International Rice Research Institute forecasts 20 per cent reduction in yields over the region per degree (in Celsius) rise in temperature. Rice becomes sterile if exposed to temperatures above 35°C for more than one hour during flowering and consequently produces no grain.

Impact of Climate Change on Soil Health

The warmer atmospheric temperature observed over the past decades is expected to lead to a more vigorous hydrological cycle, including more extreme rainfall events. Erosion and soil degradation is more likely to occur, creating sedimentation in streams and reservoirs. Soil fertility would also be affected by global warming. The increase in the temperature would induce a greater rate in the N mineralisation but there will be more volatilisation and denitrification loss. High soil temperature reduces soil organic matter both in quantity and quality. This may also decrease microbial population reducing soil productivity and nutrient cycling. Excess rainfall causes waterlogging, soil salinity problems and salt water ingression in coastal areas.

Impact of Climate Change on Water Resources

Climate change will modify rainfall, evaporation, runoff and soil moisture storage. In some areas, more frequent heavy downpours may cause localised flooding. Increased evaporation from the soil and accelerated transpiration in the plants will cause moisture stress. Thus, crops will need frequent irrigation. The water resources will come under increasing pressure and could become seasonally scarce as a result of regional changes in water supply due to changes in precipitation or snow and glacier melt. Climate change affects the availability of fresh water for irrigation. The over draft and non-replenishment of groundwater will lower the groundwater level permanently.

Impact of Climate Change on Pest

Global warming would cause an increase in rainfall in some areas, which would lead to an increase of atmospheric humidity and the duration of the wet seasons. Combined with higher temperature, these could favour the development of fungal diseases. Similarly, because of higher temperature and humidity, there could be an increased pressure from insects and disease vectors. An increase in temperature may accelerate the growth and multiplication of insect pests. The polycyclic diseases become epidemic with climate change. The geographical range of insects is expanded with increased risk of infestation.

Impact of Climate Change on Livestock

Risk of climate variability affects dairy, meat and wool production, mainly arising from its impact on grassland and rangeland productivity. Heat distress suffered by animals reduces the rate of animal feed intake and results in poor growth performance (Rowlinson, 2008). Climate change affects feed production and nutrition of livestock. There will be less fodder production due to increased water scarcity. Rise in temperature causes more lignifications of plant tissues reducing its digestibility. Global warming increases the requirements for water, shelter and energy to meet the projected milk demands.

Drought may threaten pasture and feed supplies. Drought also reduces the amount of quality forage available to grazing livestock. Some areas could experience longer, more intense droughts, resulting from higher summer temperature and reduced precipitation. For animals that rely on grain, changes in crop production due to drought could also become a problem. Heat waves, which are projected to increase under climate change, could directly threaten livestock. Heat stress affects animals both directly and indirectly. Over time, heat stress can increase vulnerability to disease, reduce fertility, and reduce milk production.

Climate change may increase the prevalence of parasites and diseases that affect livestock. In areas with increased rainfall, moisture-reliant pathogens could thrive. Vector borne diseases may have more impacts on livestock. Increases in carbon dioxide may increase the productivity of pastures and plants on which livestock feed, but may also decrease their quality.

Impact of Climate Change on Fisheries

Fishery enterprises already face multiple stresses, including: overfishing and water pollution. Climate change may worsen these stresses. In particular, temperature changes could lead to significant impacts. Increased water temperature affects fish breeding, migration and harvest. Many marine species have certain temperature ranges at which they can survive. Increased temperature and tropical cyclonic conditions affect capture, production and marketing cost of marine fish. Many aquatic species migrate towards colder areas of streams, lakes or ocean to avoid warm water. However, moving into new areas may put these species into competition with other species over food and other resources. Changes in temperature and seasons could affect the timing of reproduction and migration. Many steps within an aquatic animal's lifecycle are controlled by temperature and the changing of the seasons. Some diseases that affect aquatic life may become more prevalent in warm water.

In addition to warming, the world's oceans are gradually becoming more acidic due to increases in atmospheric carbon dioxide. Increasing acidity could harm shellfish by weakening their shells, which are created from calcium and are vulnerable to increasing acidity. Acidification may also threaten the structures of sensitive ecosystems upon which some fish and shellfish rely. The effects of climate change on agriculture by 2050 as predicted by Ministry of Agriculture, Fisheries and Food, Government of United Kingdom are presented in Table 7.2.

Table 6.2: Predicted effects of climate change on agriculture by 2050

Climatic Element	Expected Changes by 2050	Confidence in Prediction	Effects on Agriculture
CO_2	Increase from 350 ppm to 450-600 ppm	Very high	Good for crops; increased photosynthesis; reduced water use
Sea level rise	Rise by 10-15 cm	Very high	Loss of land, coastal erosion, flooding, salinisation of groundwater
Temperature	Rise by 1-2°C; winters warming more than summers; increased frequency of heat waves	High	Faster, shorter, earlier growing seasons, range moving north and to higher altitudes, heat stress risk, increased evapotranspiration
Precipitation	Seasonal changes by ± 10%	Low	Impacts on drought risk, soil workability, water logging, irrigation supply, transpiration
Storminess	Increased wind speeds, more intense rainfall events	Very low	Lodging, soil erosion, reduced infiltration of rainfall
Variability	Increases across most climatic variables; predictions uncertain	Very low	Changing risk of damaging events (heat waves, frost, droughts, floods) which effect crops and timing of farm operations

Source: MAFF, 2000.

Measures Addressing the Effect of Climate Change on Agriculture

The adverse effects of climate change on agriculture have become a major course of concern in recent years. The length of the growing season and the type of crop grown are both affected by changes in temperature. Climate change will also modify the availability of water, which will have a profound effect on agricultural productivity. To deal with effects of climate change, both adaptive measures and mitigation measures are to be taken.

Adaptation Strategies

As agricultural production increases resource constraints, particularly water, will become tighter. Agriculture globally accounts for about 70 per cent of the world's freshwater withdrawals. Climate change is expected to alter the seasonal timing of rainfall and snow pack melt resulting in a higher incidence and severity of floods and droughts. Both rainfed and irrigated agriculture need to be managed more sustainably to reduce production risks. The greater uncertainty from climate change can be best addressed through contingent planning. Adaptation through such measures as crop and livestock insurance, social safety nets, and research on and dissemination of flood, heat and drought resistant crops, including conservation of traditional plant varieties with those characteristics can be facilitated.

Adaptive approaches to minimise the adverse effects of climate change on agriculture include initiating reforestation and afforestation activities, developing water harvesting techniques, improving irrigation efficiency, conserving soil moisture through appropriate tillage methods. Another adaptation strategy taken by farmers is crop diversification and changing planting dates that has proven to be one of the most popular farm level responses to climate variability and change. Improved livestock management practices like providing better housing and shade, change to heat tolerant breeds, change in stocking rate, altered grazing and rotation of pasture, etc., may prove to be beneficial. Early warning systems and protection measures for natural disasters like: droughts, floods, tropical cyclones, etc., should be developed.

Mitigation Technologies

IPCC (2007) defines mitigation as the technological change and substitution that reduce resource inputs and emissions per unit of output. Significant mitigation can be achieved through improved cropland and grazing land management, restoration of degraded lands, and land use change like: agroforestry to increase soil carbon storage. Emissions from livestock production can be reduced through improved nutrition and better management of manure. Improved land management through mulching, minimum/zero tillage, intensive cropping, growing legumes, green manuring, crop residues management, improved nutrient management, improved composting including: vermicomposting can be undertaken to mitigate the climate change impact on agriculture. A large proportion of the mitigation potential of agriculture arises from soil carbon sequestration, which has strong synergies with sustainable agriculture and generally reduces vulnerability to climate change. Improved rice cultivation techniques can reduce methane gas emissions. Improved nitrogen fertiliser application techniques can also reduce N_2O emissions. Suitable energy crops should be encouraged to replace fossil fuel use.

A study was undertaken by the International Crops Research Institute for the Semi-Arid Tropics to find science based, pro-poor approaches and techniques that would enable Asia's agricultural systems to cope with climate change, while benefitting poor and vulnerable farmers. The study's recommendations ranged from improving the use of climate information in local planning and strengthening weather based agroadvisory services, to stimulating diversification of rural household incomes and providing incentives to farmers to adopt natural resource conservation measures to enhance forest cover, replenish groundwater and use renewable energy. Other mitigation measures include change in crop management practices, crop insurance, etc.

1. The crops and varieties which can withstand water logging conditions for a fairly long period should be preferred in the flood and cyclone prone areas. At present varieties for various crops, particularly for rice many varieties are available which are tolerant to flood conditions. Awareness should be created among the farmers of flood prone areas and adequate seeds of these varieties should also be ascertained.
2. In areas of perennial waterlogging where even rice cultivation is difficult, aquatic crops with economic importance such as: water chestnut can be introduced with fish farming. Colocasia can also be cultivated in flood prone waterlogged areas.
3. The contingent crop plans should be prepared for post flood and cyclone areas. Short duration pulses and vegetable crops should be encouraged and package of practices for these crops should be standardized for difficult situations.
4. In low lands under high rainfall region and flood prone areas, land modification such as: raised and sunken bed technique can be practiced. Trenches of 5-8 metre width and 1.2-1.5 metre depth with 10 metre or suitable length can be opened at a spacing of 10-15 metre in-between two trenches. The excavated soil is put on the space between two trenches to prepare raised beds. Vegetables and short duration fruit crops can be grown on the raised beds while trenches are utilised for fish farming. In dry season irrigation can be provided to the crops on the raised beds from the trenches.
5. In flood prone and waterlogged areas, the practice of bio-drainage using *Casuarina* and *Eucalyptus* plantations would act as a viable flood resilient system. Crops can be grown on the tree alleys. This increases land productivity.

Conclusion

Climate and weather is a basic input considered the most vital in agricultural production system since it affects the agricultural planning in a big way starting from land preparation to harvesting, processing and transportation. Thus, climate may be considered as the most critical factor determining the sustainability of agricultural systems. But climate variability and climate extremes are already having impacts on agricultural production systems. During the last few decades climate change has threatened the Indian food security in a big way. However, risks associated with climate change can be reduced through timely preparedness, coupled with appropriate mitigation actions and programmes. Short to medium range weather forecasts and early warning systems can be useful ele-ments for the agricultural decision-making process, leading to reduced risks and increased opportunities. Immediate attention should be given to contingency crop planning and integrated cyclone and flood management strategies for reducing the extent of damage. The projected extent of climate change and its effect on agriculture is a top priority item, which deserves due attention of planners, policy-makers, scientists, extension workers and all other interested in development of agriculture. There is also a need for intensifying research activity on this important agenda.

REFERENCES

Attri, S.D., and Tyagi, A. (2010). Climate Profile of India. India Meteorological Department, Ministry of Earth Sciences, Government of India, New Delhi, pp. 122.

Gupta, A.K., Nair, S.S. and Sehgal, V.K. (2009). Hydro-Meteorological Disasters and Climate Change: Conceptual Issues and Data Needs for Integrating Adaptation into Environment - Development Framework. *E-Journal Earth Science India* 2(2): 117-132.

IMD. (2006). Trends in Precipitation Extremes over India. *NCC Research Report No. 3/2006.*

IPCC. (1996). Climate Change (1995). The Science of Climate Change. Contribution of Group I to the Second Assessment Report on the Intergovernmental Panel on Climate Change. Cambridge University Press. U.K.

IPCC. (2007). Climate Change 2007: The Physical Science Basis. Cambridge University Press, U.K.

IPCC. (2013). *Climate Change 2013: The Physical Science Basis. Contribution of Working Group I to the Fifth Assessment Report of the Intergovernmental Panel on Climate Change.* Cambridge University Press, Cambridge, U.K.

MAFF. (2000). Climate Change and Agriculture in the United Kingdom. Ministry of Agriculture, Fisheries and Food, London, U.K.

Mall, R.K., Singh, R., Gupta, A. Srinivasan, G. and Rathore, L.S. (2006). Impact of Climate Change on Indian Agriculture: A Review. *Climatic Change,* 78: 445-478.

Patra, P.K. (2012). A Text Book on Climatology. Kalyani Publishers, Ludhiana, pp. 255.

Rowlinson, P. (2008). Adapting Livestock Production Systems to Climate Change – Temperate Zones. Livestock and Global Change Conference Proceedings, May 2008, Tunisia.

Pages 167-183

WATER RESOURCES: MAPPING, MONITORING AND MANAGEMENT
***Edited by*: Dr. Pawan Kumar Tyagi; Dr. Avnish Chauhan & Dr. Pawan Kumar Bharti**
***Edition* : 2017**
ISBN : 978-93-5056-861-3
***Published by* : Discovery Publishing House Pvt. Ltd., New Delhi (India)**

Study of Kharif Season for Changing Rainfall Scenario in Meerut District

Avadhesh Kumar Koshal[1*]
Sanjay Kumar[2]
Prafull Kumar[3]

ABSTRACT

Meerut district lies between 23°57′ to 29°02′ North latitude and 77°40′ to 77°45′ East longitude in the Upper Gangetic Plain Region of India. The districts of Uttar Pradesh state is covered most of the south-west monsoon so rice crop is grown in mostly in kharif season (monsoon crop). Monsoon clouds break during July and rains continue up to September. The present study is based on secondary sources of time series data of rainfall and rice yield data obtained 50 years from 1965 to 2014 is used for analysis. The S-W rainfall and rice yield data analysis to observed pattern of trend and develop forecasting model for future scenario. The average monthly rainfall of 50 years (1965-2014) for Meerut district is observed 689.2mm. The Post monsoon season is more stable then South-west monsoon. The positive trend of rainfall shows the favourable conditions for recharge and the negative trend of rainfall shows the unfavourable conditions for recharge. The data of annual rainfall and S-W rainfall is correlated with rice yield. The negative correlation values are -0.17 and -0.21 observed between rice yield with annual and S-W monsoon rainfall of Meerut. The annual, S-W rainfall and rice yield data of fifty years observed mean values are 689.7mm, 587.4mm and 1860 kg/ha respectively. The skewness has been computed for annual, S-W rainfall and rice yield indicates a negative trend. The R^2 value 0.089 means that only 8.90 per cent variation is observed in fifty years rainfall data analysis. Rainfall and rice correlation provides coefficient of -0.21 representing

1. P.D.F.S.R., Modipuram, Meerut (U.P.), India.
2. J.V. College, Baraut, Baghpat (U.P.), India.
3. College of Agriculture, S.V.P.U.A. and T., Meerut (U.P.), India.

negligible relationship between the two variables. The long-term data analysis of month-wise June, July August and September contributes 10.7 per cent, 33.3 per cent, 38.3 per cent and 17.8 per cent in south west monsoon rainfall season respectively. The monthly south-west monsoon rainfall variability in years is observed maximum after 21th century. It is most important period of rainfall seasonal cycle. The analysis data of S-W monsoon observed highest increase 98 per cent in August month and highest decrease in September month and decrease by 0.1 per cent during fifty years. The trend pattern of rice yield 868 kg/ha to 2852 kg/ha also observed in year 1965 to 2014 respectively. The expected rice yield is observed 3257 kg/ha in year 2024. The trend analysis gives the scenario of current to expected future situation. Our statistical result indicate that monsoon rainfall is not the only weather variable affecting the rice crop in kharif season in the study area.

The analysis of trend of rainfall and rice yield observed rainfall is declining but rice yield trend going to be rise in coming years. The source of irrigation, mechanization and knowledge of current situation of weather and climate change related pattern and adaptation of technology is maintend to yield trend. The objective for present was to identify decadal trends in south west monsoon (June to September) at various spatial scales.

Keywords: Cropping pattern, Climatic variability, El Nino, Indian summer monsoon and South-west monsoon.

INTRODUCTION

Rainfall is non-linear and vital renewable resource of hydrological cycle. Rainfall influenced on the agriculture. The rainfall based crops and their cropping systems adapted throughout a year to cyclic form. The whole year is dividing in three seasons *viz*; Kharif, Rabi and Zaid covered most of the area of Rice, wheat and Cucurbitaceae vegetables respectively. The climatic variability (rainfall, temperature, moisture, soil properties and other related factors) change the crop and cropping patterns. Agriculture systems/pattern is dependent on distribution of rainfall, so Indian agriculture is highly dependent on the spatial and temporal distribution of monsoon rainfall (1). Its process is random in nature. The districts of Uttar Pradesh state is covered most of the south-west monsoon so rice crop is grown in mostly in kharif season (monsoon crop). Rice is a water loving and C3 fixation monocot dominant crop in kharif season and rice-wheat system is a pre-dominate system of Meerut after sugarcane-wheat system (Fig. 8.1). Rice (*Oryza sativa L.*) and wheat (*Triticum aestivum L.*) contribute about 77 per cent of the total cereal production and are the backbone of India's food security. The majority of farmers adopted sugarcane-livestock-cereals-fodder system in this area. The rice crop having one of the major problematic role in the environment, rice grown area plays a significant role in methane emission, it is one of the most important source of anthropogenic methane (a green house gas) representing 8.5-10.9 per cent of total emission from all sources (2). *El Nino* effect on the Indian monsoon more than sixty per cent, it has a history of adversely impacting monsoon rain. After 1960,

India specific *El Nino* years are 1963, 1965, 1969, 1972, 1982, 1987, 1991 and 1997 having drought as well as *El Nino* affect. It is an oceanic phenomenon that emerges every three to seven years, the warm temperatures around the pacific coast of South America affecting cloud formation and weather patterns in many parts of the world. During the changing scenario of south west monsoon in India due to *El Nino* affect develop drought conditions and below normal rainfall. In India, most of the droughts are associated with *El Nino* episodes (3). and (4). In the past decade, 2002, 2004 and 2009 were drought years due to the phenomenon.

The IMD (Indian meteorology Department, New Delhi) divided Indian season in four categories (winter, Pre-monsoon, South-west monsoon and Post monsoon). IMD defines a four month period from June to September as Indian summer monsoon (ISM) period (5). About 75 per cent to 80 per cent of the annual rainfall is received during a short period. After study of IMD season observed most suitable and desirable season is south west monsoon which covered four months within a year to provide natural water to crop for good health, vegetative growth and yield. The southwest monsoon (June to September) impacts on study area is agricultural based economy and summer monsoon is critical (6). The all India summer monsoon (June to September) rainfall does not show any significant trend during the last century (7). The precipitation rise by 5 per cent and 15 per cent during September-October could adversely affect rice productivity (8). However, its decrease is positively related with rice yield. He observed an Increasing of rainfall is found to be negatively related with rice productivity (9).

Statistical techniques are essential tools for analyzing large datasets. It also helps us to identify which of the many pieces of information derived from observations of the climate system are worthy of synthesis and interpretation. The climatic research is complex, large level and long time period's process. The natural or human-induced factors are cause of climates change. The development of rice varieties having adaptation to climatic change should be the focus of future research and development. Changing monsoon rainfall pattern has directly affected on rice crop production and yield. It also affect on water resource, agricultural output and economy of the area. In the study area, the aim is to provide district level scenario of long trends of rainfall pattern with rice yield pattern.

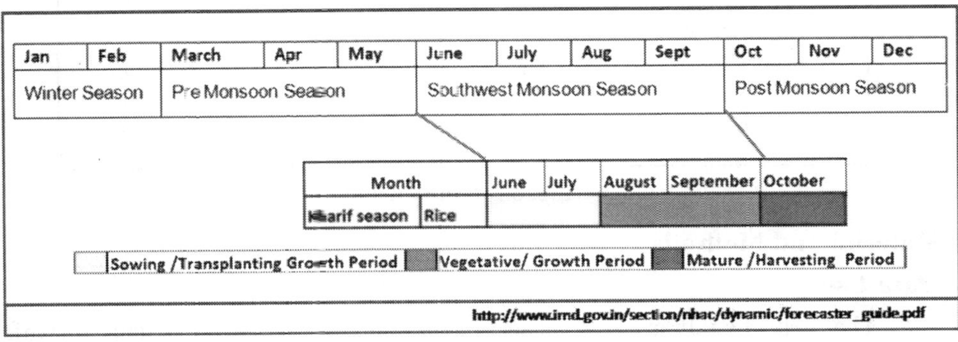

Fig 8.1: **Crop calendar of rice crop**

Objective

To understand temporal changing scenario of rainfall in monsoon season and consequently change in rice yield pattern.

Study Area

Meerut district lies between 28°57' to 29°02' North latitude and 77°40' to 77°45' East longitude in the Upper Gangetic Plain Region (Planning commission) of India and elevation of about 219 meters above the sea level (10). The geographical area of Meerut is 2,590 Sq. Km (11). It is bounds by district of Muzaffarnagar on the north, Bulandshahar on the south and Ghaziabad on the south-west. Hindon river makes its Boundary in west Direction in separates it with the Bagpat district (Fig. 8.2). Ganga and Yamuna form the natural boundaries in the east and west. It is almost an alluvial plain having very rich soil with a network of irrigation facilities. There are extremes of temperatures during winter and summer season. Monsoon clouds break during July and rains continue up to September. In this part of the country onset of monsoon occurs in the last week of June or first week of July. Meerut has a monsoon influenced humid subtropical climate characterised by cool winters and very hot summers. The average annual rainfall of Meerut is about 800mm (12). Over 80 per cent of the annual rainfall is received during the months of July to September.

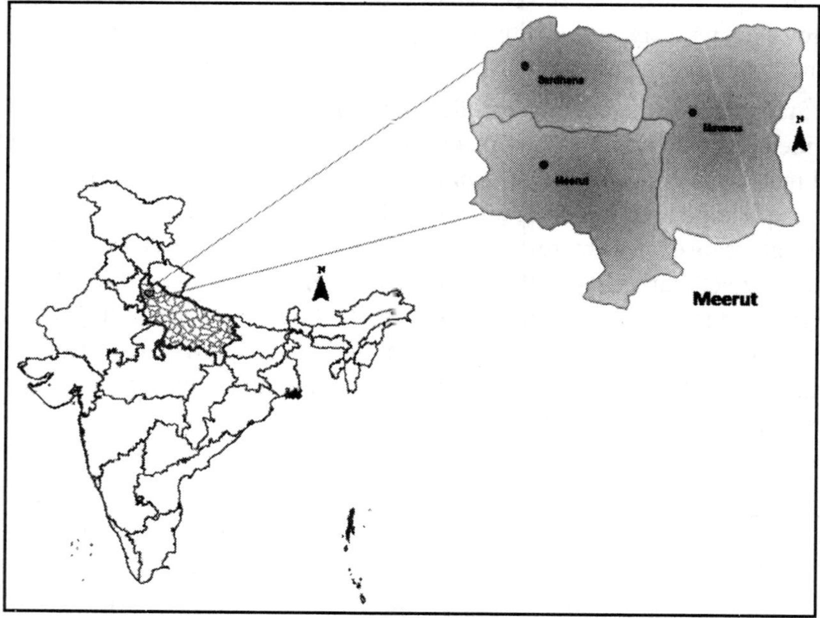

Fig. 8.2: **Study area**

Material and Methods

Data Use

The present study is based on secondary sources of time series data of rainfall and rice yield data obtained 50 years from 1965 to 2014 is used for analysis. The data set used in this study is derived from the time series of annual and monthly precipitation of Meerut district, Uttar Pradesh (Fig. 8.1). The rainfall data were collected from the published records, India Water Portal, Indian Meteorological Department, NASA/POWER Agroclimatology and other national level institutes. The different years of time series data 1960-2002 and 2004-06 from India water portal (13), year 2003 from published paper of the study area (14). Year 2007-13 from Indian Meteorological Department, New Delhi (15) and year 2014 data taken from NASA/POWER Agroclimatology (16). The fifty years rice yield data are collected from Rice – wheat consortium (17), Bulletin of the Directorate of Agricultural Statistics, ICAR-eands website, published reports and journals (18).

Methodology

A time series is defined as a set of observations arranged in time. The principal aim of a time series analysis is to describe the long-term of movements in time of some variable at a particular site. The objective is to generate data having properties of the observed long period record. To compute properties of a long period of time series is broken into separate components and analysed individually to understand the pattern of rainfall. The annual and monthly rainfall data used for observed trend during long period.

The S-W rainfall and rice yield data analysis to observed pattern of trend and develop forecasting model for future scenario. The different type of statistical data analysis *viz;* Co-efficient of Variation (CV), Standard deviation, Correlation of Co-efficient (R^2), Departure and Cumulative departure and Trend Analysis to given important scenario of change pattern of time series data. The statistical analyses are Mean, standard deviation, Co-efficient of Variation, Standard Variation, R^2, and other related analysis of data in MS Excel.

Result and Discussion

The mathematical and statistical analysis of South-west rainfall (S-W rainfall) and rice yield factors are discussed in below:

Variation of Monthly Rainfall

The average monthly rainfall of 50 years (1965-2014) for Meerut district is observed 689.2mm and the intensity of rainfall increasing from June to September (South-west Monsoon), and suddenly decreasing trend noticed from October to December (Post-monsoon). The analysis of fifty years monthly data observed 224.9mm in the month of August, 195.4mm in July, and 62.6mm in June. The lowest rainfall was observed 6mm in the month of November and its maximum rainfall is 224.9mm in the month of August. The co-efficient of variation for monthly mean rainfall observed highest in the month of November and it is 195 per cent whereas coefficient of variation is minimum for the month of August and it is 49.2 per cent for the Meerut district. This shows that rainfall is more stable in the month of August and is more variable in the month of November for the Meerut district. The scenario of seasonal rainfall data observed South-west monsoon has maximum rainfall then other seasonal rainfall (Table 8.1).

Table 8.1: Statistical summary of seasonal (month-wise) rainfall of Meerut district

Season	Month	Mean	Std. Dev.	C.V.%
Winter	January	15.8	15.1	95.8
	February	18.4	18.6	101.0
Pre-Monsoon	March	13.4	13.4	100.3
	April	9.4	11.8	125.1
	May	20.4	17.6	86.3
South-west Monsoon	June	62.6	37.5	59.9
	July	195.4	100.8	51.6
	August	224.9	110.6	49.2
	September	104.4	66.4	63.5
Post-monsoon	October	11.9	17.2	144.6
	November	6.0	11.7	195.0
	December	6.6	9.9	149.4

The Post monsoon season is more stable then South-west monsoon. The R^2 value 0.026 means that only 2.6 per cent variation in rainfall is explained by time. The highly intensity trends noticed in the month of June to September month get highest rainfall in August month and it reaches its maximum peak and also its start to decreasing from month of October and lowest rainfall in the month of November (Fig. 8.3).

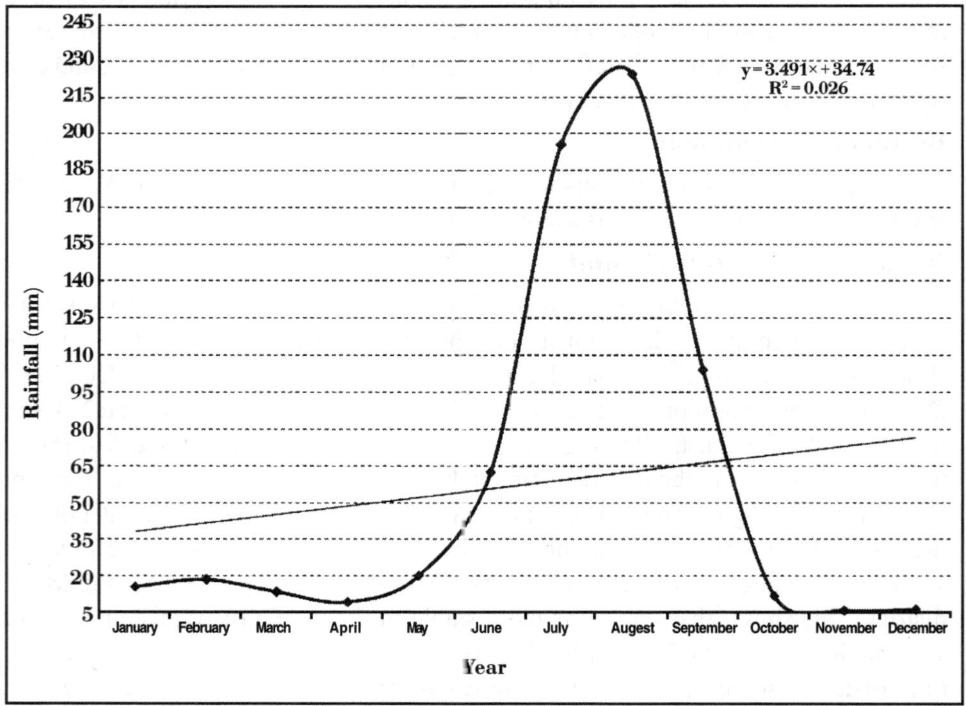

Fig. 8.3: **Average monthly rainfall of south-west rainfall (1965-2014)**

Rainfall Departure and Cumulative Departure of South-west Rainfall

The departure and cumulative departure from average rainfall for the study area has been depicted in Table 8.2. The trend of annual departure from the computed value of average annual rainfall reveals that:

(a) Years showing annual positive departure with respect to average annual rainfall were 1966-67, 1969, 1971-72, 1975-1978, 1980, 1983-1985, 1988-89, 1993-1996, 1998, 2003, 2010 and 2013. The positive trend of rainfall shows the favourable conditions for recharge.

(b) Years showing annual negative departure with respect to average annual rainfall were 1965, 1968, 1970, 1973-74,1979, 1981-82, 1986-87, 1989, 1991-92, 1997 1999-2002, 2004-2009, 2011-12 and 2014. The negative trend of rainfall shows the unfavourable conditions for recharge.

Table 8.2: South-west rainfall data and its departure and cumulative departure from average South-west rainfall in Meerut district (1965-2014)

Year	South-West Rainfall (mm)	Departure from Average Rainfall	Cumulative Departure from Average Rainfall	Year	South-West Rainfall (mm)	Departure from Average Rainfall	Cumulative Departure from Average Rainfall
1965	486.9	-100.4	100	1990	768.3	180.9	1530
1966	613.5	26.1	127	1991	541.0	-46.4	1484
1967	833.0	245.7	372	1992	442.3	-145.1	1339
1968	529.2	-58.2	314	1993	792.0	204.7	1544
1969	658.5	71.1	385	1994	725.9	138.6	1682
1970	494.6	-92.8	292	1995	802.4	215.1	1897
1971	802.2	214.9	507	1996	792.2	204.9	2102
1972	684.0	96.6	604	1997	482.4	-104.9	1997
1973	577.9	-9.4	594	1998	692.5	105.1	2102
1974	459.7	-127.6	467	1999	336.6	-250.8	1851
1975	958.0	370.6	837	2000	574.1	-13.2	1838
1976	866.5	279.1	1117	2001	474.3	-113.0	1725
1977	673.5	86.2	1203	2002	405.7	-181.7	1544
1978	871.1	283.7	1486	2003	885.8	298.4	1842
1979	326.3	-261.1	1225	2004	451.4	-136.0	1706
1980	820.6	233.2	1459	2005	573.0	-14.4	1692
1981	523.0	-64.4	1394	2006	272.3	-315.1	1377
1982	572.8	-14.5	1380	2007	289.3	-298.1	1079
1983	667.7	80.3	1460	2008	381.6	-205.8	873
1984	617.9	30.5	1490	2009	216.1	-371.3	502
1985	789.7	202.3	1693	2010	661.7	74.3	576
1986	470.3	-117.0	1576	2011	499.0	-88.4	487
1987	248.1	-339.3	1236	2012	328.2	-259.2	228
1988	896.7	309.3	1546	2013	696.3	108.9	337
1989	391.0	-196.4	1349	2014	450.9	-136.4	201
South-west average rainfall (mm) = 587.4							

Statistical Parameters of Annual Rainfall, South-west Rainfall and Rice Yield

The statistical analyses of fifty years (1965-2014) annual, monthly rainfall and rice yield are observed in mean value (Table 8.3).

Table 8.3: Annual, South-west monsoon season rainfall and rice yield (Kg/ha) of Meerut district (1965-2014)

Year	Annual Rainfall	South-west Monsoon (Total)	Rice Yield (Kg/ha)	Year	Annual Rainfall (Total)	South-west Monsoon	Rice Yield (Kg/ha)
1965	541.6	486.9	1204	1990	890.5	768.3	2135
1966	707.5	613.5	952	1991	658.0	541.0	1985
1967	943.6	833.0	1020	1992	554.1	442.3	2231
1968	585.1	529.2	875	1993	844.2	792.0	2424
1969	715.9	658.5	1086	1994	797.4	725.9	2388
1970	646.4	494.6	1023	1995	925.7	802.4	2430
1971	913.0	802.2	1179	1996	867.5	792.2	2174
1972	747.6	684.0	1160	1997	647.2	482.4	2483
1973	667.1	577.9	1096	1998	819.4	692.5	2262
1974	497.3	459.7	817	1999	407.7	336.6	2147
1975	1035.4	958.0	873	2000	691.0	574.1	2271
1976	956.8	866.5	1843	2001	583.4	474.3	2334
1977	800.6	673.5	1128	2002	465.0	405.7	2504
1978	929.5	871.1	1154	2003	1056.2	885.8	2246
1979	437.4	326.3	850	2004	722.3	451.4	2519
1980	884.7	820.6	1365	2005	639.4	573.0	2359
1981	655.4	523.0	1107	2006	352.7	272.3	2299
1982	771.9	572.8	1529	2007	373.7	289.3	2559
1983	861.7	667.7	1682	2008	437.4	381.6	2193
1984	671.0	617.9	1654	2009	223.7	216.1	2608
1985	898.0	789.7	1777	2010	701.9	661.7	2747
1986	596.9	470.3	1815	2011	556.2	499.0	2712
1987	355.9	248.1	1543	2012	395.4	328.2	2747
1988	970.5	896.7	2140	2013	923.8	696.3	2712
1989	503.4	391.0	1961	2014	634.7	450.9	2700
Average Rainfall (mm) and Yield (Kg/ha)					689.7	587.4	1860.0
Correlation (Annual rainfall and Yield) -0.17							
Correlation (S-W rainfall and Yield) -0.21							

The data of annual rainfall and S-W rainfall is correlated with rice yield. The negative correlation values are -0.17 and -0.21 observed between rice yield with annual and S-W monsoon rainfall of Meerut (Table 8.3). The annual rainfall during 50 years ranged from 223.7mm in year in 2009 to 1056.2mm in year 2003 with an average of 689.7mm. The important season cycle of rainfall observed in South-west rainfall during 50 years ranged from 216.1mm in year in 2009 to 958mm in year 1975 with an average of 587.4mm. The analysis of kharif rice crop is observed during fifty years ranged from 817 kg/ha in year 1974 to 2747 kg/ha in year 2010 with an average of 1860 kg/ha.

Table 8.3: Computation of statistical parameters of south-west rainfall data of Meerut district

Statistical Parameters	Computed Value		
	Annual Rainfall (mm)	South-west Rainfall (mm)	Rice Yield (Kg/ha)
Mean	689.2 mm	587.4 mm	1860 (Kg/ha)
Min	223.7 mm	216.1 mm	816.5 (Kg/ha)
Max	1056.2 mm	958 mm	2746.9 (Kg/ha)
Median	681.0 mm	573.6 mm	2059.6 (Kg/ha)
Mode	-	-	2747 mm
Std. Dev.	202.3	193.0	633.8
C.V.%	29.3	32.9	34.1
Co-efficient of skewness	-0.20224	-0.00078	-0.27
Correlation*	-0.17	-0.21	-

**Annual Rainfall + Rice Yield and South-west Rainfall + Rice Yield.*

The annual, S-W rainfall and rice yield data of fifty years observed mean values are 689.7mm, 587.4mm and 1860 kg/ha. respectively. The compound value of the mode 2747 kg/ha indicates ideal yield of rice crop. The calculated value of standard deviation reveals that deviation of annual, S-W rainfall and rice yield is of 202.3mm, 193mm and 633.8 kg/ha respectively over a period of 50 years. The co-efficient of variation (%) was observed for annual, S-W rainfall and rice yield values are 29.3, 32.9 and 34.1 respectively. The skewness has been computed for annual, S-W rainfall and rice yield indicates a negative trend (Table 8.4). Fig. 8.4 shows that the trend of rainfall is a negative linear relationship between rainfall and time. The R^2 value 0.089 means that only 8.90 per cent variation is observed in fifty years rainfall data analysis.

Trend Analysis of S-W Monsoon Rainfall and Rice Yield

Rainfall and rice correlation provides coefficient of -0.21 representing negligible relationship between the two variables. The regression analysis indicates R^2 value of 0.110 for rainfall and 0.867 for rice yield implying that 11 per cent rainfall only accounts for 86 per cent of rice yield. (Fig. 8.5)

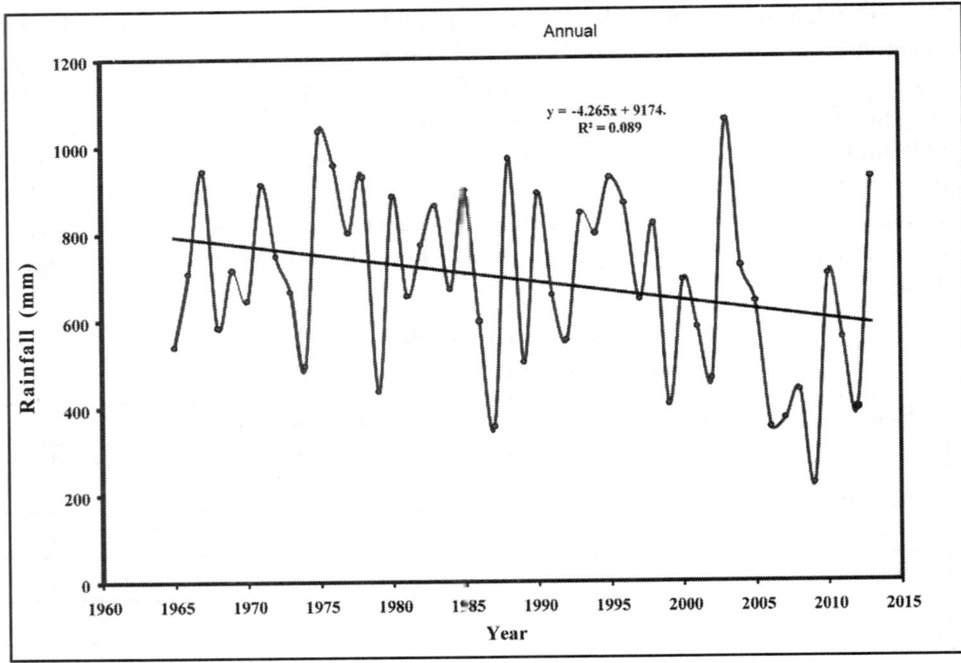

Fig. 8.4: **Trend analyses for annual rainfall of Meerut during period last fifty years (1965-2014)**

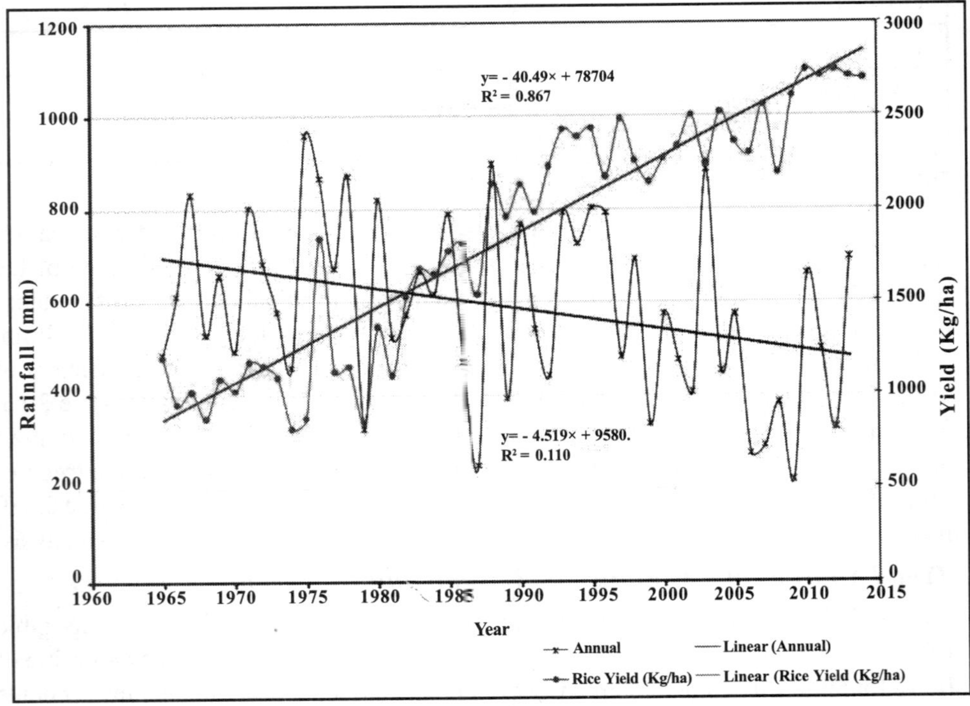

Fig. 8.5: **Relationship between annual rainfall and rice yield**

Monthly Variation of South-west Monsoon

The long-term data analysis of month-wise June, July August and September contributes 10.7 per cent, 33.3 per cent, 38.3 per cent and 17.8 per cent in south west monsoon rainfall season respectively, the results of the analysis are given in Table 8.5. The mean maximum rainfall is 224.9mm observed in August month whereas minimum rainfall is 62.6mm observed in June month. The minimum rainfall is observed in June, July, August and September month 0.30mm, 36.4mm, 16mm and 9.7mm in year 2012, 2004, 2006 and 1974 respectively, whereas the maximum rainfall is observed 157.8mm, 419.8mm, 500.1mm and 289.7mm in year 2013, 2003, 1995 and 2005 respectively. The monthly south-west monsoon rainfall variability in years is observed maximum after 21th century. It is most important period of rainfall seasonal cycle.

Table 8.5: Monthly south-west monsoon rainfall and distribution per cent of rainfall in Meerut district (1965-2014)

Year	South-west Monsoon Rainfall (mm)								
	June	July	August	September	Year	June	July	August	September
1965	6.5	172.9	189.0	118.6	1990	54.7	206.4	305.1	202.1
1966	114.7	149.5	259.8	89.4	1991	46.5	80.8	334.9	78.8
1967	26.7	208.7	500.1	97.5	1992	21.3	109.4	222.0	89.6
1968	38.9	248.1	223.1	19.1	1993	134.9	307.4	140.6	209.2
1969	44.4	230.0	177.3	206.8	1994	48.5	387.8	256.6	33.0
1970	91.2	78.7	219.8	104.9	1995	35.9	98.9	492.3	175.4
1971	76.2	221.5	364.1	140.4	1996	150.0	174.6	314.4	153.3
1972	30.1	267.4	291.6	94.9	1997	128.2	94.5	193.4	66.4
1973	45.4	136.6	323.8	72.2	1998	72.8	180.1	260.1	179.5
1974	26.8	308.1	115.1	9.7	1999	66.6	101.2	81.9	86.8
1975	82.1	361.7	269.3	244.9	2000	107.3	259.3	171.4	36.1
1976	62.0	299.2	430.3	74.9	2001	89.2	155.0	190.9	39.2
1977	82.1	357.6	118.2	115.6	2002	37.2	41.4	142.8	184.2
1978	86.9	234.6	356.2	193.4	2003	89.8	419.8	228.4	147.8
1979	65.6	129.3	90.3	41.1	2004	32.0	36.4	348.7	34.3
1980	85.1	416.9	207.0	111.6	2005	69.0	149.4	64.9	289.7
1981	124.3	258.7	78.7	61.2	2006	16.5	145.3	16.0	94.5
1982	56.7	204.3	297.5	14.3	2007	92.0	70.9	109.4	17.0
1983	61.6	236.2	200.9	169.0	2008	58.7	190.6	95.7	36.6
1984	45.6	190.6	285.7	96.0	2009	5.1	99.8	51.2	60.0
1985	59.3	373.1	271.0	86.4	2010	18.5	240.0	188.7	214.5
1986	46.9	155.6	177.5	90.4	2011	93.7	206.3	172.6	26.4
1987	15.4	46.1	156.5	30.1	2012	0.3	68.4	189.3	70.2
1988	57.1	283.3	418.5	137.8	2013	157.8	143.8	313.8	80.9
1989	37.1	107.7	147.1	99.1	2014	37.0	127.7	189.6	96.7
Average Rainfall (mm)						62.6	195.4	224.9	104.4
per cent of Rainfall						10.7	33.3	38.3	17.8
Minimum Rainfall						0.3	36.4	16.0	9.7
Maximum Rainfall						157.8	419.8	500.1	289.7

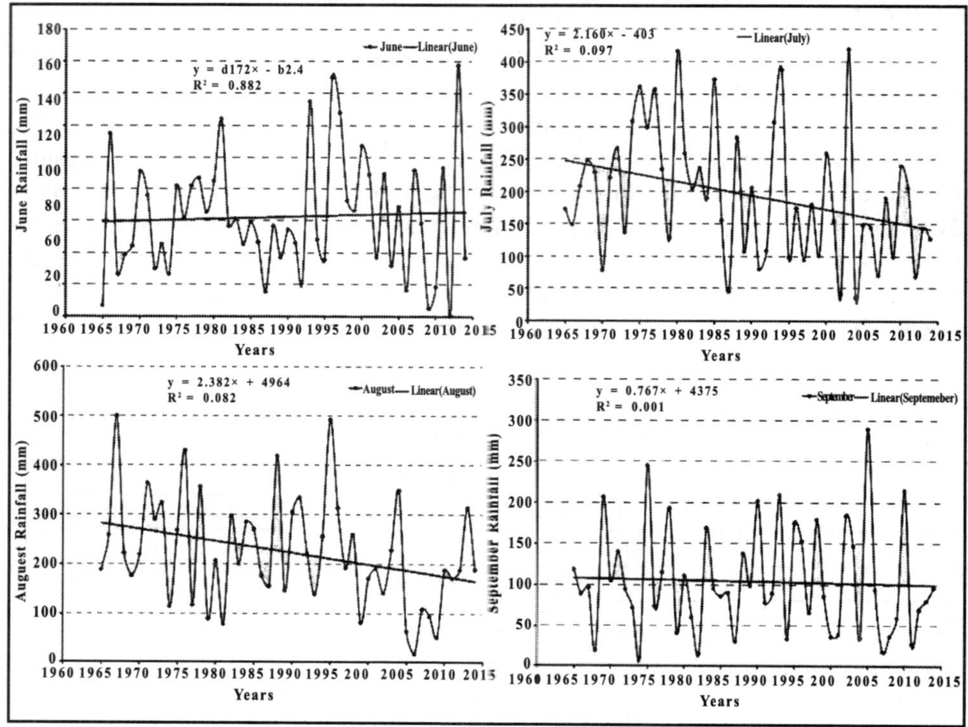

Fig. 8.6: **Monthly rainfall trend of south-west Monsoon season (1965-2014)**

The trends of monthly mean of south west monsoon rainfall over fifty years were obtained using linear regression best fit lines. The linear regression trends with their linear regression equations and coefficient of determinations for four month from June to September are represented in Fig. 8.6 and summarised in Table 8.6 below. The analysis data of S-W monsoon observed highest increase 98 per cent in August month and highest decrease in September month and decrease by 0.1 per cent during fifty years.

Table 8.6: Linear regression equations of South-west monsoon, annual rainfall and rice yield

Linear Regression Equations of Rainfall and Yield			
South west Monsoon	Month	Regression Line	R2
	June	y=0.128×-192.4	0.002
	July	y=-2.160×+4493	0.097
	August	y=-2.382×+4964	0.098
	September	y=-0.167×+437.5	0.001

Trend Analysis of South-west Rainfall (Monsoon season)

A trend analysis of the average south west rainfall of Meerut district for 50 year period from 1965 to 2014 was statistical test MS Excel in Table 8.7. Fig. 8.6 shows the plots of seasonal and annual rainfall for the study area; trends lines for the data have also been drawn. The monsoon season (S-W) is least scatter then annual rainfall. It does not show much scatter. It gives valuable trend information of series observations. Trend analysis was also performed on seasonal scale to examine if there are trends in the data at this scale. The trend analysis helps to measure the deviation from the trend and also provides information pertaining to the nature of trend. The analysis can be used as a tool to forecast the future behaviour of the trend. The method of least square fit for straight line has been used for trend analysis of the behaviour of annual rainfall, south west rainfall and rice yield. After trend analysis of data observed rainfall trend is going to decline pattern whereas rice yield data analysis observed in upside pattern. The rainfall dependent rice crop is not more dependent on rainfall other factors (hybrid varieties, mechanization and management pattern) also include for increasing of rice yield. Meerut is non-poor vulnerable in Leurs approach district of Uttar Pradesh (19) and the rice yield is found to be negatively correlated with the amount of rainfall (20).

Table 8.7: Time series analysis of South-west rainfall (mm) data of Meerut district

Year	X	Y	X2	XY	Trend	Year Value	X	Y	X2	XY	Trend Value
1965	-24	486.9	576	-11686.6	699.6	1990	1	768.3	1	768.3	585.1
1966	-23	613.5	529	-14109.5	695.0	1991	2	541.0	4	1082.0	580.5
1967	-22	833.0	484	-13326.5	690.4	1992	3	442.3	9	1326.8	575.9
1968	-21	529.2	441	-11113.0	685.9	1993	4	792.0	16	3168.0	571.3
1969	-20	658.5	400	-13169.5	681.3	1994	5	725.9	25	3629.6	566.7
1970	-19	494.6	361	-9396.6	676.7	1995	6	802.4	36	4814.7	562.2
1971	-18	802.2	324	-14439.9	672.1	1996	7	792.2	49	5545.7	557.6
1972	-17	684.0	289	-11627.4	667.5	1997	8	482.4	64	3859.5	553.0
1973	-16	577.9	256	-9246.9	663.0	1998	9	692.5	81	6232.5	548.4
1974	-15	459.7	225	-6896.1	658.4	1999	10	336.6	100	3365.7	543.8
1975	-14	958.0	196	-13412.1	653.8	2000	11	574.1	121	6315.5	539.3
1976	-13	866.5	169	-11264.2	649.2	2001	12	474.3	144	5691.8	534.7
1977	-12	673.5	144	-8082.2	644.6	2002	13	405.7	169	5273.5	530.1
1978	-11	871.1	121	-9581.9	640.0	2003	14	885.8	196	12401.2	525.5
1979	-10	326.3	100	-3262.9	635.5	2004	15	451.4	225	6771.0	520.9
1980	-9	820.6	81	-7385.1	630.9	2005	16	573.0	256	9168.0	516.3
1981	-8	523.0	64	-4183.7	626.3	2006	17	272.3	289	4629.1	511.8
1982	-7	572.8	49	-4009.8	621.7	2007	18	289.3	324	5207.4	507.2
1983	-6	667.7	36	-4006.0	617.1	2008	19	381.6	361	7250.4	502.6
1984	-5	617.9	25	-3089.3	612.6	2009	20	216.1	400	4322.0	498.0
1985	-4	789.7	16	-3158.7	608.0	2010	21	661.7	441	13895.7	493.4
1986	-3	470.3	9	-1410.9	603.4	2011	22	499.0	484	10978.0	488.9
1987	-2	248.1	4	-496.2	598.8	2012	23	328.2	529	7548.6	484.3
1988	-1	896.7	1	-896.7	594.2	2013	24	696.3	576	16711.2	479.7
1989	0	391.0	0	0.0	589.6	2014	25	450.9			475.1
							Σ=0	Σy= 28917.008	Σx 2=9800	Σx2= - 44295.397	

In year 1965 rice yield observed 1204 kg/ha and in year 2014 rice yield observed 2700 kg/ha during fifty years. The trend pattern of rice yield 868 kg/ha to 2852 kg/ha also observed in year 1965 to 2014 respectively (Table 8.8).

Table 8.8: Time series analysis of rice yield (kg/ha) of Meerut district

Year	X	Y	X2	XY	Trend	Year Value	X	Y	X2	XY	Trend Value
1965	-24	1204	576	-28884.2	868	1990	1	2135	1	2134.9	1880
1966	-23	952	529	-21884.8	908	1991	2	1985	4	3969.0	1921
1967	-22	1020	484	-22438.9	949	1992	3	2231	9	6691.9	1961
1968	-21	875	441	-18367.7	989	1993	4	2424	16	9697.7	2002
1969	-20	1086	400	-21727.6	1030	1994	5	2388	25	11939.9	2042
1970	-19	1023	361	-19432.1	1070	1995	6	2430	36	14577.1	2083
1971	-18	1179	324	-21218.1	1111	1996	7	2174	49	15220.7	2123
1972	-17	1160	289	-19724.1	1151	1997	8	2483	64	19863.5	2164
1973	-16	1096	256	-17539.1	1192	1998	9	2262	81	20355.8	2204
1974	-15	817	225	-12248.9	1232	1999	10	2147	100	21469.5	2245
1975	-14	873	196	-12226.8	1273	2000	11	2271	121	24979.7	2285
1976	-13	1843	169	-23957.1	1313	2001	12	2334	144	28008.1	2326
1977	-12	1128	144	-13530.7	1354	2002	13	2504	169	32547.1	2366
1978	-11	1154	121	-12695.5	1394	2003	14	2246	196	31443.9	2407
1979	-10	850	100	-8499.4	1435	2004	15	2519	225	37784.9	2447
1980	-9	1365	81	-12288.0	1475	2005	16	2359	256	37744.2	2488
1981	-8	1107	64	-8856.8	1516	2006	17	2299	289	39082.8	2528
1982	-7	1529	49	-10704.4	1556	2007	18	2559	324	46062.4	2569
1983	-6	1682	36	-10094.8	1597	2008	19	2193	361	41667.3	2609
1984	-5	1654	25	-8271.1	1637	2009	20	2608	400	52160.4	2650
1985	-4	1777	16	-7107.1	1678	2010	21	2747	441	57686.5	2690
1986	-3	1815	9	-5444.9	1718	2011	22	2712	484	59664.0	2731
1987	-2	1543	4	-3085.2	1759	2012	23	2747	529	63180.4	2771
1988	-1	2140	1	-2140.4	1799	2013	24	2712	576	65088.0	2812
1989	0	1961	0	0	1840	2014		2700			2852
							Σ=0	Σy= 90300.31	Σ×2 =9800	Σ×2= 400651.66	Trend value

Forecasting of S-W Rainfall and Rice Yield

On the basis, the future forecast of rainfall and yield amount for a period of ten years from 2016 to 2024 has been made (Table 8.9), which shows a negative trend for the coming years but yield shows a positive trend for the coming years. In future, expected annual and south west rainfall may be less in year 2024 observed 546.2mm and 429.3mm in Meerut district. So in view of future rainfall is not more important for rice yield it may be cause of drought tolerant with high yield varieties and water knowledge resource development (mainly water use management). The expected rice yield is observed 3257 kg/ha in year 2024. The trend analysis gives the scenario of current to expected future situation. Our statistical result indicate that monsoon rainfall is not the only weather variable affecting the rice crop in kharif season in the study area. Monsoon rainfall is one of the key factors but other climatic factors *viz;* temperature, sunshine hours, extreme rainfall, flood, drought condition, wind direction, heat and other parameters are also affect on the rice yield.

Table 8.9: Expected future annual, South-west rainfall (mm) and yield (Kg/ha) trend of Meerut district

Year	Expected Future Rainfall Trend (mm)		Expected Future Yield Trend (Kg/ha)
	Annual	South-west Monsoon	
2016	579.4	465.9	2933
2017	575.2	461.4	2974
2018	571.1	456.8	3014
2019	567.0	452.2	3055
2020	562.8	447.6	3095
2021	558.7	443.0	3136
2022	554.5	438.5	3176
2023	550.4	433.9	3217
2024	546.2	429.3	3257

Conclusion

Rainfall is major source of irrigation especially for south west monsoon for water loving crops mainly rice which are grown in large area then other crops. The S-W rainfall and rice yield data analysis to observed pattern of trend and develop forecasting model for future scenario. The positive trend of rainfall shows the favourable conditions for recharge and the negative trend of rainfall shows the unfavourable conditions for recharge. The data of annual rainfall and S-W rainfall is correlated with rice yield. The negative correlation values are -0.17 and -0.21 observed between rice yield with annual and S-W monsoon rainfall of Meerut. The monthly south-west monsoon rainfall variability in years is observed maximum after 21th century. It is most important period of rainfall seasonal cycle. The analysis data of S-W monsoon observed highest increase 98 per cent in August month and highest decrease in September month and decrease by 0.1 per cent during fifty years.

The analysis of trend of rainfall and rice yield observed rainfall is declining but rice yield trend going to be rise in coming years. The source of irrigation, mechanization and knowledge of current situation of weather and climate change related pattern and adaptation of technology is maintend to yield trend. Water is a vital component for rice crop cycle. In abnormal period for rice crop cycle, rice crop irrigated by available source (tubewell, submersible, canal, irrigation channel). Today rainfall is not regular fashion so farmers are not more dependent on rainfall.

REFERENCES

1. Kumar, V., Jain, S.K. and Singh, Y. (2010). Analysis of Long-term Rainfall Trends in India. Hydrol. Sci. J. 55(4), 484-496.
2. Manjunath, K.R., Panigrahy, S., Adhya, T.K., Beri, V., Rao, K.V., Parihar, J.S. (2009). Rice – Ecosystems of India in the Context of Methane Emission. ISPRS Archives XXXVIII-8/W3 Workshop Proceedings: Impact of Climate Change on Agriculture, December 17-18,2009, Ahmedabad, India.
3. Keshavamurty, R.N. (1982). Response of the Atmosphere to Sea Surface Temperature Anomalies over the Equatorial Pacific and the Teleconnections of the Southern oscillation. *J. Atmos. Sci.*, 39, 1241-1259.
4. Kripalani, R. H.; and Kulkarni, A. (1996). Assessing the Impacts of El Niño and non-*El Niño*-Related Droughts over India. Drought Network News. 8 (3):11-13.
5. Attri, S.D. and A. Tyagi (2010). Climate Profile of India. India Meteorological Depar tment, Ministry of Earth Sciences, New Delhi: Met Monograph No. Environment Meteorology - 01/2010.
6. *Mooley*, D.A. and Parthasarathy, B. 1983). *Indian Summer Monsoon* and *El Niño*. Pure and Applied Geophysics PAGEOPH 121:2, 339-352.
7. Guhathakurta, P. and Rajeevan, M. (2008). "Trends in Rainfall Pattern over India." *International Journal of Climatology*, 28, 1453-1469.
8. Mahmood, N., Ahmad, B., Hassan, S., Bakhsh, K. (2012). Impact of Temperature and Precipitation on Rice Productivity in Rice-wheat Cropping System of Punjab Province. *The Journal of Animal and Plant Sciences*, 22(4): 993-997.
9. Saseendran, A. S.K., Singh, K.K., Rathore, L.S., Singh, S.V., and Sinha, S.K. (2000). Effects of Climate Change on Rice Production in the Tropical Humid Climate of Kerala, India. Climate Change, 44, 495-514.
10. Meerut info: http://en.wikipedia.org/wiki/Meerut_district
11. India Forest Report (2011). Forest Survey of India, Ministry of Environment and Forests, Government of India, pp. 230-235. http://www.fsi.org.in/cover_2011/uttara pradesh.pdf
12. National Conference on Climate Change: Socio-economic and Environment Issues-problems and Challenges Souvenir April 21-22, 2013, Department of Botany, Meerut college, Meerut. pp. 1-12.
13. Rainfall data of Meerut (1901 to 2002).

    http://www.indiawaterportal.org/articles/meteorological-datasets-download-entire-datasets-various-meteorological-indicators-1901 to 2002

14. Rainfall data of Meerut (2004 to 06)
http://www.indiawaterportal.org/met_data/

15. Rainfall year: 2003.
http://shodhganga.inflibnet.ac.in/bitstream/10603/41261/6/06_chapter%202.pdf

16. IMD (Indian meteorology Department, New Delhi): (2007 to 2013). Hydromet Division, India Meteorological Department, District rainfall (mm) for last five years (2007 to 2013).

17. NASA/POWER Agroclimatology Daily Averaged Data: (2014).
http://power.larc.nasa.gov/common/AgroclimatologyMethodology/Agro1d0_Methodology_Content.html and http://power.larc.nasa.gov

18. Sobha Rani, N., Prasad, GSV., Sailaja, B., Muthuraman, P., Meera, S.N., and Viraktamath (2010). Rice almanac-India, DRR Technical Bulletin No. 50, Directotare of Rice, Rajendra Nagar, Hyderabad, A.P., India. and A.

19. Kavikumar, K.S. and Viswanathan, B. (2010). Climate Variability and Agricultural Productivity: Case Study of *Rice Yields in Northern India. Working Paper 54/2010.* WORKING PAPER 54/2010. *www.mse.ac.in/pub/WORKING%20PAPER%2058.pdf*

20. Singh, V.P. *et al.* (1996). Physiology of Stress Tolerance in Rice. Proc. of International Conference on Stress Physiology of Rice, 28 February - 5 March, 1994, Lucknow, Uttar Pradesh, India 239p.

Index

*****